Domestic Contradictions

PRIYA KANDASWAMY

Domestic Contradictions

Race and Gendered Citizenship from Reconstruction to Welfare Reform

Duke University Press | *Durham and London* | 2021

Project editor: Lisa Lawley
Designed by Matthew Tauch
Typeset in Whitman by Westchester Publishing Services

Library of Congress Cataloging-in-Publication Data
Names: Kandaswamy, Priya, [date] author.
Title: Domestic contradictions : race and gendered citizenship
from Reconstruction to welfare reform / Priya Kandaswamy.
Description: Durham : Duke University Press, 2021. | Includes
bibliographical references and index.
Identifiers: LCCN 2020046887 (print)
LCCN 2020046888 (ebook)
ISBN 9781478013402 (hardcover)
ISBN 9781478014317 (paperback)
ISBN 9781478021629 (ebook)
Subjects: LCSH: United States. Personal Responsibility and Work
Opportunity Reconciliation Act of 1996. | United States. Bureau
of Refugees, Freedmen, and Abandoned Lands. | Racism in public
welfare—United States. | Welfare recipients—Legal status, laws,
etc.—United States. | Public welfare—United States—History—
Sources. | African American women—Social conditions. |
Womanism. | United States—Social policy—1993–
Classification: LCC HV95 .K345 2021 (print) | LCC HV95 (ebook) |
DDC 362.83/56108996073009034—dc23
LC record available at https://lccn.loc.gov/2020046887
LC ebook record available at https://lccn.loc.gov/2020046888

Cover art: Delita Martin, *Six Persimmons*, 2019. Acrylic,
charcoal, decorative papers, hand stitching, and relief
printing, 72 in. × 51½ in. Courtesy of Delita Martin and
Galerie Myrtis.

Contents

Acknowledgments

I am writing these acknowledgments in the midst of a global pandemic that disproportionately steals Black life by structural design and in the aftermath of the police murders of George Floyd, Breonna Taylor, and Tony McDade. Over the many years I have worked on this book, we have witnessed countless Black lives be taken by state violence alongside the continued whittling away of social supports for working-class people in the name of privatization, individual responsibility, protection of taxpayers, and so-called American freedoms. A modest contribution to thinking about the history that informs these phenomena, this book is possible only because of the centuries of anticapitalist struggle for Black liberation and decolonization that have kept other worlds on the horizon. I could not ask the questions in this book without the intellectual and political ancestors who have made it possible for me to exist and think in the ways that I do. This book owes a particular debt to the welfare rights movement, domestic workers' organizing, reproductive justice organizing, and abolitionist movements of the past and present and to the remarkable individuals whose efforts to survive and flourish I caught fleeting glimpses of in the archives. More than anything, I hope that this book might lift up the power, resilience, and brilliance of these struggles by documenting the great lengths to which state institutions have had to go to contain them.

I could not have written this book without the amazing teachers, colleagues, students, friends, and family who have supported me. I am deeply appreciative of Evelyn Nakano Glenn's wisdom and mentorship. Not only did she give me the tools to do this research, but her own groundbreaking scholarship on women of color, labor, and citizenship has been a model for the kind of work I aspire to create. The opportunity to study with Ruth Wilson Gilmore as a graduate student has been one of life's greatest gifts.

Ruthie thoroughly transformed the way I see the world, and many years later I still think about and find new meaning in the questions she asked me then. Many of those questions were the spark for this book, and my own thinking owes so much to her genius and the lovingly high expectations she has of her students.

At the University of California, Berkeley, I also had the tremendous privilege of learning from Paola Bacchetta, Wendy Brown, Michael Burawoy, Catherine Ceniza Choy, Barbara Christian, Gina Dent, Elaine Kim, Michael Omi, Raka Ray, José Saldivar, and Charis Thompson. I especially want to thank my undergraduate teachers: Jerry Sanders for seeing potential in me and encouraging me to pursue an academic path, Ishmael Reed for affirming that I could write and impressing on me the importance of using my voice to say something important, Carol Stack for introducing me to feminist methodology, and Trinh T. Minh-ha for opening a door to women of color feminisms and queer of color theory that transformed my life.

This project was conceptualized, and the initial stages of research done, while I was a faculty member at Portland State University. I have so much appreciation for the thoughtful and generous community of scholars who made me feel at home in Portland. Words cannot express my gratitude to Patti Duncan, who has been the best friend and colleague I could ask for. Her support and encouragement kept me working on this project through difficult times, and I am so appreciative of the courage, intelligence, and kindness that she brings to everything she does. Thank you to Hillary Jenks for being the best of comrades in tough circumstances. My Portland writing group—Jade Aguilar, Reshmi Dutt Ballerstadt, Patti Duncan, Hillary Jenks, Marie Lo, Sudarat Musikawong, and Patti Sakurai—offered insightful feedback on my early writing as well as laughter, community, and delicious food. Patricia Schechter helped me craft a way of doing history as a nonhistorian, and the much-missed Peggy Pascoe's encouragement affirmed that I was on the right track. Lynn Fujiwara's support, guidance, and insight have been invaluable throughout this process. Thank you also to Veronica Dujon, Maude Hines, Ethan Johnson, Priya Kapoor, Marcia Klotz, Amy Lonetree, Lee Medovoi, and Christa Orth for being wonderful colleagues.

I have been tremendously lucky to spend the past decade of my academic career with the fabulous faculty and students at Mills College in Oakland, California. Brinda Mehta has been an exceptional intellectual mentor, and I am so grateful for her confidence in me, the great conversations we have had, and the laughter we have shared. Maggie Hunter has both shown me the ropes of midcareer academia and been a wonderful friend who models grace, compassion, and groundedness in even the most challenging of situations. I am grateful to Libby Potter for welcoming me with such enthusiasm into the Women, Gender, and Sexuality Studies Department at Mills and giving me the space to grow. Mills was a much better place with Vivian Chin's eccentric brilliance and generous heart, and I am thankful for the years we got to work together. Martha Johnson and Maura Finkelstein generously read and offered feedback on drafts of chapters. I have learned so much from working with Natalee Kehaulani Bauer, Déborah Berman Santana, Judith Bishop, Diane Cady, David Donahue, Rebekah Edwards, Jay Gupta, Sabrina Kwist, Ajuan Mance, Melinda Micco, Pedro Nava, Achy Obejas, Margo Okazawa-Rey, Chinyere Oparah, Patricia Powell, Kirsten Saxton, Marianne Sheldon, Sé Sullivan, Wanda Watson, and Arely Zimmerman. Most of all, I am so grateful to my truly amazing students who keep me connected to the reasons I do this work and challenge me to learn new things and think in new ways. I have every confidence that the future they build will be, as they say, lit, and I am looking forward to it.

I am thankful for the larger community of scholars and friends whom I have had the tremendous privilege of thinking, reading, and writing alongside. While there are far too many people to name here, a few deserve particular mention. Kate Drabinski's love, brilliance, and wit have been a sustaining force in my life for more than two decades now, and I am deeply appreciative of everything that I have learned from her. Reading in conversation with Clement Lai and Sara Clarke Kaplan was formative to my thinking and an experience that I remain grateful for so many years later. I thank Erica Meiners for her fierce commitment to building abolitionist scholarship and education and for telling me that it was probably time to just finish this book. Christoph Hanssmann and Tomomi Kinukawa have been amazing writing partners and friends who made working on various stages of this project enjoyable just by being present. The National Women's Studies Association's Women of Color: Theory, Scholarship, and Activism workshop brought this project to life in its early stages. I thank Beverly Guy-Sheftall, Yi-Chun Tricia Lin, Vivian Ng, M. Jacqui Alexander, Bonnie Thornton Dill, and Andrea Smith for organizing and teaching the workshop, and all of the participants for creating such a luminous community.

Many colleagues have supported me personally over the years or contributed to this book by sharing ideas and insights. I especially want to thank Shana Agid, Patrick Anderson, Marlon Bailey, Falu Bakrania, Janet

Bauer, Cindy Rose Bello, Alisa Bierria, Eileen Boris, Renu Cappelli, Grace Chang, Piya Chatterjee, Loan Dao, Kirstie Dorr, Qwo-Li Driskell, Sora Han, David Hernández, Emily Hobson, Daniel HoSang, Zakiyyah Iman Jackson, Ronak Kapadia, Oneka LaBennett, Elizabeth Lee, David Leonard, Jenna Loyd, Eithne Luibheid, Stephanie Lumsden, Navin Moul, Soniya Munshi, Premilla Nadasen, Jeffrey Ow, Laura Pulido, Matt Richardson, Angela Robinson, Dylan Rodríguez, Don Romesburg, Shireen Roshanravan, Amy Sadao, Nayan Shah, Dean Spade, David Stein, Anantha Sudhakar, Daphne Taylor-Garcia, Emily Thuma, Craig Willse, Connie Wun, and Kathy Yep. This project is deeply indebted to the Black feminist scholarship of Cathy Cohen, Angela Davis, Saidiya Hartman, Tera Hunter, and Dorothy Roberts. The many citations in the pages that follow cannot begin to capture the influence their writing has had on my thinking, and I want to expressly thank them for the gift of their work.

I am particularly grateful to the anonymous reviewers whose thorough and thoughtful feedback made this book immeasurably better, and I have great appreciation for Gisela Fosado, Alejandra Mejía, and everyone else at Duke University Press who kept this project moving forward even during a global pandemic.

I would not be here if it weren't for my friends and family. For all the support, love, laughter, and joy they have shared with me over the years, I give special thanks to Sheila Gallagher, Nadya Abo-Shaeer, Dan Percival, Rabeya Sen, Kushlani De Soyza, Anushka Fernandopulle, Ramesh Kathanadhi, and Anantha Sudhakar. I am very grateful to my family of origin. I thank my parents for their love and for raising me to be the person that I am. My father, Kunchithapatham Kandaswamy, instilled in me the importance of living with a kind heart and generous spirit. I would not have the audacity to try and write a book if it were not for my mother, Vijaya Lakshmi Kandaswamy, who can do anything she puts her mind to and encouraged me to see myself that way too. I am grateful to my grandparents, especially K. Krishnaswami, from whom I learned at a very young age the importance of standing up for what is just, and Rukmani, who was one of the strongest and most loving women I have ever known. My brother, Sridar Kandaswamy, and my sister-in-law, Raji Sridar, have been a continual source of support throughout this process, and it has been a gift to live most of my adult life in close proximity to them. I am so grateful to my nephew, Shiva Sridar, and my niece, Harini Sridar, for all the ways they have made our family better. They have been bright lights in my life, and it has been remarkable to watch them grow into such thoughtful, kind, and loving people. My cousins Maya Sethuraman and Vasu Sethuraman are like an additional set of siblings to me, and I am thankful for all the love, support, and mischief over the years. I can't wait to see what the future holds for Devon, Zamir, and Bodhi.

Finally, my deepest thanks and appreciation go to Leslie Griep. She has not only patiently suffered through all the drama of book writing and loved me regardless but also filled my life with far more than my fair share of joy. I am profoundly grateful for the beautiful life we have made together, and I feel so lucky that I get to continue living it with you.

ONE

Welfare Reform and the Afterlife of Slavery

The central idea is that of the palimpsest—a parchment that has been inscribed two or three times, the previous text having been imperfectly erased and remaining therefore still partly visible. . . . The idea of the "new" structured through the "old" scrambled, palimpsestic character of time, both jettisons the truncated distance of linear time and dislodges the impulse for incommensurability, which the ideology of distance creates. It thus rescrambles the "here and now" and the "then and there" to a "here and there" and a "then and now," and makes visible what Payal Banerjee calls the ideological traffic between and among formations that are otherwise positioned as dissimilar.

—**M. Jacqui Alexander**, *Pedagogies of Crossing* (2006)

On August 22, 1996, President Bill Clinton signed into law the Personal Responsibility and Work Opportunity Reconciliation Act (PRWORA), concluding a protracted struggle to "end welfare as we know it."[1] A watershed moment in U.S. history, the law instituted the most dramatic transformation in the welfare state since the New Deal. It ended the federal entitlement to Aid to Families with Dependent Children (AFDC) and replaced it with Temporary Assistance to Needy Families (TANF), a state block grant program in which assistance would be time limited, contingent on work, and subject to a range of stricter eligibility requirements. At the signing, Lillie Harden, an African American single mother and former welfare recipient from North Little Rock, introduced President Clinton. Harden was one of only two Black women in a sea of white male politicians, and her story was deployed as evidence of the potential successes the new law might bear.[2] After she was laid off from her job in the early 1980s, Harden had participated in Arkansas's Project Success, an experimental welfare-to-work program that served as a prototype for the federal law. She told the audience how the program had enabled her to leave the welfare rolls and begin work as a cook to support her family. Harden spoke of how leaving welfare and modeling hard work for her children led to their educational achievement, marriage, and familial stability, breaking what was often described by sociologists and policy makers as an intergenerational cycle of poverty.[3]

When Clinton took the stage, he described his first encounter with Harden at a governor's meeting on welfare-to-work programs ten years earlier. Clinton recounted their conversation as follows:

> I said, "Lillie, what's the best thing about being off welfare?" And she looked me straight in the eye and said, "When my boy goes to school, and they say what does your mama do for a living, he can give an answer." I have never forgotten that. And when I saw the success that she's had in the past 10 years—I can tell you, you've had a bigger impact on me than I've had on you. And I thank you for the power of your example, for your family's. And for all of America, thank you very much.[4]

Clinton went on to praise the new law as an opportunity for "overcoming the flaws of the welfare system for the people who are trapped on it," as a way of replacing "a never ending cycle of welfare" with "the dignity, the power, and the ethic of work." With these changes, he argued, welfare would from now on be as it was intended, "a second chance, not a way of life."[5] Echoing the public discourse about welfare reform that dominated the 1980s and 1990s, these comments situated welfare rather than economic inequality as the problem to be solved.[6] Welfare was seen not as an economic support for low-income families but rather as a barrier to economic advancement that fostered dependency and degraded family values. Escaping welfare was the key to both assimilation and freedom, and the clearest pathway out was through low-wage work.

Harden's presence at this historic moment signified not only her accomplishments but also the threat of what she might have become without the push to work, a threat most famously embodied in the mythical figure of the welfare queen. An invention of the Reagan era, the welfare queen was imagined as a Black woman who lived large off hardworking white taxpayers. She personified everything that was supposedly wrong with welfare. She had too much sex and too many children, consumed too much, and was pathologically dependent on the government to support these bad habits, which she in turn passed to her children. A queer figure, the welfare queen was the racialized and gendered embodiment of the excesses associated with public assistance, a quintessential sign of what was wrong with big government. Despite a strategically color-blind language of welfare reform, Harden's own body communicated as much as the story that she told and that was told about her. Her welfare-to-work success story was significant because it demonstrated that the unruly dangers her Black female body posed to the nation could be domesticated through forced labor.

However, the positioning of Harden as an example for other similarly situated women also revealed significant tensions within the law itself. Notably, PRWORA first and foremost framed its mission as protecting and preserving the heteronormative family to protect and preserve the nation. The law opened with the proclamation that "marriage is the foundation of a successful society," its preamble is littered with references to the horrors of teenage pregnancy and female-headed households, and its passage was linked to a promise that restructuring the welfare system would restore the nation to its original family values.[7] This framing resonated strongly with a history of maternalist federal and local policies that organized welfare provision through the family wage and linked public assistance for women specifically to their work as mothers of future citizens. At the same time, this framing was also a poor fit for describing the changes that the law institutionalized. Certainly, marriage-promotion programs and penalties for teenage mothers were part of the law, and the law reinforced marriage as an institution simply in the ways that it punished single mothers. However, the strong emphasis on moving recipients from welfare to work diverged significantly from earlier social welfare policy that sought to protect women from the degradation of wage labor so that they could devote their time to raising future citizens. Rather, the "power of Harden's example" was in the reframing of good mothering for working-class women as not the work of raising children but rather the modeling of disciplined labor and economic self-sufficiency for future generations. In a society that frequently fixates on the need to protect and nurture an abstract figure of the child and despite the law's own obsessive rhetorical concern for the plight of children not in two-parent heteronormative households, it is notable that the implicit message of the policies enacted by the law is that impoverished children do not need care as much as they need role models in labor discipline.[8] The actual labor of mothering is not only not recognized but also rewritten as participation in the low-wage labor market. Highlighting the futures the law imagines for these children and their mothers, George W. Bush underscored this point when he declared at the 2002 reauthorization of PRWORA that "a work requirement isn't punishment. A work requirement is part of liberation in our society."[9]

The signing of PRWORA took place on the White House lawn against the backdrop of American flags and a placard that read "A New Beginning: Welfare to Work." However, despite the continual framing of this moment as the start of something new, this book is interested in making visible the "seething presence" of the past at this particular historical juncture.[10] Following Avery Gordon's incitement to attend to ghosts, I examine how another story haunted this scene. This is a story about a fraught transition between slavery and freedom, about the paradoxes that have structured the meaning of Black women's citizenship since emancipation, and about how race, gender, and sexuality have been a persistent force in shaping the meaning of public assistance in the United States. Rather than view Black women's citizenship as incomplete or as a not yet fully realized version of white citizenship, I am interested in the theory of citizenship that emerges from Black women's experiences navigating the contradictions that have defined their subordinated position within the nation. To highlight this understanding of citizenship, this project reexamines the restructuring of the welfare state at the end of the twentieth century by juxtaposing the discourse about welfare reform with the conflicts that marked the Freedmen's Bureau's efforts to incorporate newly emancipated populations into the institutions of citizenship in the aftermath of the Civil War. The Freedmen's Bureau was established to restore social and economic order and mediate the transition from being property to being citizens for freedpeople. Like advocates of welfare reform, bureau officials addressed vast systemic inequalities through the promotion of individual responsibility. Like the threat posed by the welfare queen, the threat of vagrancy among freedpeople loomed large in the postemancipation national imagination and became a primary problem that bureau officials sought to address through both the promotion of marriage and forced labor.

The tensions between promoting marriage and forcing women to work that characterized welfare reform echoed this earlier moment in U.S. history in a way that M. Jacqui Alexander might call palimpsestic.[11] These resonances demonstrate the ways that the contradictions among a range of state interests are displaced onto Black women's bodies and the central role that the reform, surveillance, policing, and punishment of those bodies have played in producing the appearance of state power as coherent despite its many fractures. Highlighting the ways that state efforts to promote marriage and enforce labor discipline in the late 1990s reiterated the dynamics of this earlier moment, I draw attention to important historical continuities in how sexual economy, racial liberalism, and national identity have been articulated in the spectacle of making Black women work outside of the home. Relocating the Freedmen's Bureau as a central institution in U.S. welfare history demonstrates the contradictory ways in which discourses of domesticity and forced labor converge in efforts to regulate Black women's bodies, thereby challenging the belief that women's citizenship has been defined primarily by domestic confinement and that the compulsion to work has been most strongly enforced on men.

While most feminist histories of the U.S. welfare state begin with the development of mothers' pensions during the Progressive Era, this project focuses on the Freedmen's Bureau because the anxieties and questions that were central to late twentieth-century debates about welfare policy resonate strongly with those that emerged in debates about the bureau.[12] For example, questions about how to make the newly emancipated into good citizen subjects and how to encourage them to enter particular kinds of low-wage work surfaced alongside and were often expressed in terms of deep anxieties about promoting dependency, giving aid to undeserving populations, cultivating the ideals of domesticity within the Black family, and expanding the reach of the federal government. As one of the first federal-level Americanization programs, the Freedmen's Bureau demonstrates how the desire to maintain Black subjugation despite formal emancipation was a driving force in the development of state practices that employed gendered discourses of domesticity to regulate Black workers. Although the Freedmen's Bureau did not specifically target single mothers and was not a direct institutional antecedent to AFDC in the same way that mothers' pensions were, examining the techniques of government employed by the Freedmen's Bureau in response to the crisis of Reconstruction offers important insights into the ways that state practices have both shaped and been shaped by a racialized-gendered understanding of domestic space.

In analyzing the linkages between these two historical moments and centering Black women's history with the welfare state, this book makes three significant contributions. First, by turning to the Reconstruction era, I argue for a rethinking of gendered citizenship as a modality of enforcing racial subjugation. I conceptualize citizenship as consisting of both an imposed legal relationship that defines rights and obligations associated with belonging in the nation-state and a dynamic process through which the meaning of that legal relationship is negotiated and struggled over. While citizenship has often been thought of as securing universal membership within the nation, this project views citizenship as a technology for producing differentiated state subjects. What citizenship has meant in practice for different groups has varied tremendously. These differences, however, are often understood as exclusions from citizenship or signs of a promise that has not yet been fully realized. In contrast, this project challenges progressive, liberal narratives that position full citizenship at the end of a path toward equality for marginalized groups by engaging with the ways that citizenship functions as a vehicle for domination. Rather than viewing the newly emancipated as excluded from full citizenship, this project highlights the ways that legal inclusion into citizenship reiterated their subordination and curtailed the ways that they could practice freedom. Similarly, the targeting of Black women as welfare queens focused on their perceived failures to live up to citizenship ideals and the demand that they be held accountable by enforcing an obligation to work that was not imposed on other citizens. Attention to these differentiated ways that citizenship functions challenges liberal beliefs that citizenship could be universal if particular barriers were overcome. This project instead argues for a relational understanding of citizenship in which the meanings of citizenship are defined not just against those who are not citizens but also through constructed differences within the category of citizenship.[13]

Throughout the book I show how gender plays a fundamental role in naturalizing unequal forms of citizenship. More traditional engagements with gendered citizenship have focused on how the rights and obligations of citizenship have been stratified along gender lines, drawing attention to the inequalities between masculine and feminine constructions of citizenship. For example, dominant feminist histories emphasize the role that maternalist social movements played in laying the foundation for a bifurcated welfare state that defined benefits for male workers as entitlements and benefits for dependent mothers as charity.[14] These historical accounts describe the ways that Progressive Era maternalists' deployment of a discourse of domesticity that exalted motherhood and emphasized women's natural difference from men worked to forge a pathway for women into the state while simultaneously institutionalizing principles of gendered citizenship that reproduced their subordination. While many scholars have shown how maternalism was not simply a gendered project but rather was deeply engaged in the production of racial hierarchies, my project takes a different approach by turning to another historical moment altogether.[15] Situating the Freedmen's Bureau within feminist welfare history identifies the experiences of Black women with state regulation and coercion as a central thread in the development of social welfare programs and thereby challenges the assumption that the dominant thematics that define women's relationship to the domestic sphere and to the welfare state are inclusion, protection, maintenance of the family wage, and the cultivation of idealized motherhood.

By turning to the Freedmen's Bureau, *Domestic Contradictions* posits an alternative way of theorizing gendered citizenship as grounded in, rather than separable from, social relations of race and class. By mapping roles associated with the heteropatriarchal family onto membership within the nation-state, gendered constructions of citizenship naturalized a hierarchical ordering of difference. While this secured the subordination of women and children to men, gender also became a reference point for naturalizing other hierarchies.[16] Because normative gender was white, gender embedded race into citizenship in ways that persisted long after explicit racial exclusions were lifted. Entering institutions of citizenship entailed demonstrating one's deservingness by performing normative gender roles. However, Black people often found that regardless of their performance, their Blackness persistently marked them as deficient in some way. For Black women, gendered citizenship required embodying a femininity that was often in stark contradiction with the requirement that they work outside the home and with the sexualized meanings ascribed to Blackness. Because Black people were denied reparations for slavery, a family wage, the right to privacy, the right to familial autonomy, and any form of state support, heteropatriarchal gender roles were materially difficult for them to achieve. As a result, gendered citizenship worked to situate Black women as perpetually deficient and undeserving in ways that rationalized a wide range of reform and surveillance projects. Notably, these projects expanded and transformed state apparatuses by constituting gender as a terrain of cultural reform and obscuring the material supports that enabled white citizens to more easily achieve heteropatriarchal ideals of the family. In this context, figures like the domestic worker during the Reconstruction era and the workfare worker in the late twentieth century emerged as alternate tropes of gendered citizenship for Black women. While these figures remained entrenched in the cultural language of domesticity and motherhood, they simultaneously justified austerity toward Black families and demanded that Black women direct their labor away from their own children and communities.

The second contribution this project makes by turning to the Freedmen's Bureau is to build on and elaborate feminist theorizations of how domestic space has been constituted in the history of the U.S. welfare state. Within dominant feminist histories of the welfare state, the point is often made that maternalists both transcended the boundaries of the domestic sphere by making political demands on the state and reinscribed those boundaries by asserting motherhood and care of the home as women's natural vocation.[17] This argument rests on a conception of domestic space as the singular, static, internal, and private space of the familial home, a gendered sphere of confinement that entrance into politics necessarily transcends, even when domesticity is itself constructed as the basis for political power. Throughout the chapters that follow, I argue that this limited way of thinking about domestic space derives from a methodology that assumes the domestic to be simply a gendered construction through which men dominate women. In contrast to the white female subjects of histories of maternalism, Black feminist scholarship highlights that the domestic lives of Black women have rarely been private. Rather, as was clearly demonstrated in the display of Harden's personal life at the PRWORA signing, the domestic sphere that Black women inhabit is often a highly visible space that is the subject of public debate and state surveillance. Given that domestic spaces are constructed differently for differently racialized populations, the question of theoretical importance becomes not how to transcend the boundaries of domesticity but rather how power operates in the production of different kinds of domestic space for differently racialized and gendered subjects.

Throughout this book I engage the ways that the concept of domesticity and the spaces associated with it simultaneously invoke three interrelated meanings of the term *domestic*, all of which have been operative in the building of the U.S. welfare state. In its first sense, *the domestic* signifies the internal realm of the nation. Managing the poor, regulating racialized populations, and ensuring national well-being are major functions of welfare institutions and key components of *domestic policy*. In its second sense, *the domestic* signifies the internal realm of the household, and welfare apparatuses have often focused their attention on the regulation of family life in the *domestic sphere* as a means of addressing poverty and social upheaval.[18] Finally, the term *domestic* also references the *domestic worker*, whose labor is a precondition for the production of both of the above spaces.[19] Historically, the practices of welfare institutions have prioritized ensuring not only that some women perform domestic labor in their own homes but that other women remain available as a low-wage reproductive labor force. While these three meanings of *the domestic* are usually separated in common parlance, drawing attention to their interconnectedness reveals the reciprocal processes through which the making of the state and the making of families have historically been intertwined. Looking at these three connotations of *the domestic* together highlights how the language of domesticity, often invoked in efforts to build and transform welfare institutions, produced and reproduced overlapping meanings of the home as a simultaneously national place, familial place, and workplace.[20]

Grounding my analysis in Black feminist engagements with domesticity and the related concepts of privacy, surveillance, and gendered labor, I am particularly interested in how these multiple meanings of *the domestic* link racial subordination to differential access to a private sphere. As discussed in more detail in the next chapter, the home has been a central site of struggle for Black women. Although frequently denied privacy and surveilled within the home, Black women have also constructed home spaces as important sites of abolitionist practice. In addition, while frequently demonized in public discourse as bad mothers and irresponsible homemakers, Black women have also been expected to care for white children and maintain white homes as domestic workers. Taking into account these different registers of meaning, I argue for a more situated concept of domesticity. I do this by looking at how ideas of domestic space have been invoked in moments of crisis in order to further various state-building projects and at how these state practices simultaneously produce and regulate norms around the family in their efforts to secure racial and gendered hierarchies. By turning to the case of the Freedmen's Bureau to illustrate the contradictory ways discourses of domesticity were employed in efforts to regulate newly emancipated people in the Reconstruction South, I hope to suggest an alternative genealogy of domesticity that is grounded in Black women's experiences. I am interested in highlighting how attention to the postemancipation moment might enable a more nuanced reading of gendered stratification within the U.S. welfare state as a simultaneously racialized process.

Finally, through a grounded analysis of the Freedmen's Bureau's and PRWORA's efforts to promote marriage and forced labor, this project demonstrates the multiple ways in which state power and the heteronormative family are mutually constitutive. As demonstrated in the next chapter, these two historical moments offer powerful examples of how the state produces the heteronormative family as a seemingly natural organization of kinship and how naturalized ideas of the family simultaneously reinforce state power. In highlighting a reciprocal relationship between the making of state power and the making of heteronormativity, my analysis brings a queer approach to the history of the welfare state and points to the ways that destabilizing heteronormativity potentially destabilizes state power as well. Inspired by Cathy Cohen's conception of queer as a potentially coalitional category and her specific naming of the welfare queen as a queer figure, this project makes visible the multiple structures of domination that are articulated through the welfare state's emphasis on heteronormativity.[21] In the chapters that follow, I explore how constructions like the vagrant and the welfare queen in their refusals of settlement, marriage, conventional gender roles, and contractual forms of labor point toward queer possibilities that have been marginalized by a heteronormative vision of history. In doing so, I hope to also queer history by adopting methods and analyses that denaturalize liberal narratives of progress that tie history to the nation-state.

Throughout the project I approach the heteronormative family as itself a particularly dense site for the articulation of race, gender, sexuality, and class and show how discourses about domesticity and family values enabled the state to navigate multiple, sometimes contradictory investments in structures of domination while still appearing to be a coherent, unified entity. In the context of welfare policy, I argue the family has functioned simultaneously as the basis for rights claims and as a mechanism for the privatization of responsibility. The examples engaged throughout this book show that this dual meaning of the family in political discourse has been foundational to the development of racialized and gendered stratification within the welfare state. While the next chapter elaborates my theoretical arguments about state power, in what remains of this chapter, I provide a brief overview of the historical context of the Freedmen's Bureau to illustrate its continued relevance to U.S. welfare state history. After providing a general discussion of the bureau's history, I turn more specifically to the role that marriage and forced labor played in the bureau's efforts to make freedpeople into citizens and to the methodological approaches that inform my research.

The Freedmen's Bureau and the Management
of Citizenship

As one of the first federal welfare institutions, the Bureau of Freedmen, Refugees, and Abandoned Lands was charged with reinstating order and reestablishing federal authority in the aftermath of the Civil War. The formal end of slavery had produced a profound crisis not only in the racialized economic system of production in the South but also in the very meaning of citizenship, national identity, and the concept of freedom itself. While certainly not the only actor in the struggles that ensued, the Freedmen's Bureau was an important arena in which struggles to redefine these terms took place and, even in its brief existence, had a lasting impact on how racial subjugation and the ideas of citizenship, nationhood, and freedom that accompanied it were reinvented. A highly controversial institution in its time, the bureau potentially represented a dramatic expansion of federal power to intervene on behalf of freedpeople in southern states. This potential, however, was quickly curtailed by the bureau's temporary status and limited funding. Using remarkably similar rhetoric to the antiwelfare discourse of the late twentieth century, critics of the bureau painted it as an example of a federal government that was overreaching its constitutional bounds to redistribute resources to lazy and undeserving Black people at the expense of hardworking white taxpayers. These thinly veiled racist attacks on the bureau, along with bureau officials' own narrow understandings of what constituted freedom for the recently emancipated, structured much of the work in which the bureau engaged. As a result, claims to land redistribution and guarantees of political equality receded just as struggles to enforce labor discipline and normative family structure took center stage. More than a century later, efforts to restructure the welfare system would focus on anxieties about work and marriage rather than racialized economic inequality in a way that bore a striking resemblance to these attempts to control the transition from slavery to freedom.

Emancipation was simultaneously a moment of crisis in the existing social order and an opportunity for a different kind of life for people of African descent in the United States. However, freedom was not simply an abstract and universal state of being that the formerly enslaved entered after emancipation. Rather, the meaning of freedom had been constructed out of particular social relations, and as those social relations were transformed, the construct of freedom became a site of struggle. As Orlando Patterson argues, liberal ideas of freedom gained their meaning in and through slavery, defined as a social relation of domination characterized by the slave's social death and dishonored status.[22] In centering social death in the definition of slavery, Patterson highlights how slavery was more than a labor relation. Enslaved people were stripped of kinship and could not engage independently in legally recognized relationships with others. Therefore, after emancipation, state recognition and regulation of kinship became central to efforts to make freedpeople into potential citizens. However, while legal recognition of kinship offered protections for freedpeople in theory, the use of heteropatriarchal marriage as the hegemonic mechanism of defining kinship simultaneously narrowed the possible ways that freedom could be practiced and articulated citizenship to gender and sexual norms that were racialized as white.[23]

In the United States, slavery was constituted as a racial system, with Blackness coming to be both the legal and social marker of enslavability.[24] While emancipation brought the legal institution of slavery to an end, it did not undo the "fatal couplings of power and difference" that had legitimated the practice of slavery.[25] This was most evident in the way that the question of whether Black people possessed the capacity to be citizens animated Reconstruction policy. From the more explicitly racist conviction that Blackness signified an inherent deficiency in character to the more liberal position that the dehumanizing effects of slavery had trapped Black people in an immature state, the lingering association of Blackness with enslavability tarnished their capacity to be full citizens in the eyes of most white people. Notably, these racial anxieties were frequently articulated in the language of gender and sexuality. To become a citizen meant to adopt the heteronormative gender roles associated with citizenship, such as masculine independence and feminine dependency. As discussed throughout the following chapters, Blackness, with its associations with sexual and gender deviancy, presented a persistent barrier to this kind of assimilation.

Ultimately, because citizenship and freedom had been defined against slavery and Blackness had come to be the primary marker of slave status, emancipation presented something of a contradiction. What did it mean to be both Black and formally free when freedom had in many ways gained its meaning in opposition to Black existence? In the years following the Civil War, Black and white people grappled with this question both in their everyday practices and in their efforts to shape federal policy. Black communities crafted their own definitions of freedom that emphasized the importance of landownership, autonomy from whites, freedom of mobility, and the enjoyment of their lives, all of which had been denied them under slavery.[26] In practice, freedom was exercised in a multiplicity of ways. Among other things, freedpeople fought for the right to settle and cultivate their own lands, for greater community power through the vote, and for the right to move freely in search of family members they had been forcibly separated from or better prospects for their futures.[27] For freedwomen, freedom also offered the possibility of no longer working in the fields and instead directing their labor exclusively toward their own communities and families. While, as discussed in chapter 4, white onlookers often understood this practice as laziness or an ostentatious effort to "play the lady," these efforts represented an important challenge to the reproductive economy of slavery that had denied Black women access to ties with their children specifically and to the fruits of their reproductive labor more generally.[28] In addition, as Tera Hunter notes, freedpeople's visions of freedom were fundamentally structured by the desire to own one's own body; for Black women, the context of the sexual violence that had pervaded slavery made claims to control over and pleasure in one's own body all that much more significant.[29]

While in the short term Black communities realized some aspects of this broad vision of freedom, over time the terms of Black freedom became increasingly constrained. As W. E. B. Du Bois wrote of Reconstruction, "The slave went free; stood for a brief moment in the sun; then moved back again toward slavery."[30] The Freedmen's Bureau played a key role in shaping this transition, and the interconnected rubrics of free labor and domesticity were key elements through which the meaning of freedom was rearticulated. The Freedmen's Bureau had its origins in freedmen's aid societies, nongovernmental organizations founded to assist the newly emancipated. In response to the scale and scope of the social and economic crises that the Civil War wrought, Congress established the Freedmen's Bureau in March 1865 as a temporary division of the War Department with Major General Oliver Otis Howard as its first commissioner. The bureau was initially authorized to operate for one year and was allocated no specific funding. Eventually, its lifetime was extended to six years, and some federal funds were designated to support its operations. The bureau's temporary status and its location in the War Department reflected concerns about the potentially negative effects of federal paternalism toward freedpeople. These concerns were most frequently expressed as a belief that federal assistance to freedpeople would undermine their work ethic and as an anxiety that the bureau potentially represented an overreach of federal powers in relation to individual states. These institutional limitations were a serious challenge for bureau officials and had a profound effect on the way the bureau approached its mission. Because it initially had no independent funding, the bureau was highly dependent on the War Department. Its position within the War Department defined the bureau as a temporary military operation rather than a large-scale effort at redistribution or even relief provision. In addition, as part of the War Department, the bureau was subject to presidential oversight and control, a factor that proved to be a serious impediment during the Johnson administration.[31]

The bureau was charged with reestablishing order in the South and shepherding the transition out of slavery for freedpeople. What this actually meant, however, remained an area of great struggle over the course of the institution's life. The bureau's responsibilities included introducing a free labor system to the South, registering marriages, establishing schools, providing aid to the destitute, adjudicating disputes, and ensuring fair legal proceedings for freedpeople. While its formal title suggested that managing abandoned lands was within its purview, the question of land redistribution haunted the bureau's efforts. Freedpeople expected that the bureau would provide them with land, a promise that was never fulfilled. Initially, General Howard tried to allocate some confiscated Confederate lands to freedpeople, but these efforts were ultimately undermined by President Andrew Johnson's restoration of most Confederate land to its former owners. Johnson's vision of Reconstruction greatly undermined the potentially redistributive impacts of the bureau. Johnson not only vehemently opposed federal guarantees of rights for freedpeople but also sought to secure his own reelection by procuring favor with impoverished whites in the South while pardoning much of the Confederate elite. Johnson favored the quick reintegration of southern states into the union and supported southern states in their creation of Black Codes that excluded Black people from political participation, curtailed their mobility, confined them to highly exploitative labor conditions, and denied them basic civil rights. Johnson's overt racism combined with his direct oversight of the bureau curtailed the scope of bureau activities and set the South on a path toward Reconstruction that did not include a transformation in the racial order.

In February 1866, at the close of the bureau's first year, President Johnson vetoed a bill to extend the bureau's life. Johnson cited many of the same themes that would animate antiwelfare discourse in the late twentieth century as the rationale for his veto. These themes included the necessity for fiscal conservatism, fear at the prospect of a growing federal bureaucracy that might prove an obstacle to individual rights, and an insistence that self-help, not federal assistance, was the key to freedpeople's economic advancement.[32] Johnson argued that with the end of the war, an institution like the bureau was unconstitutional because it exceeded the legitimate peacetime powers of the federal government. In a twist of logic, he reframed the bureau as a threat to rather than a protector of civil rights. According to Johnson, for white citizens, the expansion of federal power threatened individual liberty. For freedpeople, however, the threat to freedom lay in pauperization. Johnson argued that the bureau would simply replace slaveholders as a new kind of master, thereby undermining the independence and self-sufficiency that characterized freedom. In Johnson's eyes, emancipation was over, and protection from the federal government was contrary to the ideals of freedom. Instead, freedpeople needed to work and support themselves without public assistance.[33] A direct assault on freedpeople's claims to reparations and land redistribution, Johnson's position reframed any form of federal assistance or intervention as a threat to the freedom and character of freedpeople.

However, just as Johnson was trying to dismantle the bureau, the proliferation of Black Codes and racial violence in the South that Johnson had sanctioned also produced an increased demand for federal intervention on behalf of Black people, both by freedpeople themselves and by Radical Republicans in the North. After much political struggle, the life of the bureau was extended in the summer of 1866, with Congress overriding Johnson's veto. At this point, Congress also allocated some funding to the bureau as part of an effort to exert more congressional power over Reconstruction. Radical Republicans supported a stronger role for the federal government in the protection of the rights of freedpeople. However, their vision of Reconstruction also excluded land redistribution, focusing instead on Reconstruction as a civic project. Grounded in a strong belief in free labor ideology and their own political objectives of Republicanizing the South, Radical Republicans saw the bureau as a tool for achieving civil and political equality. They sought to create a strong national state that would guarantee Black suffrage, civil rights, and equal economic opportunity within the confines of a free labor economy.[34] While in many ways Radical Republicans were more sympathetic to the plight of freedpeople than Johnson was, they also did not see the bureau's mission as redistributive and believed that public assistance was contrary to the goal of cultivating Republican ideals of citizenship. During the period of increased congressional control, the relief-provision activities of the bureau actually declined dramatically. As time passed, the bureau's mission became understood as less about ameliorating the effects of the economic devastation the war had wrought and more about cultivating economic independence and putting freedpeople back to work. The categories of people who were seen as deserving of assistance shrank dramatically, and by October 1866 only orphans, the elderly, the disabled, the sick, and family members of a Union solder remained eligible for bureau aid.[35]

The Freedmen's Bureau was a site of great conflict over the entirety of its life. Anxieties that the bureau paved the way for excessive federal power while providing special privileges to freedpeople at the expense of white taxpayers dramatically limited the scope of its activities. The bureau was always intended to be a temporary institution, and no permanent, freestanding institution was ever created to address the lasting injustices of slavery. When the bureau's operations ceased in 1872, Reconstruction remained incomplete. The growing power of the Ku Klux Klan in the South, the system of Black Codes designed to keep Black labor in its place, and the ascendancy of a sharecropping system signified that Reconstruction would give way to the reinvented regime of racial terror that was the Jim Crow South. Scholars from W. E. B. Du Bois to Angela Davis have noted the lasting consequences of Reconstruction's failures. The proliferation of Black Codes throughout the South rendered Black people criminals who through chain gangs and convict lease systems were put back to work in slavery-like conditions. Jim Crow segregation denied Black people access to public spaces and to the political and civil rights they had gained in the period immediately after the Civil War, thereby entrenching a racial dictatorship that would not be undone until the civil rights movement.[36] While connections have been made between the failed project of Reconstruction and the development of the modern criminal justice system or the persistence of racial segregation into the contemporary period, less attention has been paid to the ways that anxieties from the Reconstruction era continue to shape how public assistance is conceptualized.

While the bureau had many successes, most notably supporting the formation of public schools for Black communities in the South, and many freedpeople were able to use the service offered by the bureau to their own advantage, for histories of the welfare state the bureau is an early and powerful example of the ways the articulations of anti-Black racism and hegemonic constructions of gender and sexuality operated to eclipse class solidarity and undermine potentially redistributive practices. This project focuses specifically on two practices of the bureau that illustrate these articulations of race, gender, and sexuality particularly well, the promotion of both marriage and contractual labor relations. Relief provision was by far the most controversial part of the bureau's mission, and much like in the case of welfare reform, marriage and forced labor emerged as two primary strategies for enforcing state austerity. While the Freedmen's Bureau had little choice but to provide federal relief to the formerly enslaved given the devastation and massive dislocation produced by the war, this practice provoked anxieties about the possibilities of creating a class of people permanently dependent on government support. The idea that providing material assistance to Black people would promote "pauperization" and "demoralization" surfaced repeatedly in debates about the Freedmen's Bureau.[37] Based on the idea that real freedom required self-sufficiency and adherence to a masculine ideal of independence, the Freedmen's Bureau asserted that "no greater harm can be done to the negro, than supporting those who can support themselves."[38] Prefiguring twentieth-century neoliberal discourse about welfare reform, the Freedmen's Bureau defined its purpose as not to "create a race of paupers or to encourage idleness" but rather, as the Virginia Freedmen's Bureau's assistant commissioner, Orlando Brown, argued, "to make the Freedmen into a self-supporting class of free laborers, who shall understand the necessity of steady employment and the responsibility of providing for themselves and [their] families."[39]

Marriage figured centrally in bureau efforts to transform freedpeople into properly gendered citizens who were organized into self-sufficient households. Drawing on strains of abolitionist discourse that located the primary ills of slavery in the denial of the right to marriage, bureau officials emphasized the civilizing functions of marriage and saw entrance into the institution as a fundamental precondition of citizenship. As discussed in greater detail in chapter 3, bureau officers did far more than simply issue marriage certificates. They actively promoted marriage among freedpeople as part of their efforts to stamp out practices like living together, having multiple sexual relationships, and organizing kinship in ways that did not neatly align with the heteropatriarchal nuclear family. Bureau officials used marriage as a means of promoting both sexual discipline and stable, settled, self-sufficient household economies. They frequently held people to the legal terms of marriage and strongly encouraged freedpeople to take up the gendered roles and responsibilities associated with marriage, as these were intimately connected to gendered constructions of citizenship. Bureau officials strongly emphasized the need for freedmen to be independent heads of households who could provide for their dependents. In this way, marriage rationalized austerity and displaced claims for reparations by locating the blame for freedpeople's economic hardships not in the legacy of slavery but rather within the Black family. In sharp contrast to the welfare programs of the Progressive Era and New Deal, which invested resources in sustaining white families, marriage emerged as a mechanism of privatizing responsibility for Black communities' well-being. These practices sowed the seeds for the continued use of marriage as a scaffolding for the construction of a racially stratified welfare state in the twentieth century.

In addition to promoting marriage, the bureau also saw cultivating labor discipline as a key mechanism of promoting self-sufficiency. The bureau was charged with overseeing the transition to a free labor system in the South. As the possibilities for land redistribution were eclipsed, this increasingly meant that freedpeople were expected to enter contractual labor arrangements with white employers, often on the same plantations or under similar conditions to those in which they had been enslaved. The bureau encouraged entry into long-term labor contracts and supervised the execution of these contracts in southern states; coupled with vagrancy laws, the labor contract emerged as a key mechanism through which freedom became characterized by disciplined and responsible labor. Bureau officers emphasized the need for freedpeople to demonstrate their deservingness of freedom by showing the nation that they could abide by contracts and, in doing so, implicitly defined meaningful work as work that was visible, measurable, and controlled by white employers. Eliminating vagrancy—characterized as one of slavery's lingering effects—was central to the mission of the bureau, and cultivating freedom came to be defined as cultivating the self-disciplined worker who abided by a contract.

Despite the bureau's emphasis on marriage and the cultivation of gendered ideas of citizenship that emphasized female dependency and domestic confinement, bureau officers expected freedwomen to enter into labor contracts. This presented fundamental contradictions for freedwomen. On the one hand, they were expected to conform to feminine ideals of citizenship. On the other hand, when freedwomen attempted to redirect their labor toward their own families, they were accused of vagrancy or "playing the lady." Chapter 4 explores the role that domestic labor played in mediating these gendered contradictions. While the vast majority of labor contracts the bureau supervised were agricultural, the bureau also directed freedwomen to take up domestic work in white homes by enforcing domestic workers' contracts, creating industrial schools to train freedwomen in domestic skills, and transporting freedwomen north to regions where there was a high demand for domestic workers. Relatively neglected in the history of the bureau, the experiences of domestic workers both complicate liberal constructions of contractual freedom by drawing attention to the gendered nature of contracts and demonstrate how for Black women the subordinated domestic worker rather than the mother became a model of idealized feminine citizenship.

The bureau's emphasis on marriage and work reflected norms of gendered citizenship and beliefs that were shared by both its opponents and its supporters. While there was a vast range of political opinion among white people about the work of the Freedmen's Bureau, this project is primarily interested in the gendered definition of normative citizenship that these perspectives shared. As Katherine Franke has pointed out, "African Americans did not enter civil society on their own terms and accompanied by their own values, but rather did so on the non-negotiable terms set by the dominant culture."[40] Regardless of white people's position on the bureau, a central tenet of white political discourse was that freedpeople needed to adapt to dominant constructions of citizenship that fundamentally excluded them and not the other way around. While Radical Republicans and southern planters may have disagreed about freedpeople's capacities to assimilate to dominant norms, they both maintained the value of norms that had been constructed through white supremacist logics. In the eyes of the nation, if freedpeople were unsuccessful at becoming citizens, it would be because they themselves had failed, not because of the impossibility of the standards to which they were held.

Heteronormativity functioned as a linchpin of the nonnegotiable terms of citizenship in that it linked labor discipline, sexual discipline, and state austerity through the construct of the self-sufficient and stable household. The push toward both marriage and contractual labor relations can also be understood as a mechanism by which claims to redistribution and reparation were made unintelligible by relocating responsibility in the aftermath of slavery onto the shoulders of freedpeople themselves. This was a fundamental part of what Saidiya Hartman describes as the transition from "the pained and minimally sensate existence of the slave to the burdened individuality of the responsible and encumbered freedperson."[41] As Hartman argues, the emphasis on responsibility as the hallmark of liberal individuality erased the nation's responsibility for addressing the violence of slavery and the continued marginalization of Black people and instead required that freedpeople continually demonstrate their deservingness of freedom.[42] To be free came to mean to be responsible for oneself; in the words of Hartman, "fundamentally, to be responsible was to be blameworthy."[43] In this way, race structured the balance between citizenship's rights and responsibilities. White citizenship entitled one to liberties, protections, and material benefits, whereas Black citizenship was primarily understood as a question of fulfilling obligations and demonstrating deservingness. In interrogating the practices of the Freedmen's Bureau, this project argues that the heteronormative family has been a central mechanism for elaborating this racialized structure of citizenship.

Between Reconstruction and Welfare Reform

My objective in this project is not simply to revise already existing histories of the U.S. welfare state. Instead, in centering struggles over the meaning of citizenship for Black women, I seek to shrink the ideological distance between historical moments in order to illustrate how the unresolved problematic of incorporating Black people into institutions of citizenship that were constitutively defined against Blackness continued to haunt welfare politics in the late twentieth century. In thinking about the persistence of Black inequality in the United States, mainstream scholarship has adopted one of two stances. Scholars either locate the source of continued inequality in Black culture itself or suggest that social reforms to remedy racism have not gone far enough. In contrast, this project interrogates the construction of citizenship itself as a limit on the possibility of equality and freedom. As such, I do not so much look at how groups have been excluded from citizenship but instead seek to complicate the dichotomy between exclusion and inclusion.

The hegemonic narrative that casts slavery as in the past and the post–civil rights United States as a postracial society produces an ideological distance between the conflicts and contradictions that structured emancipation and the neoliberal restructuring of the U.S. welfare state at the end of the twentieth century. Building on an understanding of history that takes seriously how what Avery Gordon calls haunting troubles linear ideas of progress, this project draws attention to continuities in how anti-Black racism structures U.S. ideas of citizenship and belonging from Reconstruction into the present.[44] In particular, turning to the Reconstruction era suggests some of the ways that anti-Black racism inheres in the terms of liberal and neoliberal discourse and makes visible the racial history of what is often seen as a race-neutral vocabulary of citizenship. In addition to targeting Black women, welfare reform was an attack on immigrants, teenage parents, and in reality the entire working class. This project highlights both the specificity and expansiveness of anti-Black racism by showing how the racialized and gendered discourses about citizenship that developed in the postemancipatory moment were employed to cast an increasingly wide net of social stratification in the U.S. welfare state.

The analytic framework of this book is deeply indebted to M. Jacqui Alexander's use of the palimpsest as a metaphor for rethinking the relationship between historical moments. Alexander argues that modernity relies on a linear conception of time in order to produce an artificial division between the "then and there" and the "here and now."[45] These divisions construct present and past as mutually exclusive and locate racial difference as of a different space and time. Tied to the dichotomous construction of tradition and modernity that Alexander critiques, the idea of progress naturalizes a particular organization of space and time in which the West constructs itself as more advanced or forward in time compared to a Third World that is rendered as traditional, backward, and of the past. As discussed in greater detail in the next chapter, heteronormativity, a key signifier of civilization, plays an integral role in locating different racialized groups within this linear trajectory. In invoking the palimpsest, Alexander develops a methodological approach that "scrambles" hegemonic constructions of space and time in order to reveal the interconnectedness of historical moments and locations that are usually understood as distinct. By juxtaposing seemingly disparate events, this method highlights the imperfect erasures of racialized and gendered violence that link seemingly separate historical moments.[46]

In the U.S. context, slavery often functioned as the "then and there" of national history against which the "here and now" of multicultural, colorblind democracy of the late twentieth century was contrasted. For the United States to define itself as a modern, progressive global force, slavery had to be understood as a closed chapter in the nation's history. Both U.S. imperial projects abroad and domestic forms of settler colonialism and racial violence rely on a liberal narrative of racial progress that consigns slavery to a past that is over and done with, an artifact of a backward southern economy that was overcome by federal intervention and the modernizing forces of northern industry. In contrast, emancipation, understood as a monumental event in a march toward increasing equality, represents a victory of liberal democratic ideals over a tarnished past. This understanding rewrites national history such that slavery is represented as inconsistent with the nation's constitutional values, and emancipation is seen as a step toward actualizing the founding vision of a nation built on freedom, equality, and democracy. This historical narrative not only obscures slavery's continued centrality to the building of the U.S. nation but also naturalizes a linear idea of progress that places racism in the past. Rather than seeing emancipation as the end of slavery, it is better understood as a transition between different modes of subjection or as marking the beginning of what Hartman calls the "afterlife of slavery." Hartman describes the afterlife of slavery as the continued effects of the "ranking of life" that slavery instituted, "skewed life chances, limited access to health and education, premature death, incarceration, and impoverishment."[47] These effects are understood not just as a legacy of slavery but rather as a continuing system of anti-Black racism grounded in the same systems of knowledge and power that enabled slavery. The afterlife of slavery is an ongoing production, and this book highlights welfare policy as one significant site in that production.

This project is particularly concerned with the role the heteronormative family plays in the afterlife of slavery. Notably, there has been a sociological and political fixation on the Black family in efforts to understand the persistence of Black inequality in the United States. Surfacing both in Reconstruction-era debates about Black people's capacity for citizenship and in late twentieth-century efforts to explain Black economic inequality, discourses about the dysfunctionality of the Black family have a central place in public discussion of racial difference. Liberals of both these periods held that one of slavery's primary harms was that it kept Black people from developing heteronormative families; they argued that nonnormative Black genders and sexualities were signs of the damage that slavery had wrought on the Black psyche. Seen as backward compared to the dichotomously gendered, liberal, free subject, Black nonnormative genders and sexualities became a sign of Black bodies' former enslavability. Structural inequality attached itself to the Black body and became understood not as an external oppressive force but rather as inhering within the body itself, most notably in the ways that gender and sexuality were embodied. In this way, the Black body can be seen as a kind of palimpsest inasmuch as the imperfect erasures of the slavery system shape how that body is read within the dominant consciousness. For example, the image of the welfare queen reiterated the optics of slavery and its immediate aftermath in its construction of Black female welfare recipients as overly sexual, emasculating, unfeminine, undisciplined, and needing to be controlled. Indeed, both Reconstruction-era discourse and the assault on the welfare system in the late twentieth century consistently pathologized individuals for trying to survive amid tremendous structural violence, and this pathologiza-tion was most frequently articulated in the language of gender and sexu-ality. In both cases, heteronormativity functioned as a way of privatizing inequality and reiterating individual responsibility in a context in which Blackness marked one as undeserving of assistance and perpetually in need of reform.

Methodologically, recognizing these intricate relationships between distant historical moments offers an important challenge for history, a dis-cipline that rests on and reproduces a naturalized, linear organization of time. The very distinctiveness of history as a discipline lies in an under-standing of the past as over, knowable in the present only through a process of excavation. Central to nation-building projects, history erects borders around national identity as well as between past and present. By troubling these borders, this project seeks to dislodge liberal narratives of progress as an organizing principle of U.S. history. My point in drawing attention to the relationship between these different moments is not so much to simply assert their similarity but rather to engage in a historical analysis that makes visible the ways in which the ideological landscape of welfare politics has been animated by the afterlife of slavery.

This book asks how the incomplete project of Reconstruction shaped the categories that were deployed in the restructuring of the welfare state at the end of the twentieth century. Rather than look at history as a linear progression of events, I approach history in terms of shifting terrains of possibility, asking how past social relations structure the possibilities that materialize in the present. In approaching history from this vantage point, I focus on the ways in which struggles to regulate the genders and sexu-alities of freedpeople circumscribe the meanings of citizenship in more recent years. As such, this project is centrally concerned with language. As Stuart Hall argues, "Language is the medium *par excellence* through which things are 'represented' in thought and thus the medium in which ideology is generated and transformed."[48] In other words, the language of citizenship employed during these periods enabled certain interpretations of social relations and foreclosed others. In turning to the Reconstruction era, this project asks how the language of citizenship upholds racial and gender stratification even as it is the primary language through which ideas of equality and freedom are articulated. This is particularly relevant in the context of color-blind discourse as it makes visible the ways in which race and gender live in the terms the state uses even when those terms actively obscure their racialized and gendered histories.

This project also gestures toward the possibilities that were not realized in the Reconstruction era by highlighting abject figures of freedom. Ways of embodying freedom that exceeded the confines of liberal terms have largely been written out of the archive, yet, I argue, these figures still haunt the political scene. In turning to the archive, I am interested both in the processes by which a particular vision of heteronormative, liberal personhood became naturalized as the ends of emancipation and in the traces of queer figures that this vision rendered ghostly. Following Anjali Arondekar's injunction that our approach to the archive move from "fact-finding" to "fact-reading," I view the archive not as a repository of information but rather as an active force that structures narratives of national belonging and normative personhood.[49] As Arondekar writes, "The possibility of such readings lies in productively juxtaposing the archive's fiction effects (the archive as a system of representation) alongside its truth effects (the archive as material with 'real' consequences)—not as incommensurate, but as antagonistically constitutive of each other."[50] Particularly with regard to the national archive, I take this to mean that rather than approach the archive as either being a repository of truth or telling just one story among many others, it is necessary to recognize the archive as producing narratives that carry the material force of state power. Throughout this project, therefore, I am less concerned with discovering what really happened than with understanding how a particular interpretation of social relations came to have the power to constitute the real. In addition, I am interested in the experiences and social phenomena that cannot be encapsulated by that interpretation. Understanding what is not there to be as important as what is there in the archive, this project asks how evidence is constituted as such and how we account for the experiences that the construct of evidence excludes.

Relying on archival sources presents particular challenges for understanding and representing the agency of freedpeople in the face of the structural obstacles that were placed between them and citizenship rights. As the available records recount history from the perspective of state officials, they offer only a distorted view of freedpeople's agency and the forms of resistance they may have practiced in response to efforts to limit the meaning of freedom. However, while it is difficult to reconstruct a coherent story of freedpeople's agency from the archive, I argue throughout the book that the Freedmen's Bureau's efforts to promote marriage and work must be understood as a response to freedpeople's desires and efforts to direct their energies elsewhere. Taking up Saba Mahmood's caution that agency not be conflated with resistance but rather be understood "within the grammar of concepts within which it resides," I argue that the effort to make freedpeople into proper liberal subjects was an effort to constitute their agency in ways that could be more easily controlled by the state.[51] Rather than view figures like the vagrant and the welfare queen as simply resistant, I argue that they make visible ways of practicing agency that do not align with liberal subjectivity. Efforts to criminalize vagrancy operated by framing vagrancy as a vestige of slavery that was contrary to freedom. These efforts might be understood as trying to erase the possibility of alternate conceptions of desire, subjectivity, personhood, and freedom altogether.

The vast majority of my research is drawn from the archives of the Bureau of Refugees, Freedmen, and Abandoned Lands contained within the U.S. National Archives. The collections contain bureaucratic records of everyday activities as well as reports and reflections from bureau officers, marriage and labor contracts issued by the bureau, and records of disputes between freedpeople and white Southerners that the bureau mediated. These records primarily catalog the perceptions and investments of bureau officials in relation to the bureau's larger mission, restoring order in the South and integrating freedpeople into systems of free labor and gendered constructions of citizenship. The narrative that emerges from these records resonates strongly with national investments in the idea of racial progress and obscures the complex ways in which racial structures of domination were reinvented rather than destroyed in the post–Civil War era. These records make visible the processes through which heteronormativity was produced as a mechanism by which freedpeople were incorporated into citizenship in subordinating ways and as a means of naturalizing state power. They show how liberal constructions of freedom were naturalized and how other ways of expressing freedom were erased by naming them as something else, such as vagrancy, crime, sexual deviancy, or vestiges of an enslaved past.

While these records offer useful insights into the relationship between state building and the construction of the heteronormative family as a basis for citizenship, they provide very little information about how freedpeople actually experienced the bureau's practices and understood its work in the transition from slavery to freedom. Because the records tell the story entirely from the perspective of the state, it is important to recognize and explore this absence as an important site of knowledge. By drawing attention to this absence, this project seeks to denaturalize the state's story as the only story and instead highlight traces of other narratives that the archive actively obscures. Rather than attempt to retrieve marginalized experiences from the archive, a process that invariably reproduces the terms and constraints of dominant discourse, I seek instead to show how state institutions work to realize certain possibilities and erase others. Exploring the absences of the archive points us to a consideration of the possibilities of a particular historical moment that remained unrealized. The hope is that engagement with these foreclosed historical possibilities might spur a broader imagination of the possibilities available in the present.

Overview of Chapters

This book moves between two historical moments in order to make visible the relationship between them. For this reason, it is not a purely chronological history but rather a historical excavation of discourses about work and marriage that developed in the Reconstruction era and that continue to haunt the late twentieth century. The next chapter elaborates the theoretical arguments that frame the book by establishing the ways that state power and the heteronormative family are mutually constitutive. I focus on three different aspects of the relationship between the state and family. First, I examine how familial metaphors ground state sovereignty by offering a model of "hierarchy within unity."[52] Pointing to the ways that the state models itself after the family, I show how naturalizing the heteropatriarchal family simultaneously naturalizes the state and vice versa. Second, I look at how the heteronormative family operates as a tool of conquest that links Native genocide and the dehumanization of Black people. Locating the welfare state as a structure of settler colonialism, I argue that the policing of vagrancy emerges as an effort to suppress forms of Black freedom that challenged settler ways of life. Finally, building on Black feminist theorizations of domesticity, I challenge the liberal constructions of public and private as separate spheres. Instead, I note the ways that the boundary between public and private is dynamic and shaped by racial as well as gender hierarchies. Pointing to the different ways that private and public have been constructed in relation to different populations, I argue that the production of a boundary between the two is constitutive of state power.

Chapters 3 and 4 form the heart of the book. Drawing on original archival research about the Freedmen's Bureau, these chapters document the bureau's efforts to contain Black freedom through marriage promotion and forced labor. Chapter 3 looks specifically at the role that marriage played in the transition from slavery to freedom. For whites, marriage grounded masculine citizenship in ideas of independence and privacy that were the basis for claims to political rights while, at the same time, defining women's citizenship through ideas of dependency and domesticity that warranted both subordination and protection. In contrast, this chapter argues that, for freedpeople, marriage and gendered constructions of citizenship became the basis for privatizing responsibility for the lasting harms of slavery, enforcing economic and social obligations, and rationalizing public surveillance. By linking African American citizenship to heteronormativity, marriage erased other ways of organizing kinship and practicing sexuality. Alternative sexualities became understood not just as deviant but as a residue of slavery that could not be contemporaneous with the free subject, a theme that would resurface virulently in the antiwelfare discourse of the late twentieth century. Much as in welfare reform, bureau officers saw marriage as a means of combating vagrancy in that it promoted settlement as the norm, emphasized the importance of moral reform, and shifted financial responsibility for the well-being of freedpeople from the federal government onto male heads of household. For freedwomen, the emphasis on adhering to domestic norms that accompanied the push toward marriage was often in blatant contradiction with the demand that they work outside the home. Given these contradictions, gendered citizenship did not serve as a basis for protection but rather positioned freedwomen as perpetually in need of reform. The chapter concludes by turning to examples of freedwomen who refused or subverted the institution of marriage to elucidate alternative understandings of belonging, kinship, and domestic space that existed among freedpeople.

Chapter 4 delves deeper into the contradictions that gendered ideas of citizenship produced for freedwomen by focusing on the domestic worker as a central figure through which Black women's citizenship was defined during the Reconstruction era. In locating the welfare state's origins in Progressive Era maternalist movements, feminist scholarship has emphasized the centrality of motherhood to gendered constructions of citizenship. In contrast, Freedmen's Bureau officials frequently viewed freedwomen's efforts to withdraw from the labor force and direct their labor toward their own families as indulgence, laziness, and an effort to "play the lady." In this context, the chapter argues that the figure of the domestic worker played a key role in mediating the contradictions inherent in gendered ideas of citizenship that idealized domesticity in a context where freedwomen were still forced to work outside the home. Analyzing long-term labor contracts for domestic workers that were registered with the bureau in the South as well as bureau efforts to recruit and train freedwomen to serve as domestic workers in northern cities, the chapter shows how domestic work was framed not just as an economic opportunity but also as a mechanism for instilling normative sexuality, cultivating the desired qualities of female citizens, and preserving the nation. Frequently contrasted with the vagrant figure of the prostitute, the domestic worker offered a model of feminine citizenship that invoked the cultural characteristics of motherhood without a simultaneous regard for the well-being of Black children.

The final chapter of the book explores how the discourses and state practices developed to contain vagrancy in the Reconstruction era haunt twentieth-century welfare history. The chapter begins by reading the history of the Progressive Era, the New Deal, and the welfare rights movement in relation to the history detailed in chapters 3 and 4. I argue that juxtaposing the practices of the Freedmen's Bureau with the welfare state that emerged in the twentieth century reveals the ways that the heteronormative family has functioned to secure racial inequality. While during Reconstruction the family was a mechanism of privatizing responsibility for Black families, welfare programs that were designed to cultivate and serve white families offered state support. As welfare rights organizing challenged racial barriers and won greater access to AFDC for Black women, public sentiment toward welfare receipt shifted. In the post–civil rights era, anxieties about Black citizenship from the Reconstruction era resurfaced, and the vagrant reemerged in the figure of the welfare queen, as a threat to be contained. Like the Freedmen's Bureau before it, welfare reform posited marriage promotion and forced labor as a pathway from the dependency of welfare receipt to independence and full liberal personhood. Similar to the figure of the domestic worker during the Reconstruction era, the workfare worker invoked gendered ideas of citizenship grounded in motherhood while directing women's labor away from the care of their own children. Demonstrating the lingering afterlife of the racially stratified concepts of citizenship forged during Reconstruction, the chapter highlights the ways that the language of gender and sexuality continued to signify racial difference despite the formal color blindness of antiwelfare discourse.

TWO

Making State, Making Family

Throughout this book I consider the vagrant and the welfare queen as queer figures that make visible the centrality of racialized heteronormativity to the development of the U.S. welfare state. Strikingly similar, these two figures linked racialized fears of moral degeneracy, anxieties about gender and sexual normativity, and a desire to manage populations through the cultivation of settled and privatized families. While the vagrant and the welfare queen were fictions that bore little resemblance to the actual lived experiences of freedpeople in the late nineteenth century or welfare recipients in the late twentieth century, these narratives hyperbolized the anxieties these groups provoked in the national imagination and mobilized them toward a reconfiguration of state power. As such, they offer a useful starting point for thinking about the ways that anti-Blackness and heteronormativity have been articulated in the development of the welfare state. In invoking the term *queer*, my intention is not to ascribe a queer identity to the populations that these figures ostensibly represent in an ahistorical or decontextualized way. I am not suggesting that people labeled as vagrants and welfare queens necessarily identified themselves as queer or that in the Reconstruction era *queer* even functioned as a category in the way it does today. Rather, I use the term *queer* to describe a mode of analysis that I believe is particularly generative for theorizing the operations of the welfare state. This mode of analysis is grounded in and builds on key insights that have emerged specifically from Black feminist, Black queer, and queer of color critique.

Domestic Contradictions is particularly indebted to Cathy Cohen's rethinking of the subject of queer studies and queer politics in her groundbreaking essay "Punks, Bulldaggers, and Welfare Queens." Cohen critiques how "queer politics has served to reinforce simple dichotomies between heterosexual and everything 'queer,'" arguing that these simple dichoto-mies derive from the privileging of the experiences of those for whom sexu-ality was the primary and often exclusive site of nonnormativity.[1] Drawing on the work of other Black feminist scholars, Cohen emphasizes how het-eronormativity functions as a structure of power that links race, gender, class, and sexuality and argues that the radical potential of the term *queer* lies in the possibility of forging coalitions among the multiple populations that heteronormativity marginalizes. Cohen highlights the welfare queen as a particularly powerful example of a figure who embodies sexual devi-ance despite her ostensible heterosexuality and in doing so makes visible the role heteronormativity plays in securing oppression based on gender, race, sex, and class simultaneously. Drawing attention to the long history of pathologizing and criminalizing Black family forms and Black expressions of gender, Cohen points to the ways that Blackness is cast as a form of gen-der and sexual deviance. Given that promoting the heteronormative family has been an anchor of U.S. welfare policy since its inception and that pub-lic discourse about poverty and public assistance is frequently expressed through the language of gender and sexuality, Cohen's understanding of *queer* firmly locates welfare politics within the terrain of queer politics. For Cohen, a queer analysis is not just about recognizing and expanding sexual diversity and freedom. Rather, queerness challenges heteronormativity as a structure of power and signifies a coalitional politics that aims to dismantle the multiple forms of oppression that heteronormativity secures.

By drawing attention to the ways that the making of the heteronorma-tive family as natural fact is interwoven with the production of state power, this project points to how figures like the vagrant and the welfare queen potentially destabilize or "make strange" the normative ways of being and uneven distributions of life chances promoted by the welfare state.[2] This deconstructive project simultaneously seeks to turn attention toward what José Esteban Muñoz describes as a queer horizon of possibility. As Muñoz writes, "Queerness in its utopian connotations promises a human that is not yet here, thus disrupting any ossified understanding of the human."[3] Both the state and the family are central to the constitution and normaliza-tion of liberal subjectivity, and one of the central purposes of settled domes-ticity has been to cultivate and universalize particular forms of gendered humanity.[4] Therefore, the vagrant and the welfare queen do queer work in their respective historical moments not just because they are signs of sex-ual deviance but because they challenge the naturalization of state power, heteropatriarchal families, and liberal subjectivity that has been central to citizenship and governance in the United States. These figures, which both emerged in moments of intense racial retrenchment, make visible how gender and sexuality have been deployed to estrange Blackness from citizenship rights and have subversive potential in that they suggest ways of being that exceed the constraints of the heteronormative family and liberal constructions of citizenship. The virulence with which vagrancy and welfare fraud have been policed indicates just how threatening these alternate possibilities have been to the dominant order.

Finally, this project is queer in the sense that it denaturalizes a tendency to view gender, race, class, and sexuality as separate and instead focuses on understanding their interconnections within a particular social formation. While most histories of the welfare state have looked at its racial, capitalist, and heteropatriarchal dimensions in isolation, this project, building on Roderick Ferguson's framework of queer of color critique, refuses these ideologies of discreteness. Rather, as Ferguson writes, "Queer of color analysis . . . opts instead for an understanding of nation and capital as the outcome of manifold intersections that contradict the idea of the liberal nation-state and capital as sites of resolution, perfection, progress, and confirmation."[5] Ferguson's framework highlights that not only are race, nation, capital, gender, and sexuality inseparable, but the relationships among these structures of power are coconstitutive, converging, and also at times in contradiction with each other. For example, Ferguson notes the way that capital's demand for an exploitable labor force produced a kind of diversity that was in tension with a white supremacist vision of national identity. These tensions became understood through the production of racial difference, which depended on the construction of people of color as having deviant genders and sexualities.[6] In the cases examined in this book, the incorporation of formerly enslaved people into citizenship produced contradictions between the gendered ideals that organized liberal personhood and the settler colonial and anti-Black foundations of the nation. Figures like the vagrant and the welfare queen emerged out of these contradictions, and the anxieties they provoked both shored up the heteronormative family and elicited significant moments of state building.

This chapter examines the relationship between the production of state power and the production of the heteronormative family, arguing that figures like the vagrant and the welfare queen make visible a mutually constitutive relationship between state power and racialized heteronormativity that is central to the constitution and regulation of multiple forms of difference. I highlight the processes through which state building and the naturalization of the heteronormative family have been intertwined, showing how discourses about the natural family legitimate and reinforce the expansion of state power, while state practices simultaneously entrench the family as a naturalized way of organizing kinship, gender, labor, and race. This reciprocal relationship not only enables tremendous stratification in the allocation of the rights, resources, and responsibilities of citizenship but also situates the family as a key scale at which the contradictions that might emerge between racialized, heteropatriarchal, and capitalist interests become apparent.

In my analysis, I take the state to be a historically specific way of organizing governance that developed in western Europe and was universalized through processes of colonialism. What distinguishes the state, which is neither natural nor universal, from other forms of political organization is its recognized sovereignty over a bounded territory and its "monopoly of the legitimate use of violence" within the borders of that territory.[7] In addition to repression and the direct exercise of violence, state power is also productive, invested in the constitution of subjectivities and populations.[8] The state consists of a collection of institutions, agents, discourses, and practices and is not a singular actor or thing despite a semblance of unity. While liberal theories position the state as a neutral arbitrator of conflict, the state is produced through and invested in maintaining social hierarchies. However, the state's interests are neither identical to those of dominant groups nor distinct from them. Rather, the state has relative autonomy, which requires balancing investments in maintaining multiple structures of domination and securing the state's own legitimacy in a democratic society.[9] While the state is not a singular entity from which power emanates, the accumulation of discourses, technologies, and practices that makes up state power produces the semblance of the state as a concrete, unified agent. Therefore, it is important to consider not only how the state brings together white supremacist, heteropatriarchal, capitalist interests in a particular moment but also how the state maintains its own coherence and legitimacy when these interests diverge or are in tension with each other. The capacity to appear as above and encompassing of society is central to legitimizing state power, and the ability to present an appearance of unity and coherence despite internal tensions and nebulous, pervasive, and diverse localized practices is a distinctive feature of the state.[10]

Like the state, the heteronormative family is a ubiquitous and familiar presence in political discourse whose role can be difficult to define. Within liberal political theory, the heteropatriarchal family is understood as a private sphere in contrast to the public realm of the state. However, despite this veneer of privacy, the family operates as a construction through which politics is waged. Nineteenth-century discourses about domesticity and late twentieth-century discourses about family values both mobilized a particular representation of the family in an effort to distribute power and resources along racial, gendered, class, and national lines. Building on Michael Omi and Howard Winant's concept of the racial project, a framework that emphasizes the way representations are linked to struggles over resources centers the question of what work the family does within a given political landscape.[11] In turning to two interconnected moments in the history of the U.S. welfare state, this project highlights the different ways the family operates to naturalize state power.

Building on feminist and antiracist scholarship on the U.S. welfare state, I argue that the family is not just a site of state regulation but rather is actively produced by and productive of state power. The family's capacity to link different kinds of differences is key to these operations. As Patricia Hill Collins has argued, the traditional family ideal has been a "privileged exemplar of intersectionality" in that it links race, gender, class, sexuality, and nation in multiple ways.[12] Not only do discourses about the family naturalize heteropatriarchal relationships within the home, but the family is simultaneously embedded within a constellation of ideas about race, civilization, settlement, a sexual division of labor, citizenship roles, and national identity. In this way, the traditional family functions as a linchpin for many interlinked and coconstitutive forms of structural oppression. While the term *intersectionality* circulates differently in different contexts, in this project I adopt Grace Kyungwon Hong's definition of intersectional analysis as "an analytic mode that does not privilege one site of identification over another, but insists on the importance of race, class, gender, and sexuality as interlocking and mutually constitutive."[13] In Hong's formulation, intersectionality is not an area of study but rather a methodological approach or "a reading practice, a 'way of making sense of' that reveals the contradictions of the racialized and gendered state."[14]

The remainder of this chapter lays out a theoretical framework for understanding the relationship between the production of state power and the naturalization of the heteronormative family. I focus on three aspects of this relationship that are particularly significant to understanding the historical examples presented in later chapters. While these aspects overlap and in many ways are inseparable in the historical cases considered, I distinguish them here to clarify the ways in which the heteronormative family and state power are mutually constitutive. I begin by examining how familial metaphors ground state sovereignty, national identity, and citizenship roles by offering a model of social organization grounded in both hierarchy and unity. Next, I look at the role the heteronormative family plays in securing relations of conquest that are fundamental to the development and reproduction of the settler colonial state. While settler colonialism is often neglected within theories of the welfare state, I argue that centering it as a structure grounded in both Native genocide and slavery complicates the idea of population that emerges from biopolitical understandings of the relationship between the welfare state and the heteronormative family. Third, I explore the shifting boundaries between state and family through the theoretical lens of the public-private divide. Drawing on Black feminist theorizations that show the contingent and constructed nature of this boundary, I point to the ways that the public-private divide is not a limit on state power but rather is constitutive of it. Critically examining the relationship between state power and the heteronormative family makes visible the ways that the family operates as a vehicle that enables the state to establish an appearance of unity and coherence while navigating interests that sometimes diverge. The contradictions that emerge from the state's simultaneous investment in multiple structures of domination are displaced onto the scale of the family, a move that is key to maintaining state legitimacy. In my historical analysis of the figures of the vagrant and the welfare queen in the chapters that follow, I build on the theoretical framework developed here to suggest that these constructions reveal the actual tenuousness of the seemingly natural and stable relationship between state and family. Because the vagrant and the welfare queen refuse the basic presumptions that underwrite this relationship, they operate as queer threats that potentially destabilize racialized heteronormativity and the different modalities of state power that sustain and are sustained by it.

Naturalizing Hierarchy

The first aspect of the relationship between state and family that I consider is the way that familial metaphors ground the construction of state sovereignty, national culture, and citizenship roles. These constructions deploy the family as a template for state power while actively producing and reinforcing the heteropatriarchal family as a model of natural hierarchy. Anne McClintock argues that as a signifier of "hierarchy within unity," the family has been a powerful trope for sanctioning inequality. She notes that "because the subordination of woman to man and child to adult were deemed natural facts, other forms of social hierarchy could be depicted in familial terms to guarantee social *difference* as a category of nature."[15] The family plays a unique role in reconciling hierarchical power relationships between its members with an ostensible unity of interests. The subordination of women and children, as well as enslaved people and free domestic workers, as discussed in later chapters, is understood not only as a natural fact but as in the shared best interests of the family as a whole. In this way, the heteropatriarchal family serves as a reference point for the constitution of state power and national identity. The state can function as a family, hierarchically organized for the benefit of all. At the same time, this use of familial metaphors to naturalize state power reiterates the naturalness of the family, thereby enabling policy and practices that promote heteropatriarchal family formation and the elimination of alternative ways of organizing kinship.

Familial metaphors are central to dominant constructions of state sovereignty. Like the patriarch of a household, the state takes on the role of both protector and unquestioned authority within a territory. Just as a patriarch exercises absolute dominion over a household, the state exercises absolute sovereignty over its territory, and it is the naturalization of patriarchal forms of domination within the family that legitimates this exercise. As Wendy Brown notes, the prerogative powers of the state are both modeled after the patriarchal family and secured through a promise that every man will continue to be "king in his own castle," thereby entrenching the patriarch's monopoly on legitimate violence within the home while establishing the state's monopoly on legitimate violence within a territory.[16] In both cases, hierarchical social relations are understood as emanating from a unity of interests. While the patriarch might wield violence within the family, he also represents the entire family unit within the political sphere. Similarly, the state's capacity for unchecked violence derives from the idea that it is a singular representative of the will of the people.

One example of how familial metaphors are employed to establish state authority in the United States is the frequently invoked language of "founding fathers" to describe the authors of the Constitution. This metaphor constructs the will of the father as the basis of sovereignty and the foundation of law. Literally positioning the citizenry as children who must obey the law as they would obey a father, the metaphor invokes familial bonds to constitute unity and identification with the state despite this hierarchical relation. Notably, the founding fathers metaphor is frequently invoked when questions arise about the future path of the nation as a way of looking to the past in order to chart a way forward. Both in the realm of constitutional interpretation and in cultural politics, the argument that an idea aligns with what the founding fathers would have wanted is used as evidence that it is good for the nation as a whole, even though the authors of the Constitution sanctioned slavery, the genocide of Native people, and the exclusion of women from political and economic life. In this way, the language of founding fathers functions to constitute the interests of white men as the interests of the nation as a whole while simultaneously reinscribing racial and gender hierarchies.

Familial metaphors have also been significant in defining and differentiating citizenship roles. Reference to the heteropatriarchal family as a natural organization of gender, sexuality, and kinship has had the effect of naturalizing hierarchies within the nation-state. Gendered roles within the family formed the basis for gendered roles within the nation. The heteropatriarchal family constructs binary gender and a sexual division of labor as natural, situating men and women as fundamentally different and embodying complementary but unequal positions. Men are figured as independent heads of households, decision-makers, and providers who engage in economic and political life, whereas women are understood to be dependent caretakers and nurturers who tend to the domestic sphere. Constructed as biological nature, these familial roles become the basis for gendered constructions of citizenship and national belonging. Whereas masculine citizenship is defined through rights and entitlements that enable men to be independent actors in civil society, feminine citizenship is defined through women's roles as mothers and reproducers of the nation. For the first part of the U.S. nation's history, all women were excluded from political participation, and in the early twentieth century the case for some women's inclusion was often based on their status as mothers and the moral force associated with domesticity. Maternalist movements that grounded political claims on behalf of women in motherhood were central to the construction of the U.S. welfare state. These movements argued for protective labor legislation for women and pensions for single mothers on the grounds that the nation's future depended on the work that mothers did to raise the next generation of citizens. While often successful in securing resources for some women, these efforts also reiterated hierarchy within unity by tying women's citizenship to their subordinated status as mothers. Rights or protections for women were not to guarantee their own individual well-being but rather to guarantee the health of their children and the future of the nation. As a result, women whose actions did not align with dominant gender norms were required to modify their behavior to receive benefits or were excluded from them entirely.

The heteropatriarchal family not only formed the basis for stratified forms of gendered citizenship but also offered a metaphor for reconciling racial inequality with the values of national unity. Patricia Hill Collins notes that "racial inequality becomes explained using family roles," with people of color often being positioned as undeveloped children while white people are understood as mature, complete adults.[17] Historically, this is evident in the discourses that rationalized slavery by arguing that it was part of a civilizing mission that served the best interests of Black people. While legally treated as property, enslaved people were often conceptualized as dependents within the slave owner's household.[18] This understanding rewrote slavery as like the care of children in that it provided for the enslaved's material need for food and shelter and their moral need for labor discipline. While these discourses were challenged, infantilization remains a key mechanism for constructing racial difference. For example, in the late twentieth century, representations like the welfare queen cast Black women as having a childlike inability to control themselves that led to pathological dependency, and federal welfare programs were often likened to poor parenting that supported indulgent behavior. Antiwelfare activists suggested that instead the state needed to take a more disciplinary approach of forcing welfare recipients to grow up and become responsible citizens by requiring that they work.

Collins observes that, in addition to enabling stratification in how the rights and obligations of citizenship are allocated, familial metaphors also shape who is viewed as contributing to the nation.[19] In the heteropatriarchal family, men are understood to be the primary providers, while women's labor often remains invisible. Children are viewed as being provided for but not necessarily as contributing materially to the well-being of the family. It is easy to draw parallels to how race and gender structure how different groups' contributions to the nation are measured. For example, white men's contributions are rarely if ever challenged. They are seen as the makers of the nation and the unquestioned drivers of political and economic life in the present. In contrast, while some women may gain social recognition as mothers, the feminized labor of reproduction is often undervalued or erased entirely. Finally, people of color are often viewed as using the resources of the nation without giving anything back. For example, in discourse about welfare, an ostensibly white taxpayer who contributes their fair share is contrasted with an ostensibly Black or immigrant welfare recipient who simply takes. These deeply entrenched ideas about who can be a contributor are also reflected in the way that the centrality of enslaved labor to the building of the nation or the U.S. economy's dependence on immigrant labor are conveniently ignored in national discourse.

Historically, programs like mothers' pensions and AFDC were both modeled on and designed to reinforce the heteropatriarchal family. Maternalist social movements built a case for these programs by arguing that single motherhood was a threat to future citizens and envisioned that the state would take up the role of patriarch within families where a male head of household was absent. They saw the state as providing for, protecting, and regulating single mothers within the confines of the home. In this way, maternalist social welfare policy constituted new forms of state power by naturalizing the heteropatriarchal family and the gendered hierarchies that structured it. As a result, the relationship the welfare state cultivates with subjects often mirrors hierarchical relations within the family. National Welfare Rights Organization leader Johnnie Tillmon drew attention to this dynamic in her 1972 essay about the experiences of women on welfare in which she observed, "The truth is that AFDC is like a super-sexist marriage. You trade in *a* man for *the* man."[20] Noting how the welfare state controlled how women spent their money, invaded their privacy, and regulated their sexuality, Tillmon drew strong parallels between the welfare state and a domineering husband. In making this comparison, Tillmon illustrates how being on welfare feels like being in an abusive relationship, thereby highlighting how the patriarchal hierarchy within the family functioned as a model for how welfare institutions treated their clients.[21]

Although the heteropatriarchal family appears as natural within nationalist discourse, the state does a great deal to produce this appearance. The policies and practices discussed throughout this book demonstrate how the state both actively cultivates a particular family form and seeks to eliminate alternatives. For example, as discussed in the next chapter, when freedpeople entered into citizenship, they were forced to define their family relationships through the heteropatriarchal family. These practices had the effect of erasing other ways of organizing kinship and thereby naturalizing and universalizing the heteropatriarchal family. In addition, the unequal status given to freedmen and freedwomen by the federal government produced or at the very least exacerbated inequalities within the Black community. Ways of being and relating to others that did not conform to heteronormativity were criminalized as vagrancy. Understood as the remnants of the damage wrought by slavery, nonheteronormative genders, sexualities, and kinship among freedpeople were thought of as an anterior state to civilization, and their proliferation was linked to a threat of national degeneracy that needed to be contained. Similarly, in the late twentieth century, the idea that AFDC undermined the heteropatriarchal family constituted it as a threat to the well-being of the nation itself. Anti-welfare discourse claimed that restoring family values was key to restoring the health of the nation. As discussed in chapter 5, the discourse of family values thus deployed familial metaphors to reinforce social hierarchies as in the continued unified interests of the nation-state.

Heteronormativity, Settlement, and the Welfare State

In this section I turn to the specific historical relationship that has developed between the heteronormative family and state power in the context of settler colonial and anti-Black violence in the United States. Drawing on scholarship from indigenous, Black, and queer of color studies, my analysis situates welfare history in relation to the state's mandate to naturalize and perpetuate the genocide of Native peoples. First, I establish that heteronormativity has been central to the establishment and continuation of a settler colonial state and that state efforts to cultivate the heteronormative family must be understood as part of a project of naturalizing settlement and genocidal violence. Settler colonialism has largely been disregarded in theories of the welfare state. While a more elaborated history of the treatment of Native people in welfare policy is beyond the scope of this project, I contend that the heteronormative imperatives that structure the welfare state must be understood in relation to the imperative to cultivate a settler population and eliminate life that does not align with settler norms. Second, I argue that settler imperatives have shaped the articulation of anti-Blackness and heteronormativity in welfare policy. I contend that efforts to promote marriage and compulsory labor did not seek to make Black people into settler subjects but rather sought to contain the potential threats that Black freedom posed to settler colonial society. Finally, in highlighting the relationship between Native genocide and anti-Blackness, I argue that one of the ways the family is productive of state power lies in its ability to link various structures of domination into a seemingly cohesive formation.

Patrick Wolfe defines settler colonialism as "a structure not an event."[22] Wolfe's definition challenges a tendency to view settlement as something that happened in the past, drawing attention instead to the ongoing processes that produce and naturalize settlement in the present and as the future. The emphasis on settler colonialism as structure locates state institutions like the Freedmen's Bureau, AFDC, and more contemporary welfare programs not as what came after settlement but rather as continually engaged in an ongoing process of occupation.[23] Wolfe argues that settler colonialism has both a "negative and positive dimension" in that it seeks both the elimination of indigenous societies and the construction of a new settler society on occupied territory.[24] The negative dimensions of settler colonialism include genocide, removal, forced assimilation, and other mechanisms that violently erase Native peoples, cultures, and land claims, whereas the positive dimensions include processes of state building, the construction of settler national identities, and the production of settler populations that sustain continued colonial occupation.

Tiffany Lethabo King has raised important concerns about the language of settler colonialism and its ascendancy as a theoretical framework. Drawing on the work of Joanne Barker, she notes that the language of settlement with its connotations of repair and agreement often sanitizes colonial violence. Additionally, King argues that settler colonial studies tends to rely on dichotomous constructions of the settler and the Native that exclude a consideration of slavery's role in the colonization of the Americas and notes that the turn toward settler colonial studies often marginalizes engagements with colonial violence within Native and Black studies.[25] King returns to the language of conquest instead in order to problematize the ways that "The preoccupation of North American and Oceanic White settler colonial studies with settlement, settler subjectivity, and land make[s] it increasingly difficult to register the far-reaching and ongoing violence of conquest in everyday life."[26] While I agree with these critiques, in relation to both the Freedmen's Bureau and twentieth-century welfare policy, I am interested in the specific idea that settlement plays in defining the kinds of domesticity the state seeks to cultivate and the forms of kinship and social relations that get marked for elimination. As the examples detailed in later chapters of this book illustrate, I emphasize that while settled domesticity may appear natural or benign, it is constituted through violence and should be understood as a mechanism of conquest.[27] In this sense, I share the concern with how the violence of conquest manifests in everyday life and hope to show how the welfare institutions of the state perpetuate that violence.

Constructions of gender and sexuality grounded in the heteropatriarchal family play a central role in both the genocide of Native Americans and the cultivation of settlement as a naturalized right that aligns with white domesticity. Numerous scholars have demonstrated that efforts to eliminate Native peoples have been intimately connected to the normalization of modern forms of sexuality, and as Chris Finley argues, "heterosexism and the structure of the nuclear family needs to be thought of as a colonial system of violence."[28] Nishnaabeg scholar Leanne Betasamosake Simpson uses the word *queer* to signify the difference between indigenous political orders and colonial, heteropatriarchal political orders, noting that in her indigenous nation queerness was so normal that it did not have a name. Simpson writes, "Queerness provides for and celebrates variance, including straightness, whereas heteropatriarchy sets out to destroy, control, and manipulate difference into hierarchies that position white, straight, cisgendered males as normal, and everyone else as less."[29] For Simpson, indigenous queerness is not simply a sexual identity but rather "a web of supportive, reciprocal, generative relationships" that exceed heteropatriarchal social organization.[30] As a colonial project, heteropatriarchy sought to eliminate not just queer sexualities but this entire web of relationships and the way of life they fostered.

European encounters with queer indigeneities in the Americas potentially destabilized their own understandings of what constituted natural gender and sexuality. Colonists fixated on gender and sexual variance as a sign of a lack of civilization, thereby organizing difference into a temporally structured hierarchy. Within this evolutionary logic, Native genders and sexuality were constructed as primitive or backward in time in contrast to the more advanced, modern expressions of gender and sexuality that Europeans embodied.[31] Not only did this hierarchy construct Native genders and sexualities as remnants of the past that needed to be eliminated, but modern sexuality simultaneously emerged as normative through its juxtaposition with these nonnormative, primitive sexualities.[32] Settler colonial efforts to eradicate the Native were efforts to eradicate both the sexual and gender variance that challenged heteronormativity and also the web of social relations that fostered that variance. These efforts produced modern sexuality as an instrument through which settler colonial aspirations are realized. As Scott Lauria Morgensen argues, "Modern sexuality arose in the United States as a method to produce settler colonialism, and settler subjects, by facilitating ongoing conquest and naturalizing its effects."[33] The normalization of modern categories of sexuality is thus inseparable from and instrumental in continued processes of naturalizing settlement.

Read alongside Simpson's description of indigenous queerness as a web of social relations or a way of life that exceeds Western ideas of sexual orientation, Morgensen's framing of modern sexuality as a method or tool of conquest highlights the role that settler constructions of gender and sexuality play in genocide. This happens both through the killing of those whose existence challenges heteronormativity and through practices and policies that seek to eradicate the web of relations among people, nonhuman life, and land that makes queer indigeneity possible. Historically and in the present, genocide takes many forms, and conquest is a highly gendered and sexualized process.[34] For example, Morgensen notes the ways that gender and sexual transgression elicited violence in accounts of Vasco Núñez de Balboa's massacres. In these accounts colonial aggression becomes refigured as an effort to eliminate sodomy, nonbinary expressions of gender, and other sinful or unnatural acts and establish patriarchy and binary gender as normative and natural.[35] The incredibly high numbers of murdered and missing indigenous women reiterate the role gendered and sexualized domination play in conquest. In these cases, representations of indigenous women as sexually promiscuous, engaged in sex work, or otherwise deviant are often used to justify their murders.[36]

The federal government's policy of allotment, instituted through the Dawes Act of 1887, offers a particularly powerful example of how heteronormativity functions not just in the killing of individuals but also in efforts to eradicate a way of life. By linking the heteropatriarchal family and private property, the Dawes Act sought to eliminate collective land claims by dividing Native lands into individual allotments granted to male heads of households. This practice simultaneously restructured kinship and land relations, transforming diverse understandings of kin into legally recognized heteropatriarchal family units headed by men and transforming collective claims to land into private property. Not only did allotment "free up" for non-Native settlement any lands that remained in excess of individual allotments, but it also established private property, a legal construct of the settler colonial state, as the universal framework through which relationships to land would be negotiated. By privatizing kinship, the Dawes Act sought to remake Native peoples in the image of the heteropatriarchal nuclear family, transforming diverse structures of belonging into governable male-headed households that were easily recognized and controlled by the settler colonial state.[37] A vivid example of the reciprocal relationship between the making of national and familial domestic spaces that I highlight in this book, the Dawes Act demonstrates how state efforts to organize Native peoples into heteropatriarchal family units enabled the expansion of the settler colonial state and vice versa.

Boarding schools also functioned as primary institutions through which colonists sought to eliminate queer indigeneity. Perhaps most succinctly expressed in Richard Pratt's philosophy of "kill the Indian, save the man," the objective of boarding schools was to eradicate Native cultures and civilize Native children by inculcating them with settler colonial norms.[38] In doing so, they devalued Native reproductive labor, working to curtail the reproduction of Native communities by disrupting both those communities' claims to their children and Native children's sense of belonging within their communities. A primary aspect of the boarding school's civilizational project was enforcing heteronormative gender. Boarding schools not only sought to eradicate gender expression that did not conform to binary gender roles through violence directed at Two-Spirit children but also disciplined Native children into properly gendered girls and boys through education into the gendered forms of labor that characterized Western domesticity.[39] As Morgensen notes, for Native children, this process required "internalizing a possibility" that life outside of the strictures of heteronormative gender and sexuality was impossible and thereby consigning Native genders and sexualities to the past.[40] In light of these practices, the idea of "kill the Indian, save the man" warrants a more explicitly gendered reading. To "kill the Indian" was to eliminate the possibility of ways of being that exceeded heteronormative gender and sexuality, and to "save the man" was to cultivate a singular gendered subjectivity as the totality of what it meant to be human. These practices disrupted Native kinship ties, rendered Native genders and sexualities as of the past, and fractured Native practices of belonging while subjecting Native children and their families to tremendous violence and trauma. By disappearing Native ways, boarding schools naturalized settlement as the inevitable progress of civilization. In addition to the distinct impact they had on Native communities, boarding schools also provided a model for the Reconstruction-era industrial schools for freedwomen discussed in chapter 4 and the Americanization programs of the early twentieth century that specifically targeted family life as a site of intervention.

Engaging with settler colonialism as a constitutive aspect of the welfare state makes visible the degree to which the naturalization of the heteronormative family and the naturalization of state power are intertwined.

The family figured prominently in efforts to secure conquest, and, in turn, the policies of the settler colonial state reinforced the naturalization of heteropatriarchy. A linear construction of time in which modern sexuality and kinship organized through the heteronormative family are figured as more advanced than Native practices represented settlement as natural evolution rather than violent occupation. In this schema, gender and sexuality were also markers of racial difference, and the elimination of gender and sexual variance was linked to both the elimination of Native life and the cultivation of a settler society. A broad range of Native feminist scholarship has not only made visible the linkages between colonial domination and heteropatriarchal violence but shown how decolonization and self-determination require the dismantling of heteropatriarchy. This work articulates visions of sovereignty, relations to land, membership and belonging, and mappings of space that are not tied to the nation-state or to heteropatriarchy.[41] These scholars demonstrate that just as the making of the settler state is tied to the production of the heteropatriarchal family, its undoing is tied to the deconstruction of heteropatriarchal ways of being.

Although this book's primary arguments focus on the centrality of the regulation of Black women to the development of the welfare institutions of the state, theories of settler colonialism and conquest are particularly important to this project in two ways. First, centering the violence of conquest makes visible the limitations of biopower as a frame for understanding the working of the welfare state. Michel Foucault argues that the modern state is characterized by the emergence of biopower or the power to "make live."[42] In contrast to sovereign power, which is exercised as the power to kill, and disciplinary power, which works specifically on the individual body, biopower's primary concern is the regulation of the population as a primary resource of the modern state. The development and expansion of state apparatuses to promote the general welfare are clear examples of the working of biopower, and biopower has been an incredibly useful concept for understanding the operations of the welfare state and the central role constructions of family have played in the regulation of populations. At the same time, however, Foucault's theory of biopower fails to engage with the colonial social relations that underwrite biopower's emergence and does not grapple with the specificities of settler colonial states at all.[43] Managing the health of the population takes on a different significance in this context because the settler population secures conquest, and cultivating the settler population is key to reinforcing the legitimacy of the settler state's claim to territory and facilitating Native genocide.

Foucault's analysis of biopower resonates with the "negative and positive dimensions" of settler colonialism identified by Wolfe in some ways. For Foucault, sovereign power does not simply disappear with the emergence of biopower; rather, it is relegated to the realm of state racism. Foucault argues that racism constructs a "break between what must live and what must die," and racially othered populations become the target of sovereign power.[44] For Foucault, the relationship between sovereign power and biopower operates through a eugenic logic in which the elimination of the subordinate race is necessary to make the population stronger. Sovereign power is understood as purging inferior elements to protect the health and purity of the population as a whole.[45] One might describe biopower in its efforts to cultivate and manage a settler population as the positive dimension and the killing of Native populations through sovereign power as the negative dimension. However, as Morgensen points out in the case of boarding schools and other seemingly assimilationist projects, biopower actually works to facilitate a genocidal project.[46] In this case, the enforcement of norms is not about assimilation or making Native people live in a particular way. Rather, norms shore up and propagate settler ways of life by eliminating the alternatives. As Finley argues, "The logics governing Native bodies are the same logics governing non-Native people. . . . The colonizers may feel bad, stressed, and repressed by the self-disciplining logics of normalizing sexuality, but Native people are systematically targeted for death and erasure by these same discourses."[47] This more nuanced understanding of how gender and sexual norms operate is also useful in thinking about the treatment of freedpeople and the racialization of welfare receipt.

Second, while theories of settler colonialism and anti-Blackness have frequently developed independently of each other, Tiffany Lethabo King locates slavery and anti-Blackness as firmly within the logic of conquest and emphasizes that Black studies and Black radical struggles have long contested Native genocide.[48] King's analysis is particularly useful to my own thinking about heteronormativity and the welfare state because she challenges the tendency to reduce genocidal violence against Native peoples to questions of land, and anti-Blackness to questions of labor. Rather, King points to a logic of conquest and shifts the focus to "the way the settler also becomes the conquistador/a (human) through Native genocide and Black dehumanization."[49] Drawing on the work of Sylvia Wynter, King argues that both Native genocide and the violent enslavement of Black people are prerequisites for the production of the liberal human subject who embodies modern sexuality.[50] This is a particularly important point for understanding the paradoxes that structured the moment of emancipation. On the one hand, the Freedmen's Bureau was charged with facilitating a transition from having the legal status of property to having the legal status of human. On the other hand, humanness was defined through anti-Blackness and Native genocide.

Throughout the book I show how the figure of the vagrant (and her later incarnation in the welfare queen) emerged from this paradox. Freedpeople's dreams of freedom were wide ranging and among other things entailed desires for mobility, reunification with kin, ownership of one's own body, control over one's time and labor, and pleasure. These conceptions of freedom were often opposed to and threatened the liberal concepts of the human that had been forged through genocide and slavery. In addition, they signaled a refusal to equate freedom with becoming liberal subjects. Throughout the examples I engage in the next chapters, I show how these refusals and alternate conceptions of freedom were rewritten in dominant discourse as vagrancy. The vagrant can be read as a sign of Black fungibility in the way the figure links a broad range of anxieties. King notes that "fungibility is, in fact, a product of White anxiety and representation, an attempt to 'get in front of' or anticipate Black fugitive movement."[51] For King, fungibility, or "the unfettered use of Black bodies for the self-actualization of the human and for the attendant humanist project of the production and expansion of space" rather than labor exploitation, is the cornerstone of anti-Blackness.[52] While this project pays particular attention to labor, the concept of fungibility makes visible the ways that efforts to force Black women to work have been about more than just exploitation.

As detailed in the following chapters, the Freedmen's Bureau sought to combat vagrancy and make newly emancipated people into proper citizens through the promotion of marriage and long-term labor contracts. Both work and marriage were significant because of their potentially settling effects on a potentially transient population. Not only did bureau officials seek to keep freedpeople in one place in order to maintain a stable supply of agricultural labor, but transience itself was seen as antithetical to civilized, liberal, heteronormative subjectivity. In his history of early twentieth-century South Asian migrant workers, Nayan Shah argues that establishing permanence over transience was central to the elaboration of heteronormative ideals of citizenship. As Shah notes, engaging in proper forms of intimacy that were grounded in settled domesticity was essential to the cultivation of liberal subjects. He writes:

In liberal political philosophy, men gathered the capabilities of self-possessive individualism through their emotional, intimate, and ethical training in households. The public attributes of intimacy include the capacity to be the author of one's own life direction; to possess the ethics to manage coupled relationship and domestic dependents; to engage with the demands of contract and the ownership of property; and to be a sovereign political subject able to negotiate freely with others in the political debate that sustains democracy.[53]

Proper intimacy within the private sphere was foundational to the liberal social and political order. As the domestic sphere was where one learned how to properly be a free subject, the production of domesticity through the institution of marriage was thought to be central to the integration of newly emancipated people into citizenship. Shah's study focuses primarily on male subjects and, in doing so, highlights the role the heteronormative household played in settling men into the responsibilities associated with working, participating in politics, and providing for dependents. It is important to note, however, that efforts to promote proper intimacy were also central to cultivating a different modality of settlement for women. Domesticity produced women's citizenship as defined primarily through dependency and confinement within the private sphere. If men acquired the skills to practice citizenship in the home, women theoretically anchored that process by tying men down.

By cultivating proper forms of intimacy and settled households, the Freedmen's Bureau employed marriage and labor discipline as a mechanism to contain freedom and reassert settler colonial norms. Rather than assimilate freedpeople, these practices reiterated heteropatriarchy as normative, natural, and civilized and in doing so fortified the dichotomy between the modern and the primitive. Many freedpeople refused to comply with the dictates of heteropatriarchy, and even when they may have attempted to, racial difference still marked them as lacking. If the Native represented that which needed to be eradicated to secure the settler colonial state, the vagrant signified an alternative to modern sexuality that needed to be policed and contained. As Shah demonstrates, the vagrant functioned as a key figure through which the dangers associated with improper forms of intimacy were understood. If proper intimacy linked normative sexuality with individual sovereignty and economic independence, the vagrant threatened to unravel all those things. The definition of vagrancy was notably vague. As a crime, male vagrancy simultaneously signified a failure to engage in wage labor, loitering in public space, homelessness, panhandling, homosexuality, and a generalized lack of discipline. While each of these specific crimes is quite different, by bringing them together the construct of vagrancy conflated economic dependency, nonnormative sexual practices, and a lack of the self-control that distinguished the liberal individual.

While anxieties about male vagrancy tended to focus on the threat that vagrancy posed to masculine ideals of independence, dependency was already defined as a key aspect of women's citizenship. Efforts to combat vagrancy among women therefore focused not on cultivating independence so much as cultivating proper forms of dependency. When directed at women, charges of vagrancy frequently connoted prostitution or displays of sexual excess in public spaces and often signified transgressing the boundaries of the domestic sphere. Whereas for men a lack of independence was associated with being out of control, for women too much independence warranted these same fears. The solution to these concerns was confinement within the domestic sphere, returning women to their proper place within the heteronormative family. The gendered construction of female vagrancy, however, was complicated by race. For Black women, in particular, the idea that women should be confined to domestic roles directly contradicted desires to keep Black women engaged in agricultural and domestic work in the South. As discussed in chapter 4, freedwomen who chose to redirect their labor toward their own families by taking on the gendered roles of housewives were deemed to be "playing the lady" and frequently accused of idleness and vagrancy. In this way, the idea of vagrancy presented a double bind for freedwomen. One was vagrant if one stepped outside of the boundaries of the domestic sphere, and one was vagrant if one chose to remain within that sphere. This double bind was a direct result of the contradictory imperatives of the bureau.

This pattern continued into the late twentieth century. While welfare reform is rarely thought of in the context of settler colonialism, efforts to push welfare recipients into marriage and forced labor were also efforts to reinforce the settler colonial state and the forms of humanity it engenders.[54] The idea that welfare undermined the family emerged as the strongest argument against it, and the threat posed by welfare recipients was consistently framed in terms of their failure to settle into proper heteronormative families. Despite the spatial confinement that characterized the impoverished urban Black communities who were the targets of welfare reform, antiwelfare discourse emphasized transience in welfare recipients' lives—the transience of fathers, of sexual relationships, and of participation in the labor force—and sought to domesticate welfare recipients through the stabilizing institutions of marriage and work. The association of welfare receipt with fraud and deception legitimized the settler colonial state in the ways that it positioned that state as a victim rather than a perpetrator of theft. Constituting welfare recipients as an undeserving population in contrast to deserving taxpayers reinforced a belief that colonizing subjects who properly inhabit normative gender roles are naturally entitled to property, resources, and rights, effectively erasing indigenous peoples and their claims to land. In other words, the effort to distinguish between deserving and undeserving subjects that has been so central to debates about public assistance in the United States legitimized the foundational premise that at least some settlers were truly deserving.

At the same time, Morgensen's observations about the potentially genocidal effects of biopower are very applicable to the case of welfare reform. On the one hand, efforts to inculcate sexual and labor discipline sought to produce subjects who would live in ways that aligned with racialized heteronormativity and capitalist interests. On the other hand, these efforts were coupled not with state investment in a population's well-being but rather with neglect and the withdrawal of resources. With its specific emphasis on making welfare recipients into better mothers by enforcing labor discipline, welfare reform directed women's reproductive labor away from their own children while also instituting limits on reproduction, like the family cap, that had clear roots in eugenics.[55] Unlike New Deal programs, where compulsory heteronormativity was linked to state support and incorporation into the nation, in both the case of the Freedmen's Bureau and that of welfare reform, compulsory heteronormativity was articulated to austerity and the production of Black lives as disposable. In these examples, biopower functioned not as an effort to "make live" but rather as a coupling of intense forms of regulation and normalization with profound material deprivation and violence.

When viewed through the lens of settler colonialism, the relationship between state and family can be seen as constituted at the intersection of multiple racial, gendered, and sexual hierarchies. The naturalization of heteropatriarchal gender and sexuality as civilized and modern justified the elimination of Native ways of living. Genocidal violence, allotment, and boarding schools were all justified as efforts to eliminate primitive genders and sexualities and cultivate civilization. These practices were essential to both building the settler colonial state and naturalizing the heteropatriarchal family through the elimination of alternatives. Emancipation was also structured by settler colonial constructions of citizenship, and as Black visions of freedom potentially threatened settler colonial norms, the policing of vagrancy emerged as a technique of containment. The fight against vagrancy further entrenched the cultivation of settlement as the ostensible goal of welfare programs. However, these programs invested in some families while disinvesting in others. The result was that the state supported white families in successfully meeting the ideals of heteropatriarchy. However, this support was often obscured so as to make the heteropatriarchal family itself seem natural. Black families, however, were held to the same ideals without being given the same forms of state support. This worked to reinforce the dichotomy between modern, civilized white families and primitive, culturally deficient Black families. Modern sexuality linked racisms in that it constituted Native peoples as needing to be eliminated and Black people as needing perpetual surveillance, policing, and reform. Both of these constructions secured the legitimacy of the settler colonial state as protecting the heteropatriarchal family from these multiple threats.

Constituting Public and Private Spaces

A third way that the heteropatriarchal family and state power mutually constitute each other is through the construction of shifting boundaries between public and private spaces. Liberal political theory constructs a clear division between the public realm of the state and economy and the private sphere of the family. In this construction, the public operates as the domain in which independent subjects engage in political and economic life, and the private functions as a space beyond state intervention. Many feminist critics have correctly highlighted the multiple ways that the public-private divide, conceptualized within liberalism as a limit on state power, sanctions violence and exploitation within the home by positioning it outside of the political sphere. However, like liberal theorists, these critics tend to map the boundary between public and private onto the boundary between the state and the family while treating it as static and uniformly experienced across the many differences among women.[56] In contrast, Black feminist engagements with the public and private have attended to the shifting and contextually specific meanings of public and private spaces as well as the dynamic nature of the boundaries between them. Historically, Black women have had to negotiate both dominant white constructions of public and private space and also efforts to curb the formation of more autonomous Black publics and privates. As a result, their experiences, particularly for those working as domestic workers within white homes, underline the contingent and relational nature of divisions between public and private space. By centering these experiences, I argue that it is necessary to examine the ways the boundaries between public and private spheres are constituted differently in relation to multiple, interconnected structures of power. Instead of viewing the private sphere as a familial space outside the reach of the state, I argue that the construction of a boundary between public and private is constitutive of state power. The production of this dynamic boundary enables the state to impose responsibilities and bestow privileges in differentiated ways that reinforce racial, capitalist, and gendered structures of power while reiterating the naturalness of the heteropatriarchal family.

While liberal theoretical frameworks tend to abstract the organization of public and private spaces from the context of settlement and slavery, these processes were foundational to how those spaces developed in the United States. As discussed in the previous section, settler colonialism was anchored in domestic norms and the transformation of land into private property. Similarly, public came to mean the space of the settler colonial state, a space that required the erasure or exclusion of Native peoples. Legally constructed as private property, enslaved people were excluded from the rights and privileges associated with both public and private space. Mobility restrictions barred their presence in public without permission from their masters, and a vigorous apparatus designed specifically to contain and police Black movement worked to confine the enslaved to plantations.[57] The labor of enslaved people, both through the production of wealth and through domestic service, enabled the construction and maintenance of white domestic spaces, although the fact of that labor was frequently erased.[58] Subsumed within the private space of the plantation, enslaved people were denied a right to a private sphere of their own. The enslaved were considered both property and dependents within the plantation household, and unfettered access to their bodies, time, and labor was guaranteed to white slaveholders by the construct of the private sphere.[59]

Despite the totalizing nature of the institution of slavery, enslaved people still reconfigured space in ways that reflected their own needs and desires. Stephanie Camp uses the concept of "rival geographies" to describe the alternative ways that enslaved peoples used and experienced space within the plantation economy. Retooling Edward Said's concept, she shows how enslaved people responded to spatial restrictions by reconstructing space in dynamic ways that served their own needs. Camp argues that in contrast to planters' efforts to fix space, "the rival geography was characterized by motion: the movement of bodies, objects, and information within and around plantation space."[60] By producing alternate possibilities, these rival geographies challenged the power of the state and the plantation to define and control space. Camp documents the way enslaved people laid claim to public space through practices like truancy and social gatherings, finding ways to both elude white surveillance and constitute their own provisional publics within the rigid plantation system. The context of slavery also complicated the meaning of domestic space for enslaved people. Slave quarters were highly contested spaces that were simultaneously "public spaces of labor reproduction and private spaces of community formation and family life."[61] While the quarters themselves were very much a part of the life of the plantation, and the labor performed within them was essential to the reproduction of enslaved people as a labor force and subject to planters' surveillance and intervention, the quarters were also the closest enslaved people had to private homes. Camp documents the processes by which Black women claimed those domestic spaces as their own, for example, by hanging abolitionist posters in their homes. These kinds of actions reflected enslaved women's commitment to actively remaking slave quarters into their own domestic spheres despite the contingency of those spaces and the power that planters held to separate families and communities through the slave trade and other forms of violence.

While domestic spaces have often been conceptualized as sites of confinement within feminist theory, Angela Davis argues, in her essay "Reflections on the Black Woman's Role in the Community of Slaves," that for enslaved Black women the domestic sphere took on a very different meaning. Davis observes that within the system of slavery it was only in the domestic sphere of the slave quarters that enslaved people "could attempt to assert the modicum of freedom they still retained."[62] The home, which was furthest removed from white surveillance and was where basic needs were met, was the only place where one's labor was not exclusively in the service of the oppressor, and thus the home, and more specifically Black women's work within it, formed the backbone of resistance to slavery. Davis argues that in the context of the dehumanizing violence of slavery, "the community gravitating around the domestic quarters might possibly permit a retrieval of the man and the woman in their fundamental humanity."[63] In this way, the domestic sphere of the slave quarters was private in that it was at least minimally shielded from the masters' watchful eyes but also functioned as the basis for community among Black people on the plantation.

The multiple and shifting boundaries between private and public that developed during slavery continued to shape the racialized and gendered meanings of public and private space after emancipation. In the Reconstruction era, limitations on mobility were rewritten as vagrancy laws that criminalized Black people's presence in public space, and as Jim Crow segregation in the South solidified, public space became synonymous with racial exclusion.

Claiming ownership of one's body in public was an important way of expressing freedom for Black women, but it also had potentially high costs, and many forces emerged that sought to contain Black women's participation in public culture.[64] The racialized constructions of Black women's sexuality that anchored the system of slavery persisted after emancipation, and as a result Black women were subject to a hypersexualizing white gaze in public space. Those who asserted their presence in public were frequently read as prostitutes, were subjected to gendered and sexualized violence, or found their behavior policed in other ways. In response to this, Black communities often adopted a politics of respectability that attempted to erase or hide any sign of gender or sexual deviance.[65] As a result, many Black women experienced the public sphere not as a place of free expression but as a place where one's persona had to be carefully crafted in relation to the dominant gaze. Despite this larger context, Black communities also produced alternate public spheres that had more expansive norms around participation. As Elsa Barkley Brown shows, during the Reconstruction era, churches became central spaces of public engagement within the Black community. Women often wielded a great deal of power within these spaces, and even when dominant society excluded women from political participation, Black communities constituted Black men's vote as a collective community vote that included women and children, thereby challenging the gendered organization of the public sphere.[66] While these efforts were eroded with the intensification of segregation and racial violence in the late nineteenth century, they represent an important rival geography of public space that emerged from the experiences and visions of the formerly enslaved.

The meaning of the private sphere was equally if not more contested during the Reconstruction era than during slavery. With emancipation, Black people sought to secure the privacy and kinship relations that had been denied them under slavery through the constitution of their own domestic spheres. The institution of marriage played a central role in this. As Tera Hunter establishes, marriage functioned as a public institution that secured the private home. In other words, at least theoretically, legally recognized marriage constituted a boundary that shielded the household from public intervention. In practice, however, this boundary appeared porous in some contexts and rigid in others. Marriage did not shield Black families from surveillance within the home or from the mandate that Black women work outside the home, and parental and other kinship relationships, while perhaps more secure, could still be easily disrupted by state intervention. However, marriage did secure a privatized family that was expected to be self-sufficient, and in this context the boundary between public and private delineated survival as a private rather than public responsibility.

For many Black women, their experiences of the domestic sphere were also complicated by the fact that they crossed boundaries between their own homes and the white homes they worked within. After emancipation, large numbers of Black women were concentrated in domestic work, and their labor was essential, though often unrecognized, in the maintenance of idealized white domestic space. White employers frequently referred to their domestics as "part of the family" and used ideas of familial responsibility and love to secure highly exploitative working conditions. In this context, the privacy of the white home produced a greater vulnerability to abuse for Black workers by shielding employers who mistreated them. This made Black women particularly vulnerable to sexual harassment, physical violence, and emotional abuse from their white employers. Notably, much of this abuse and exploitation was administered by white women, and Black women's relegation to domestic work was rooted in the belief that idealized white women needed to be protected from difficult or dirty work. While they were frequently denied privacy within their own homes, Black domestic workers saw how the privacy of the white home enabled their exploitation. In their efforts to assert their rights, domestic workers challenged the public-private divide by reframing their employers' private homes as public workplaces. They emphasized that domestic workers operated in an employment rather than a familial relation by setting boundaries around their time, clearly defining their responsibilities, highlighting their technical skill, and, when necessary, quitting.[67]

Sarah Haley's discussion of domestic carcerality provides a particularly harrowing example of how the private sphere of the white home functioned as a site of state violence against Black women. Haley documents the way white homes were used as an extension of the penitentiary through the practice of paroling Black female prisoners into domestic service for white families in Georgia during the Jim Crow era. Designed to address a demand for Black domestic labor, this practice produced slavery-like conditions within white homes as an extension of the racist criminal justice system. Socially isolated, paroled women worked under the threat of being sent back to prison or the chain gang, and their future freedom was dependent on the white family for whom they were forced to work. As a result, they were subject to extreme forms of surveillance and control and had no recourse against violence and abuse. This practice illustrates the way that boundaries between public and private space are constructed dynamically in the interest of maintaining racialized and gendered forms of domination.[68] That a private home simultaneously operated as an extension of state institutions destabilizes the idea that public and private space are necessarily separable and thereby fundamentally challenges liberal and mainstream feminist conceptions that the public-private divide serves as a limit on state power.

When Black women's experiences are taken as central to theorizing the public-private divide, it becomes clear that the tendency to see that divide as a fixed separation between state and family is flawed. Rather, these historical examples all illustrate the way that the division between public and private is dynamically constituted in relation to multiple structures of power. In a different context, Anannya Bhattacharjee has described this as the "mirage-like" character of the division between public and private spaces in order to illuminate the way this division is constituted not just through heteropatriarchy but through racial, class, and national hierarchies as well. That both the state and the family can be experienced as public by some and private by others suggests that the state and the family are not opposites, as liberal discourse constructs them; rather, the boundaries between them are contextually determined and functional to state power. Once the mirage-like character of the public-private divide is acknowledged, the key questions become, How does the appearance of a division between public and private get mapped onto the state and the family in a particular moment, and what work does this appearance of a boundary do in relation to state power?[69]

While political theorists have engaged more substantively with the elusiveness of the division between state and society, the public-private divide still tends to be theorized as a static and stable boundary. Black feminist history suggests, however, that the boundary between public and private has always been dynamic and constructed in ways that are instrumental in securing racial and gender subordination. To borrow from the work of Timothy Mitchell, this history suggests that the state's boundaries should be understood as "structural effects" that shift and change in order to generate "resources of power" for the state.[70] The production of a difference between the state and the private sphere is central to the workings of the state. However, these differences are not stable but rather shift to enable specific operations in particular contexts. In this way, the division between public and private might be viewed as a flexible boundary that enables rather than simply limits certain operations of state power. For example, in some contexts defining the family as private reinforces patriarchal hierarchies within the home that might advance state interests, while in other contexts viewing the quality of family life as of national concern enables expanded state surveillance.

Historically, racial difference has been the basis for denying Black people both the right to a private sphere and access to the public sphere. As the examples engaged in this book illustrate, from the Freedmen's Bureau to welfare reform, home life within Black communities has been the subject of intense public scrutiny. In contrast, for white families, the domestic sphere has been constructed as the basis for a right to privacy, and state investment in white families has been a means of shoring up access to private space. For example, New Deal–era efforts to secure homeownership and a family wage for the white working class extended the guarantee of privacy along racial lines. State investment, in this context, was framed as a necessary and legitimate way of respecting claims to the heteropatriarchal family. The idea that this family was natural and should be supported underwrote state investment while that state investment secured a particular familial form as natural. In contrast, in relation to Black communities, the state has both denied access to the private sphere as a right and used the public-private divide as a mechanism for enforcing obligations. While the Freedmen's Bureau encouraged the formation of a domestic sphere in its efforts to promote marriage, the domestic sphere of freedpeople was not a site of state support. Freedpeople did not receive economic benefits for adopting heteropatriarchal family forms, and often the conditions that they were subject to undermined efforts to adhere to the ideals of domesticity. However, gender and sexual relations within freedpeople's homes were made a national concern, enabling state surveillance and reform projects that made the ostensibly private sphere a site of public debate and intervention. At the same time, in relation to questions of public assistance, the public-private divide emerged in the expectation that freedpeople's families be self-sustaining. While marriage and family recognition did not guarantee privacy in the domestic sphere, they did become a vehicle for the privatization of economic responsibility. For white working-class families, the private sphere could be employed as a claim to resources, whereas for freedpeople the private sphere worked to rationalize state austerity. The shifting character of the public-private divide enabled the privatization of social responsibilities while continuing to deny freedpeople basic rights to privacy in their familial relationships. These examples suggest that the division between public and private not only is flexible but is constituted to advance particular political projects in different historical moments.

Conclusion

The state and the heteronormative family are coconstitutive and do important work to naturalize each other through at least three interrelated processes. First, the family provides a metaphor that naturalizes hierarchy within unity. Because the hierarchies that organize the heteronormative family are seen as natural, references to the nation in familial terms work to naturalize hierarchies within the nation-state. At the same time, the state itself cultivates a particular way of organizing kinship while suppressing others, thereby producing the heteronormative family as a naturalized reference point. Second, the family and the forms of gender and sexuality it fosters play a central role in conquest and the ongoing structures of the settler colonial state. Heteronormative gender and sexuality were constituted through and operated as a method of Native genocide while also being deployed to cultivate a primary resource of state power, the settler population. Upon emancipation, freedpeople were subjected to settler norms of gender, kinship, and sexuality, and the enforcement of these norms was key to defining freedom in terms that reinforced the settler colonial nation-state. Vagrancy emerged as a vehicle for white anxieties about how Black freedom might threaten settler colonial norms, and the policing of vagrancy operated as a means of containing this threat. While biopower functioned in the settler colonial context as a way of cultivating the settler population, efforts to reform vagrants and, later, welfare recipients show how biopower could also couple intense forms of regulation and normalization with austerity and structural violence. Third, the shifting nature of public and private space is important to the constitution of state power.

While the private and public spheres are often thought to be distinct and the boundary between them static, Black feminist histories reveal that this boundary is actually contingent and shifting. Grappling with the ways that public and private space are simultaneously racial and gendered constructions makes visible how the production of the boundaries between them is constitutive of state power and enables racialized and gendered forms of domination.

The following chapters build on and extend this analysis by showing the specific ways these processes manifested in the regulation of freedwomen's sexuality and labor during the Reconstruction era and of welfare recipients in the late twentieth century. I begin by looking at the role that marriage played in constituting freedpeople's families in particular ways and the way the cultivation of the heteronormative family became a vehicle for establishing hierarchy, producing settlement, and privatizing social responsibility. I then turn to efforts to force freedwomen into domestic service to show how state officials worked to reconcile gendered constructions of domesticity with the mandate that freedwomen work outside their own homes. Finally, I look to the more recent past to explore how these processes resurface in late twentieth-century efforts to transform the welfare system.

THREE

Marriage and the Making of Gendered Citizenship

In June 1866, "Marriage of a Colored Soldier at Vicksburg by Chaplain Warren of the Freedmen's Bureau" appeared in *Harper's Weekly* magazine (figure 3.1). The image depicts a young couple who stand with hands clasped and eyes cast downward as an official of the Freedmen's Bureau performs their marriage ceremony. The chaplain, the largest figure in the picture and the only individual named, stands just to the right of the anonymous soldier. His arm is outstretched in what appears as both a blessing of the union and a transfer between the men of patriarchal authority over the many women who surround them. Invoking the nationalist trope of the soldier returning home from war to marry the woman he left behind, the image itself links military service, marriage, and gendered citizenship. The soldier, having demonstrated his masculinity in war, has earned freedom from slavery and the freedom to marry. Given the ways that slavery was rationalized through discourses that represented the enslaved as childlike, the image frames marriage as a passage into adulthood not just for the individuals involved but also for the race as a whole.

However, while marriage plays this dual role in marking a monumental event in both the lives of individuals and the collective situation of the race, the moment itself appears not as a joyous celebration of freedom but rather as a scene of great restraint. Everyone in the picture stands in his or her proper place, and in positioning himself as emancipator, the state official remains the unchallenged center of authority in the frame. The spectators who surround the wedding are formally dressed, with the men in military uniforms and the women in modest, nearly identical white dresses. Their dress and demeanor suggest a highly gendered performance of respectability

Figure 3.1 Alfred R. Waud, *Marriage of a Colored Soldier at Vicksburg by Chaplain Warren of the Freedmen's Bureau. Harper's Weekly*, June 10, 1866, p. 412. https://www .loc.gov/pictures/item/2009630217/.

and a subtle awareness that they are all in fact being watched. After all, the image is first and foremost an image for a nation of spectators whose relationship to emancipation was marked primarily by concern rather than joy. The image does not emerge from a celebratory discourse on emancipation but rather intervenes in a long-standing debate among whites about whether or not Black people were prepared for the responsibilities of freedom, whether freedom was even in their best interests. In creating a picture of emancipation that reflects white civilization, the representation assuages white anxieties that emancipation might beget chaos and unruliness. As such, it reiterates ideas about the benevolence of slavery, suggesting that the institution of slavery had civilized the enslaved and now, under the continued supervision of the state, they were ready to proceed as freedpeople.

This image quite literally places heteronormativity at the center of the emancipatory moment as the institution of marriage both marks and mediates the transition from the time of slavery to the time of freedom. The question of time is central to the image as it speaks to two prominent white anxieties about emancipation. Were freedpeople ready for citizenship? And, now that they were free, how could their time be directed back toward the essential labor they had performed while enslaved? Marriage offered an answer to these anxieties as both a step forward on the path toward civilization and a means of settling and stabilizing a potentially transient population. In the singular moment of the wedding, the image from *Harper's Weekly* captures a relationship among the making of heteronormative families, the making of racialized and gendered citizens, and the remaking of the nation in the aftermath of the Civil War. The simultaneity of becoming free, becoming citizens, and becoming married is indicative of the vital role that marriage would play in the transition from legal property to racially subordinated citizenship—a role that would have a lingering impact on late twentieth-century debates about welfare policy.

Throughout this chapter I demonstrate how marriage functioned as a rubric through which gendered citizenship as a mode of racial stratification was constructed and institutionalized. Marriage was uniquely situated at the nexus of racial and settler colonial constructions of civilization that upheld sexual dimorphism and kinship organized through heterosexual reproduction as the pinnacle of human evolution, contractual understandings of freedom and liberal individualism, a belief that settlement and domestic responsibilities would promote self-sufficient families reliant on wage labor rather than state support, and a narrative of progress that absolved the nation of responsibility for slavery by situating it firmly in the past despite its lingering effects. Given this particularly dense locus of meaning, marriage operated as a complex and often contradictory sign of freedom. While, for white men and women, marriage functioned as the basis for privacy and the exercise of rights, for freedpeople, access to marriage enabled surveillance in the private sphere, privatized social responsibility for slavery, and criminalized or erased sexual practices and structures of kinship that exceeded the heteronormative family. This dual meaning of the private sphere complicates conventional distinctions between private and public and contributed to the development of gendered constructions of citizenship that maintained racial inequality.

I begin by focusing on the role the legal prohibition of marriage under slavery played in linking heteronormativity to ideas of freedom. I then turn to abolitionist arguments that both cast the absence of marriage as one of the primary horrors of slavery and situated marriage as key to mediating the transition from slavery to freedom. These arguments demonstrate how discourses about marriage that linked former enslavement with sexual deviance were central to the rearticulation of racial difference and the production of slavery's afterlife in the Reconstruction era. While entering into marriage contracts was an important sign of freedom, it also required the adoption of liberal forms of personhood and heterosexual structures of kinship that sought to produce and direct freedpeople's agency in the service of state interests. As a key moment in the entry into citizenship, marriage secured the transition to wage labor, cultivated gender hierarchy within Black communities, provided new grounds for criminalization, and justified austerity toward freedpeople. The obligations of marriage were rigorously enforced on freedpeople. However, when freedpeople sought to claim rights associated with marriage, their efforts were often frustrated. Finally, turning to Civil War widows' pension claims, I explore how freedwomen resisted efforts to enforce marital norms and how this resistance reveals potentially queer conceptions of freedom, belonging, and agency.

Slavery, Freedom, and the Family

Because slavery depended on the genealogical isolation of the enslaved, the prohibition of slave marriage was fundamental to the institution. Through its prohibition, marriage was constituted as a normative marker of civilized, free life and became a vehicle through which dichotomous gender was constructed as a sign of racial progress. Abolitionist discourse frequently reiterated these same ideas about civilization, and as the federal government began to grapple with how formerly enslaved persons might be transformed into citizens, marriage and its civilizing potential took center stage. The consequent push toward marriage marginalized other ways of organizing kinship and sexuality by casting them as out of time with liberal citizenship. In this way, race, heteronormativity, and citizenship worked to simultaneously anchor racial hierarchy in gender, and freedom in marriage.

Given marriage's central role in establishing and legitimating kinship within the U.S. legal system, the denial of the right to marry was critical to the production of enslaved people as socially dead.[1] Marriage was a contract relation in a society in which "contract marked the difference between freedom and coercion."[2] Thus, the inability to marry was one of the distinguishing markers of slavery, and marriage was a principal sign of freedom. Even though, as considerable historical evidence demonstrates, enslaved people practiced various kinds of kinship, these relationships were not legally recognized or protected, which meant they did not carry with them the privacy, political standing, security, and stability that white families enjoyed.[3] The threat of forced separation through the interstate slave trade or hiring-out practices hung over all enslaved families. Enslaved people responded to this threat in a variety of ways, often developing more short-term or contingent forms of relationship or modifying the commitments of marriage to accommodate the precarity of their situations. As Tera Hunter argues, enslaved people "developed and articulated gradations of intimacy that were quite complex and not visible to those judging them through the conventional lenses of heterosexual marriage."[4]

While slavery produced sometimes insurmountable barriers to family formation, slaveholders frequently used the idiom of family to rationalize slavery, and slavery alongside marriage was understood to be a domestic affair.[5] Enslaved people were situated as dependents within the households of their white masters and mistresses. For masters in these households, having dependents verified their independence and secured their political power.[6] For mistresses, the power they wielded over enslaved workers within the home secured their domestic status and enabled the performance of proper femininity.[7] As dependents within their masters' households, enslaved people could not make autonomous political demands or assert the independence of their own households. Even if they engaged in informal practices of marriage, enslaved men and women remained trapped within the private jurisdiction of their masters' families and so could neither lay claim to a private sphere of their own nor exercise political power in the public realm.[8]

Finally, the prohibition of marriage was a cornerstone of the reproductive economy of slavery. Slave status passed matrilineally, meaning that any child born to an enslaved woman became the property of her owner.[9] As a legal structure, marriage guaranteed the sanctity of heteropatriarchal families. Prohibiting marriage severed legal ties between enslaved parents and their children and alienated individuals from intergenerational relationships. At the same time, by rendering Black women as outside of the parameters of marriage, the prohibition of marriage contributed to the racialized construction of Black women as perpetually sexually available and thereby rendered them more vulnerable to sexual violence and abuse in ways that were foundational to the reproductive economy of slavery.[10]

The prohibition of marriage was not simply about exclusion from the institution. Rather, it was also an important component in the constitution of marriage and the system of heterosexual kinship it secured as normative markers of freedom and civilized life. The prohibition of marriage did not just deny slaves kinship as organized through marriage. It also erased the broad range of kinship and sexual relationships that existed among enslaved people. While the heteronormative lens that structures the ways in which much of African American history has been written often invisibilizes queer sexualities within enslaved communities, many scholars have noted a diversity of sexualities and kinship formations within the African diaspora.[11] These queer relationships were also unrecognized by the state. However, they were not named in the law as a right that was denied. The prohibition of marriage alone normalized the institution as synonymous with both family and freedom. In its explicit denial, marriage was constituted as part of what it meant to be legally free. While exclusion from marriage rights was a fundamental component in producing the social death of slaves, it did not necessarily follow that the granting of those rights would negate that social death or that marriage was the only or even the preferred rubric through which freedpeople's familial relationships could have been organized. Just as Orlando Patterson argues that the meaning of freedom "emerged as a necessary consequence of the degradation of slavery and the effort to negate it," the meaning of marriage was grounded in the terms of slavery and subordination.[12] Even as it was held out as a pathway to freedom and citizenship, marriage as an institution would play a key role in securing slavery's continuing afterlife.

Discourse about marriage in the context of both slavery and emancipation linked gender and sexuality to racialized constructions of civilization. Slavery was understood by its practitioners to be part of a civilizational project, and marriage and the system of sex and gender categorization that it consolidated were key to this project. A racial construct employed to distinguish the ostensibly more advanced white population from supposedly primitive nonwhite groups, civilization asserted that the most advanced stage of human evolution was characterized by a dichotomous and hierarchical construction of sexual difference that was codified in the institution of marriage. In this way, civilization was at its core a temporal construct that relied on a linear understanding of time as defined by evolutionary progress.[13] This construct was central to the social construction of races as synonymous with different stages of human evolution and linked settler colonialism and slavery through a gendered logic.[14] As María Lugones describes, in the colonial imaginary "other human inhabitants of the planet came to be mythically conceived not as dominated through conquest, nor as inferior in terms of wealth or political power, but as an anterior stage in the history of the species, in this unidirectional path."[15]

Sex and gender were integral to a construction of civilization that defined movement toward a clearer division of the sexes as evolutionary progress and movement away from that division as degeneration.[16] Deviation from

Eurocentric heteropatriarchal gender norms marked both Black and Native people as uncivilized and deserving of enslavement, conquest, and violence. As Gail Bederman demonstrates, Victorian racial and gender ideologies posited that "as civilized races gradually evolved toward perfection, they naturally perfected and deepened the sexual specialization of the Victorian doctrine of spheres. 'Savage' (that is, nonwhite) races, on the other hand, had not yet evolved pronounced sexual differences—and, to some extent, this was precisely what made them savage."[17] Bederman's point that it is not simply the gendered meanings ascribed to the categories of male and female that are constructed through race but the dichotomous sex categories themselves is an important one. Far from being natural, sexual and gender difference emerge as significant forms of categorization in conjunction with the delineation of racial difference. Dichotomous sex categories do not simply divide those categorized as men and those categorized as women but also produce a racial division between populations that are seen as adhering to binary gender and those that are not.[18] Notably, the prohibition of marriage, the exploitation of Black women's productive and reproductive labor, and the sexualized violence of slavery made it impossible for Black people to conform to dominant gender norms, suggesting that slavery's civilizational mission was less invested in reforming the characters of the enslaved than in producing and naturalizing ideas of racial difference that were anchored in gender. By rendering enslaved people as perpetually in need of civilization, the institutions of slavery in the United States ensured their own continuity. In this context, race and gender developed as mutually constitutive systems—race became intelligible through naturalized ideas about gender, and gender gained new significance in its capacity to signify racial difference.[19]

Abolitionist discourse frequently reiterated the gendered and sexualized constructions of race and civilization that had rationalized slavery. In contrast to claims about the civilizing influence of slavery, nineteenth-century abolitionists frequently argued that slavery, and particularly the institution's undermining of heteropatriarchal nuclear family structure, kept the enslaved trapped in a backward and uncivilized state. In this context, the lack of recognition of marriage was often cited as one of the primary horrors of slavery. Frederick Douglass argued that slavery worked "to blot out the institution of marriage," and the African Methodist Episcopal Church equated slavery with "fornication, adultery, concubinage."[20] Harriet Beecher Stowe even went so far as to argue that "the worst abuse of the system of slavery is its outrage upon the family . . . one which is more notorious and undeniable than any other."[21] Indeed, as Amy Dru Stanley notes, "no abolitionist argument proved more compelling than testifying to the conflict between slavery and domesticity."[22] In their challenge to slavery, abolitionists reproduced the terms of civilization and the particular articulation of race, gender, and sexuality that had justified racial subordination in troubling ways. These terms also came to structure understandings of emancipation and the belief that marriage was an important part of cultivating freedpeople's capacity to act as responsible, respectable, and free citizens.[23]

The American Freedmen's Inquiry Commission, a committee charged by the secretary of war to detail the condition of freedpeople in the South and the steps necessary to fold freedpeople into the nation, highlighted marriage as vital to making freedpeople into good citizen subjects in ways that reflect the discursive themes that would emerge as central in the Freedmen's Bureau's practices of marriage promotion. For example, in its assessment of slavery in South Carolina, the commission described the degradation of slavery as follows:

> The slave was not permitted to own a family name; instances occurred in which he was flogged for presuming to use one. He did not eat with his children or with their mother; "there was no time for that." In portions of this State, at least, a family breakfast or dinner table was a thing so little known among these people, that, ever since their enfranchisement, it has been very difficult to break them of the lifelong habit that each should clutch the dish containing his portion and skulk off into a corner, there to devour it in solitude. The entire day, until after sunset, was spent in the field; the night in huts of a single room, where all ages and both sexes herded promiscuously. Young girls of fifteen—some of an earlier age—became mothers, not only without marriage, but often without any pretense of fidelity to which even a slave could give that name.[24]

The objective of the American Freedmen's Inquiry Commission was to assist freedpeople but only in ways that would also protect the national interests threatened by the incorporation of this population into the polity. As the preceding passage suggests, freedpeople were viewed as unprepared for citizenship, and the primary evidence for this lack of preparation was located in the domestic sphere. This description of the households fostered by slavery suggests that because of the lack of marital relationships, enslaved people remained in a backward and uncivilized state. The descriptions of the enslaved "clutching" their food, "skulking" into corners, and "herding promiscuously" and indiscriminately liken freedpeople to animals in need of domestication and suggest that while enslaved people had uncontrolled sexual relationships with each other, they lacked the meaningful social ties that characterized civilization. Not only does this representation erase the complex cultures of enslaved people and the reproductive labor that Black women performed under slavery, but it equates the lack of marital relationships with a lack of sociality altogether.[25] In other words, marriage is what distinguishes civilized humanity, what marks the difference between the slave and the citizen.

In addition, this passage must be read in the context of gendered discourses about domesticity that defined women's roles primarily in terms of caring for the home. Women were not merely seen as responsible for creating a home that was a safe haven from the cruelties of the outside world; because the home was viewed as the bastion of civilization, women's performance of domestic roles was also essential to preserving national well-being. In this context, the horrific domestic scene of slavery also marks the absence of proper gender differentiation as a problem that the state must grapple with in making freedpeople into citizens. The description situates the enslaved as backward in time in relation to white civilization, erasing the way that the material conditions of slavery were not just contemporaneous with idealized constructions of domestic space but a prerequisite for these constructions in terms of both the wealth accrued through slavery and the domestic labor performed by the enslaved. The discursive linking of racial progress to the performance of heteronormative, patriarchal gender roles enabled a complicated structure of blame in which, on the one hand, the institution of slavery itself was responsible for holding enslaved people back from civilization and, on the other hand, it became the responsibility of freedpeople themselves (under the surveillance and tutelage of the federal government) to take up their own rehabilitation.

Officials of the Freedmen's Bureau identified the absence of marriage as one of the greatest challenges to freedpeople's incorporation within the nation. Bureau officials frequently described freedpeople's choices not to comply with the institution of marriage as an evil that needed to be corrected or, as bureau officer J. P. Lee wrote, "a great stain" that ministers, teachers, and bureau officers were working to remove.[26] Bureau officers fixated on practices such as couples "taking up" together or "cohabiting" without marriage, the potential transience of freedpeople's relationships, sexual promiscuity, prostitution, and the bearing of children outside of marriage. As Mississippi bureau agent Thadeus Preuss observed in an 1867 report:

The Marital Relations of the Colored People generally I am sorry to have to state are in a most deplorable condition. They seem to pay but little attention to the sacred requirements of the marriage relation. In most instances living together and calling themselves man and wife as long as it conveniently suits them. In many instances they are the possessors of several wives and also several husbands. This deplorable state of morals has been permitted to exist amongst the Colored People in a State of Slavery yielding a large revenue to their owners. Now that they are free, some steps should be taken to remove this evil.[27]

Statements such as these suggest, in contrast to the image from the opening of this chapter, that many freedpeople did not see marriage as fundamental to their freedom and often chose to opt out of the institution even after it became legally available to them.[28] However, these choices were not understood by bureau officials as expressions of agency but rather as a sign of moral degeneracy and a lack of preparedness for citizenship. Bureau officials cited these choices as evidence of slavery's dehumanizing effects that had to be corrected for freedpeople to take on the responsibilities of citizenship. In this way, the discourse on marriage narrowly delimited what freedom might look like by constituting alternative sexual practices and forms of kinship as remnants of slavery that could not be contemporaneous with the free subject.[29]

The likening of nonnormative sexual practices to a "stain" or "evil" to be expunged reveals the way in which former enslavement cast a shadow across freedpeople's inclusion as citizens. Expressions of agency that did not align with bureau goals were reframed as deficiencies in the capacity to exercise agency as a free subject. Bureau officials consistently interpreted deviance from hegemonic sexual and gender norms as an inheritance from slavery that tarnished the characters of freedpeople and left them unsuited for the responsibilities of citizenship. In this way, sexuality played a central role in postemancipation efforts to reconstruct the meaning of race, as anxieties about the extension of citizenship to freedpeople were frequently expressed as anxieties about the threat their sexual immorality potentially posed to the nation. Just as sexuality had played a significant role in pre-emancipation racial formation, the articulation of racial difference and sexual nonnormativity in this moment worked to reconcile formal inclusion into the institutions of citizenship with continued racial subordination.

Significantly, Freedmen's Bureau officials, the Freedmen's Inquiry Commission, and other white reformers all saw slavery as having degraded the characters of the enslaved. There was no comparable concern for the characters of those who had perpetuated slavery. Situating slavery's legacies as an element of the past that lived on in the behaviors of freedpeople worked to both relocate responsibility for remedying slavery's harms onto freedpeople themselves and maintain a distinction between the formerly enslaved and the rest of the citizenry. In their own claims to freedom, freedpeople frequently drew attention to the wealth their labor had produced for the nation as the basis for redistributive claims to land, holding former slaveholders and state and federal governments responsible for redressing the harms of slavery. In contrast, bureau officers and white reformers emphasized the moral, and particularly sexual, reform of freedpeople as a central concern, thereby transferring responsibility for remedying the harms of slavery from those who had profited from the institution of slavery to the formerly enslaved themselves. Notably, the writings of bureau officers demonstrate how despite emancipation freedpeople's former enslavability continued to differentiate them from other citizens. Increasingly, gender and sexuality constituted the terrain on which this racial difference was established.

Marriage Registration and the Making of Liberal Individuals

In response to these sexualized anxieties, the Freedmen's Bureau was charged with the responsibility of issuing marriage certificates. Bureau officers were authorized and encouraged to perform marriages, and some jurisdictions, such as Mississippi and North Carolina, went so far as to pass blanket statutes that legally married all cohabitating freedpeople regardless of their consent or knowledge of the law.[30] Although these activities are often conceptualized as legalizing already existing relationships, the bureau's emphasis on marriage registration is better understood as part of a process of bringing a population whose everyday lives had formerly been controlled by slave owners under the management of the state. Establishing one's identity in state records was a vital part of the transition from legal property to legal personhood, and the registration of marriages along with bureau-certified labor contracts simultaneously marked freedpeople's entrance into the institutions of citizenship and their entrance into the national archive as human beings. In a way, marriage certificates and labor contracts functioned like birth certificates for the formerly enslaved. They recorded the vital information of freedpeople in state records for the first time and, in doing so, marked a symbolic birth of freedpeople as liberal individuals capable of entering into contractual relations.

Citizenship required that one define one's identity by the statistical facts that constituted legal personhood. These facts were not objective truths so much as an effect of the state's need to stabilize identities and differentiate individuals for the purpose of conferring rights and responsibilities. Citizenship entailed a commitment to a singular identity that was defined by stable characteristics such as names, family heritage, age, race, and gender that could be collected and verified by the state. Often taken for granted as natural aspects of personhood, these characteristics were constituted as facts only through state practices of record keeping that stabilized them. Upon emancipation, many freedpeople had multiple names, were uncertain of their age, or could not easily define their parentage. In a context in which freedom was defined in contractual terms, this posed a significant problem in that without stable markers of identity it would be difficult to hold people to the terms of the contracts into which they entered.

While the defining characteristics that the state uses to delineate individual identity are often taken as the truest markers of who one really is, Jacqueline Stevens demonstrates that these "facts" reflect political interests rather than natural attributes.[31] In the practice of marriage registration, the Freedmen's Bureau was invested not just in recording facts about individual freedpeople's lives but in producing freedpeople as subjects of statistical information. Marriage registers and marriage certificates painstakingly cataloged details about each of the parties, recording the following beneath the designations male and female: age, color, color of father, color of mother, number of years lived with another woman (or man), reason for separation, number of children by previous companion, and the number of children together (see figure 3.2). These registers and certificates demonstrate the ways that marriage was about far more than legally sanctifying a couple's relationship. The records simultaneously served a census-like function, documenting and stabilizing basic information like a name, age, race, relationship history, and family composition. As there was no systematic way of verifying much of this information, its significance did not lie mainly in its factual accuracy. Rather, collecting these details was the basis for the recognition of individual personhood and the establishment of a new relationship between the state and the recently emancipated.

The first, and perhaps most important, facts recorded on marriage certificates were names. To participate in marriage contracts or labor contracts,

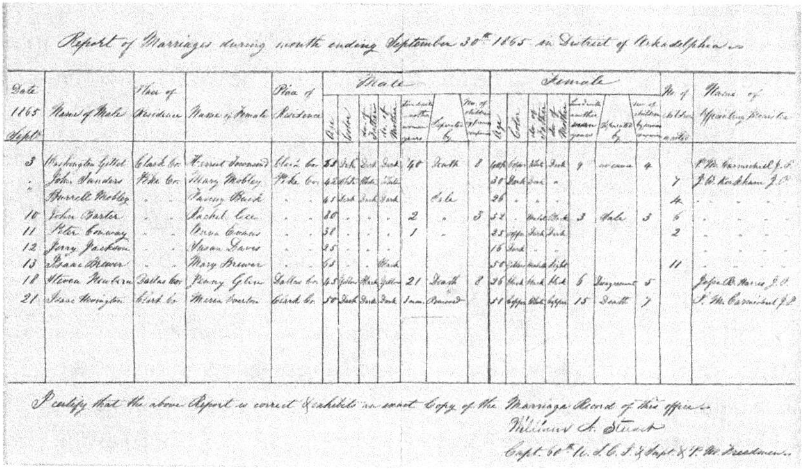

Report of Marriages during month ending September 30th 1865 in District of Arkadelphia

I certify that the above Report is correct & exhibits an exact Copy of the Marriage Record of this office.
William A. Stuart
Capt. 60th U.S.C.I. & Supt. & P.M. Freedmen

Figure 3.2 Marriage Register from Arkadelphia, Arkansas, Sept. 30, 1865. Marriage Records of the Office of the Commissioner, Washington Headquarters of the Bureau of Freedmen, Refugees, and Abandoned Lands, 1861–69.

freedpeople were compelled to adopt dominant conventions of naming by taking both a first and last name and committing to use only a single name.[32] With emancipation, standardized forms of naming became important both for supporting the integrity of state record keeping and for holding freedpeople to the terms of contracts. Therefore, in conjunction with marrying freedpeople, bureau officials required them to take a surname. As the South Carolina marriage rules outline, "Every Freedman having only one name is required to assume a 'title' or family name. . . . When once assumed, it must always thereafter be used and no other."[33]

This compulsion to adopt dominant conventions of naming was linked to the compulsion to adopt a patriarchal organization of the family. In *John Freeman and His Family*, an instructional text for freedpeople intended to cultivate the values of good citizenship, one of the first anecdotes about the protagonist's life as a freedperson is about being named. When John reports for his first day of work as a freedperson, the lieutenant in charge requests his name. John replies that his name is simply John. When asked for a last name, John replies that he is "Colchester Lenox's John" and that he has no last name. Remarking that John must have a last name, the lieutenant proceeds to name John, first offering Lenox, John's former master's last name. Upon John's objection to this name on the grounds that it would always be a reminder of his enslavement, the lieutenant names him John Freeman.

This interaction concludes with the lieutenant explaining to John, "You must give your wife the same name, then, mind, and all your children. Then we shall know you all belong together. You'll be *the Freeman family*."[34]

In this anecdote, the name individuates John as no longer the property of his master (Colchester Lenox's John) but as his own person (John Freeman) in charge of his own "Freeman family." To enter into contracts, freedpeople were required to adopt names that mirrored the structure of white naming practices. As Elizabeth Regosin notes, Black people had their own naming practices, both under slavery and after emancipation, that reflected their own understandings of kinship and belonging. The dominant structure of naming, however, organized freedpeople into easily recognizable heteropatriarchal households that "belonged together," thereby constituting kinship in very narrow ways. Because names functioned as the legal record of kinship, standardizing freedpeople's names was also a means of standardizing the kinds of family relationships that would be recognized by the state. In this way, naming was key to the formation of a public identity that connected belonging in a heteropatriarchal family to belonging in the nation-state.[35]

This anecdote also illustrates the way that naming as a practice of state record keeping linked racial subordination and wage labor to the heteropatriarchal family. A prerequisite for entry into a labor contract, the conferral of a surname solidifies John's gendered identity as an independent worker and a responsible head of household. On his way home, John reflects on his naming as follows: "He had got a *name*, and a treasure, indeed, it seemed. A new name it was, distinct, clean of slavery, savoring of the life of liberty and equal rights upon which he was entering. He was determined that he would never disgrace it by idleness or want of integrity, or by any act unworthy of freedom; and he was earnestly desirous that those who bore it with him should esteem and cherish it as he did."[36] While John's new name clearly marks the transition from being enslaved to being free, it also operates as an incitement to become a subject whose freedom is defined in opposition to idleness. Having a name and being free both require that one never falter in demonstrating one's worthiness of those things to one's emancipators. As Saidiya Hartman points out in her reading of various counsels for freedmen, these instructional anecdotes reinforced a conception of freedom that was defined by "the burdened individuality of the responsible and encumbered freedperson."[37] Naming, in particular, was fundamental to the individuation required of the liberal, rights-bearing subject, and having a singular identity was a precondition for entering into contracts and being held legally responsible. The name was a key signifier of independence and self-possession. However, because the state official retained the power to name and to define the normative structure and meaning of names, being named simultaneously marked John as a free man and subjected his freedom to the parameters determined by the state.[38]

The performance of freedom compelled by the act of naming was deeply gendered. In a complementary moment of interpellation in *John Freeman and His Family*, Miss Horton, a white teacher who acts as a benevolent reformer throughout the text, addresses Clarissa, John's wife, as Mrs. Freeman during her first visit to their home. Upon hearing this, Clarissa's response is described as follows: "Clarissa hardly knew what to do when she heard herself addressed in this unexpected and respectful manner. She had never been called Mrs. Freeman before. That sounds a heap like white folks, she thought to herself, and now I must honor the name as John says."[39] As Hartman points out, for Clarissa, naming bears a different significance as it simultaneously defines her freedom and her civil death as John's wife.[40] In contrast to the call to masculine independence, the name Mrs. Freeman compels Clarissa to emulate the norms of white femininity in her efforts to be a good citizen. Throughout *John Freeman and His Family*, however, Clarissa is also expected to work diligently outside the home. Becoming Mrs. Freeman therefore ties Clarissa to the obligations of domesticity but does not offer her the same protections from the labor market that white women enjoyed.[41] Rather, for freedwomen, marriage often meant that their labor became their husbands' to sell, as is evidenced in the widespread practice of freedmen signing labor contracts on behalf of their wives.

Read alongside the historical archive of the Freedmen's Bureau's marriage records, these anecdotes about naming reveal the political interests reflected in the listing of names on marriage certificates. Marriage as an institution was a key location for the solidification of names, and marriage certificates did not simply record names but rather produced families organized through heteropatriarchal practices of naming. While the family is often cast as prepolitical, at the moment of emancipation the state actively produced a particular family form as normative and as the precondition for political belonging through the registration of marriages. At the same time, marriage worked to constitute gender as a fundamental component of identity and as a key mechanism through which the meaning of citizenship would be defined. The compulsion to legally marry laid the foundation for holding freedpeople legally accountable for fulfilling the gendered obligations of citizenship. In her discussion of the coconstitutive character of marriage and the state, Jacqueline Stevens notes that "to be born into a family is always to be born into a larger group that made possible the family form as such."[42] The case of emancipation illustrates that the reverse is also true. To enter the nation, freedpeople needed to enter heteropatriarchal families.

Marriage did not simply recognize a relationship between two individuals. It simultaneously located that relationship within an intergenerational heteropatriarchal family tree that positioned individuals in relation to both past and future.[43] Marriage and the heteronormative constructions of kinship it secured reproduced a specific temporality—what Jack Halberstam calls *straight time*—that both organizes daily life around domestic norms and, through the rubric of generations, "connects the family to the historical past of the nation, and glances ahead to connect the family to the future of both familial and national stability."[44] While they were pushed to adopt the conventions of straight time, freedpeople's relationship to the construction was complicated. Not only was there considerable resistance on the part of whites to imagining freedpeople as part of the future of the nation, but, legally, it was difficult to navigate the past of slavery, in which freedpeople's personhood had not been recognized.

To bring the socially dead into the realm of legally recognized kinship, marriage registers had to reconstruct a genealogical past in which to locate the relationship. This process can be seen in the way that marriage certificates and registers recorded details about the parents and children of the couple, thereby constructing a heteronormative family tree within which the marriage was embedded. These registers and certificates acknowledge kinship ties between the individuals being married and their parents and children in state records for the first time. While the records themselves do not contain the names of parents and children, they ask specifically about the color of both parents of each of the individuals being married, the number of children each individual had with another companion, and the number of children the couple had together. This recording of multigenerational details about families reveals the way in which state record keeping presumed, and in doing so produced, the idea that freedpeople came to freedom already embedded in the heteronormative family, the very thing that slavery had explicitly denied access to. The recording of parental information both erases the violence of a structure that explicitly legally alienated children from their parents and makes invisible any diversity in the kinship relations practiced under slavery. In doing so, the records function to simultaneously construct and naturalize heteronormative kinship. In this way, state efforts to anchor heteronormativity across time masquerade as the simple bureaucratic recording of facts.

Just as marriage certificates distilled a heterosexual genealogy for Black families entering into freedom, they also produced a heterosexualized past for the individuals registering their marriages. Certificates listed the number of years spent with a previous companion and the reason for separation to resolve a problem of timing. The marriages registered by the Freedmen's Bureau were unique in that they frequently constituted in the present a legally binding relationship that extended into the past. For example, the North Carolina law that declared all formerly enslaved cohabiting couples to be married commenced those marriages not at the time of the passage of the law or at emancipation but rather when the individuals began living together. As Laura Edwards notes, this was significant because had the marriages begun after emancipation, all children born earlier would have been considered illegitimate, and the state would have been financially responsible for them.[45]

This retroactive recognition of marriage also posed a problem in that many freedpeople had relationships with multiple individuals who might have been legally recognized as their spouses under the law. Therefore, translating the sexual and domestic practices of enslaved people into the legally recognizable rubric of marriage required that the recognition of relationships be selective. Recording the number of years they had lived with a previous partner and the reason for separation was a means of achieving this selective recognition and preserving the monogamy of marriage. Bureau officials also recorded the number of children each spouse had with a previous partner in addition to the number of children the couple had together. This practice worked to establish parental responsibility for children from previous relationships, a primary concern for bureau officials, who sought to minimize the number of freed children who would be potentially dependent on the state. Because there was no way to record earlier relationships that did not approximate marriage, this record-keeping practice made invisible any forms of kinship that did not conform to heteronormative standards. In this way, the bureau's efforts at promoting legal marriage did not simply organize freedpeople into heteronormative family units. In doing so, these practices also actively dismantled other family forms, rendering meaningful kinship ties that did not conform to heteronormativity untraceable within the archive and impossible as the grounds for legal claims. In this sense, marriage simultaneously produced and foreclosed legal kinship relationships among freedpeople.

One of the most striking elements of the bureau's marriage records is the column for reason for separation, which is predominantly listed as sale or death. Just as the records attempt to produce a linear narrative of the past that erases the social death of slavery by retroactively recognizing previous relationships that were not seen as legitimate in their own present, the indication that these relationships frequently ended in forced separation through the sale of one of the parties defies this erasure. As a visible sign of the violence of slavery, the marking of sale troubles the genealogy the records try to produce by gesturing toward the artifice at its foundation. The marking of sale challenges the clean break between slavery and freedom that marriage certificates ostensibly signified, pointing instead to slavery's lasting effects. The record keeping that solidifies the transition from being treated as property to being treated as a population remains animated by the relations of domination inscribed by slavery.

The registration of marriages was a cornerstone in the effort to make freedpeople into liberal individuals. The practice both solidified contract relations as a sign of freedom and stabilized gendered forms of individual personhood that were grounded in the heteronormative family. A key part of the process of making freedpeople into individualized subjects constituted through statistical facts, marriage registers organized kinship through heteronormative relationships while simultaneously securing a relationship between individuals and the state. Marriage certificates reveal the ways in which entry into citizenship was predicated on the production of gendered difference. The practice of marriage registration worked to construct heteronormative kinship as a natural fact and in doing so laid a foundation for the gendered enforcement of obligations in racially stratified ways.

Enforcing the Gendered Obligations of Marriage

In addition to stabilizing identities and securing liberal forms of personhood, efforts to organize freedpeople into heteronormative families through marriage were simultaneously efforts to remake the division between public and private spheres that was fundamental to the liberal political order. As noted earlier, in the antebellum South, women, children, and enslaved people were all considered dependents located within the private sphere of the household while white male heads of households wielded political power within the public sphere. In this context, the public and private spheres were not just separate. Rather, the private sphere constituted the basis for political power in the public sphere in that having dependents secured white men's status as independent citizens.[46] The construction of the domestic sphere as a space of privacy worked to depoliticize social relations within the household. Conflicts between husbands and wives and between slave owners and the enslaved were understood as private and therefore outside of state jurisdiction, a perception that reinforced racialized patriarchy within the household. At the same time, because of their dependent status, wives, children, and enslaved people were barred from exercising political power in the public sphere.

Given this structure, the legal recognition of marriage ought to have formed the basis for political rights, privacy, and masculine entitlement for freedmen while at the same time confining freedwomen to a subordinated and protected position within the domestic sphere. However, in practice, marriage became a vehicle for exacting a different set of gendered obligations of citizenship from freedpeople and constituting the home as a site of public surveillance. While for white men and women marriage was the linchpin of a gendered system of rights and protections, for freedpeople marriage first and foremost articulated freedom to the burdens of a privatized family. Freedmen's Bureau officials strongly emphasized the need for freedpeople to form "self-sufficient" families, thereby linking masculine independence to wage labor. At the same time, while freedwomen were expected to adopt dominant norms of femininity, they were also expected to continue to work outside the home. These strategies privatized the violence of slavery, thereby absolving the federal government of responsibility for the well-being of freedpeople and justifying austerity toward them. Just as marriage situated the question of public responsibility for slavery in the private sphere, it also made a spectacle of freedpeople's private lives. Marital relations became a site of state scrutiny, intervention, and criminalization, and exacting gendered performances of citizenship in the domestic sphere was central to how the bureau envisioned addressing the legacies of slavery. While marriage established a gendered division between public and private space for freedpeople, race shaped how this boundary was drawn and what it would come to mean.

The bureau's efforts to promote marriage were part of a larger strategy to stabilize the Black labor force through the restructuring of household economies. Just as the vagrancy laws discussed in the next chapter played a significant role in this process by criminalizing movement, marriage established settlement as the desired norm.[47] A lack of respect for marriage was frequently associated with the ills of vagrancy. As bureau agent P. Marshal noted in his inspection report on Jefferson and Orleans Parishes in Louisiana:

> There are no less than seven hundred colored families living in Gretna and Algiers and the intermediate suburbs. Many of these keep groceries and boarding houses also houses of ill fame, and such places are the endeavors of the young portion of the colored people, whose ignorance and aversion to work is soon developed into vagrancy. Adultery is a prominent vice among them, during last week no less than three separate cases were brought. Many are living together as married who are bound by no other tie than the dictate of their former overseer or master.[48]

Bureau officials' complaints about aversion to work, prostitution, adultery, and the persistence of informal practices of marriage among freedpeople were frequently linked in this manner, signaling the ways vagrancy as a construct extended beyond the lack of employment or a stable home. Vagrancy was instead understood as a cultural condition characterized by laziness, lack of discipline, irresponsibility, and sexual promiscuity. Much like the culture-of-poverty discourse that would emerge in the twentieth century, vagrancy was viewed as a legacy of slavery that needed to be remedied, particularly through reform of gendered and sexual behaviors.

The discourse on vagrancy substituted cultural explanations for an analysis of the material inequalities produced by slavery and suggested that it was cultural reform, not the redistribution of resources or reparations, that was most important to freedpeople's future. This was particularly apparent in references to nonnormative sexual relations as a lingering effect of slavery that held the emancipated back. An assistant commissioner in Louisiana wrote, "Their lack of regard for matrimonial alliances is one of the great drawbacks to their progressiveness. . . . This degrading evil is one of the many which slavery imparted and fostered upon them so clearly that they cannot at once become entirely free from this disgusting practice."[49] This understanding of slavery as having left a cultural legacy among freedpeople that was the primary barrier to the exercise of liberal freedom displaced an analysis of the structural inequalities that hundreds of years of stolen labor had produced, while simultaneously pathologizing nonnormative sexual practices. Vagrancy, in this context, was not just an individual crime but a sign of a larger cultural condition of unfreedom fostered by slavery. To be vagrant was to fail to take up the responsibilities of citizenship and to continue to exist in the backward cultural conditions fostered by slavery. In this sense, the vagrant was out of step with the temporality of citizenship. Rather than moving forward toward citizenship and freedom, the vagrant remained mired in the dependency of slavery. Thus, the discourse on vagrancy functioned as a powerful technique for rewriting structural inequalities as cultural deficiencies, and it was these cultural deficiencies that needed to be overcome in order to be free. Marriage, through the ways it articulated labor and sexual discipline, offered a means of expunging these vestiges of slavery and cultivating liberal subjectivity.

In this context, marriage more than any other institution had the potential to prevent vagrancy by constituting the boundaries of a new private sphere for freedpeople. However, this private sphere was not so much a space outside the realm of public jurisdiction as it was a space in which gendered liberal subjects might be cultivated. As discussed in the previous chapter, Nayan Shah has shown how the legitimation of forms of intimacy that are linked to settlement and permanence forms "the cornerstone of the social and political order."[50] Shah shows how forms of intimacy grounded in the heteronormative family were seen as central to the development of the possessive individualism and independence that characterized the normative masculine liberal subject. Conversely, feminist historians have argued that women's dependent position confined them to the sanctity of the home and defined their value as citizens in terms of dependency, motherhood, and the intergenerational transmission of national values.[51] Significantly, the valuation of settlement as necessary to a home life that would produce properly gendered citizens developed alongside the naturalization of settler colonialism and the occupation of Native lands. In relation to these constructions, deviant sexuality and gender transgression were frequently associated with a lack of self-determination and social disorder. Bureau officials believed that marriage could correct this by forcing freedpeople to take responsibility for themselves and transforming former slaves into citizens. As Katherine Franke shows, marriage functioned as a "domesticating technology" that linked citizenship status to specific ways of embodying gender and sexuality.[52] This process of domestication put forward settler colonial constructions of gender and sexuality as naturalized ideals. However, in practice, these ideals worked not as a facilitator of assimilation but rather as a measure against which freedpeople would consistently be deemed undeserving. In this way, settler domesticities worked not to make freedpeople into a settler population but rather to deploy heteronormativity in ways that linked their subordination to the ongoing process of settler colonialism.

The duties of bureau officials went well beyond encouraging freedpeople to marry and legally sanctifying heteronormative kinship relations. Officials were also expected to cultivate the specific gendered behaviors that accompanied marriage in their efforts to make the domestic sphere an anchor for citizenship. The manual for officers of the Freedmen's Bureau in Mississippi directed officials as follows on the subject of marriage:

> You will require husbands to live with and support their wives and children. For this purpose apply to the officers of the civil law when you think a case requires compulsion.
>
> Visit the families of freedpeople, for the purpose of inquiring into their domestic relations; give them all needed information; teach them that marriage has all the sanctions of the Divine Law; repress, by all means in your power, "taking up together"; and, when you find it practicable, apply the vagrant law as a check to the course of lewd women.[53]

Bureau officials' jurisdiction went well beyond requiring legal marriage, extending into the domestic sphere to dictate what behaviors and relationships within the home should look like. For freedmen, this meant settling down and providing for their dependents. For freedwomen, this meant sexual restraint and the subordinated position of a wife within the domestic sphere. The domestic economy of marriage was defined by labor discipline and sexual restraint and worked as an economic and cultural safeguard against vagrancy by establishing male heads of households as financially responsible for themselves and their dependents and containing sexuality within the heteronormative home. Notably, just as bureau officials worked to produce a domestic sphere modeled after a white ideal of the civilized family, for freedpeople the domestic sphere was significantly different in that it did not include a claim to privacy. Rather, the home became a site of particularly intense surveillance and regulation.

While the bureau's marriage-promotion practices opened up freedpeople's domestic and sexual relations to public scrutiny, they simultaneously privatized responsibility for freedpeople's material well-being, locating it in the nuclear family. The promotion of marriage was closely linked to anxieties that freedpeople might become public charges. An important rationale for both requiring men to adopt the role of head of household and confining women's sexuality and reproduction to the nuclear family was the idea that Black families should be self-sufficient and require no public support. While the bureau did provide limited forms of short-term material assistance to freedpeople in the immediate aftermath of the war, this assistance quickly waned, and claims to land and other forms of wealth redistribution went unrealized. Instead, as discussed in chapter 4, the bureau concentrated its efforts on securing labor contracts, under the belief that free labor was the path to both self-sufficiency and true freedom.

Marriage and the legal responsibilities it conferred on male heads of households were key to rationalizing austerity toward freedpeople. The Freedmen's Inquiry Commission argued that the marriage ceremony, "while it legitimizes these relations, imposes upon the husband and father the legal obligation to support his family."[54] Rooted in an ideal of masculine citizenship that grounded male power and independence in the capacity to care for dependents, marriage for freedpeople became interwoven with a disproportionate emphasis on obligation.[55] Marriage secured legally recognizable households with male heads responsible for dependent wives and children. However, for freedmen, dependents became the basis on which to exact discipline rather than a foundation for political power. Marriage guarded against vagrancy in that it instilled in freedmen an obligation to stay in one place and engage in wage labor. Taking on this obligation was understood as a necessary part of the transition from being a slave to being a man. As Representative William Kelley of Pennsylvania argued, freedmen would become industrious citizens once "the freedman [can] feel that he is a man with a home to call his own, and a family around him, a wife to protect, children to nurture and rear, wages to be earned and received, and a right to invest his savings in the land of the country."[56] By providing an investment and incentive to hard work, marriage and family were central to constructions of masculine independence and freedom grounded in settlement, provision for dependents, and wage labor.

The way bureau officials approached the problem of desertion illustrates this. The desertion of women and children was a central concern of the bureau, and holding fathers legally and financially responsible for their wives and children was frequently presented as an important reason for encouraging legal marriage among freedpeople. Bureau officials expressed anxiety that the continued practice of informal marriage would allow freedmen to shirk their responsibilities as husbands and fathers. As one official noted, legal marriage needed to be required because "while many consider sacred the marriage vows taken while slaves, others take advantage of the manner in which they were married, desert their families and contract new obligations, procuring legal license."[57] Another official, noting numerous complaints from wives about husbands who had deserted them or failed to provide adequate support for their children, pointed out that without the strict enforcement of the legal obligations of marriage, "a man's wife here is in a worse condition than his baker or grocer, for they can enforce the payment of the debts due them but she for the debts contracted at the altar is without remedy."[58] Marriage was used as a tool to secure financial obligations and prevent transiency by holding men responsible for the material needs of their dependents. The bureau not only encouraged marriage but also worked to enforce marriage contracts in much the same way as it worked to enforce labor contracts. Bureau agents encouraged husbands who left their wives to return and invoked vagrancy laws against men who abandoned their families and their jobs by moving to another location.[59] The Freedmen's Inquiry Commission even recommended that freedmen who refused to support their children be forced to contribute a portion of their wages to their care, an early precedent to late twentieth-century child support enforcement practices.[60]

Bureau officials expressed similar anxieties about the fathers of children born outside of marriage. In his report on the condition of freedpeople in Alexandria and Fairfax Counties in Virginia, Captain Lee wrote, "I desire to call your attention to the necessity of compelling the fathers of illegitimate children to support them. At least three fourths of the applications for assistance come from women with children, but who have no husbands. The fathers of these children can usually be reached—but in the absence of any means of compelling them to support their children the evil continues to exist."[61] Lee's statement demonstrates bureau officers' concerns that federal assistance was going to women and children who should be supported by freedmen and the officers' belief that holding fathers accountable was a necessary response to the large number of freedwomen and children who found themselves impoverished after the war. These beliefs resonated with those of local governments as well, some of which adopted strict bastardy laws designed to force fathers to support their illegitimate children and to communicate that "the state would not pick up the tab."[62] Part of the broad effort to criminalize Black mobility and bind freedpeople to long-term labor contracts with white planters, these laws were harshly enforced, often with little or no evidence. As even one bureau official observed of the use of bastardy laws in North Carolina, "The apparent object of the Bastardy Law is to relieve the County from the support or the liability to support the illegitimate children. . . . There had been many complaints from Freedmen who have been arrested under this law as the putative fathers of children nearly three years of age and who, in order to give them security were obliged to sell themselves or their services for periods from one to seven years."[63]

These examples illustrate how the legal transition from slavery to citizenship for freedmen coincided with the emergence of the figure of the irresponsible father—what today might be called the "deadbeat dad"—as a criminalized subject. The constitution of marriage both as the normative family form and as a legally enforceable contract worked to settle potentially transient freedmen into family obligations and laid the ground for the criminalization of those who did not appear to comply. In this way, emancipation signaled an important transition in how Black families were treated by the state. Before emancipation, the law constituted the boundary between private and public in such a way as to guarantee slaveholders absolute power over the lives and social relations of the enslaved by both denying enslaved people access to their own private sphere and reinforcing the power of white male heads of households. In this context, questions about fatherhood and the legitimacy of children were largely irrelevant to the state. All children born to an enslaved mother inherited her enslaved status and were thus property, natally alienated from their parents. After emancipation, the emphasis on marriage shifted the boundaries between private and public, constituting a domestic sphere for freedpeople that was simultaneously public and private. On the one hand, gendered behaviors within the domestic sphere were the subject of much public scrutiny. On the other hand, the nuclear family became a privatized locus of responsibility for freedpeople's material needs.

Once freedpeople could potentially claim public assistance, it became very important to tie them to heteropatriarchal families that would supplant those claims. Hence, desertion, illegitimacy, single motherhood, and other nonnormative sexual practices and forms of kinship emerged as problems to be solved. While most explicitly discussed as problems of gender and sexual normativity, these questions were fundamentally about withholding resources from freedpeople. For freedmen, particular weight was placed on the obligations that marriage produced, particularly the obligation to engage in wage labor. While emancipation marked a legal transition from natal alienation to citizenship, citizenship came to connote privatized responsibilities rather than public entitlements. As Laura Edwards argues, citing the widespread practice of apprenticing Black children to whites, marriage did not "make African American men household heads with the power to protect the interests of their dependents. It simply obligated them to support their dependents because it was inconvenient and unprofitable for white planters to do so."[64]

Notably, the construction of the U.S. welfare state during the Progressive Era and New Deal relied heavily on discourses that naturalized and idealized the heterosexual nuclear family in very similar ways to the discourses invoked by the Freedmen's Bureau. However, in relation to primarily white citizens, gendered conceptions of citizenship served as a vehicle for demanding that the state intervene in the conditions of labor so as to better align them with cultural constructions of masculine independence and feminine dependence.[65] While this of course reproduced and even expanded heteropatriarchal domination, it also forged a relationship between white citizens and the heteropatriarchal family that was characterized by material support from the state and redistribution through the normalization of the family wage. In contrast, for freedpeople, gendered constructions of citizenship had little impact on labor conditions. Rather, enforcing gender norms was relegated primarily to the terrain of cultural reform and did not warrant government support for creating the conditions that might actually make heteronormative family life possible. This divergence between cultural constructions of gendered citizenship and the labor demands placed on freedpeople constituted an impossible predicament. Successfully becoming a citizen required men to be independent providers, but freedmen generally did not have access to wages on which they could support a family. Successfully becoming a citizen for women required them to perform idealized femininity, but freedwomen were simultaneously required to participate in forms of labor that rendered them outside of the protections of womanhood. In this way, gender became a vehicle for constituting freedpeople as perpetually failing as citizens and therefore perpetually in need of reform.

The bureau's efforts to promote marriage also instilled and reinforced gender hierarchy within Black families. While it is difficult to generalize about freedpeople's own conceptions of gender roles, numerous examples indicate that the newly emancipated's vision of freedom included forms of gender equality. For example, Edwards shows how freedpeople and working-class whites employed different conceptions of gender that allowed women greater access to the public sphere.[66] Elsa Barkley Brown documents the ways that Black communities subverted the extension of suffrage exclusively to Black men by using men's votes as community votes over which women exercised considerable power.[67] Similarly, in her analysis of Black political discourse in Arkansas during Reconstruction,

Hannah Rosen notes that even relatively privileged Black male political leaders shied away from invoking masculinist constructions of citizenship despite the vast lexicon that grounded political rights in manhood.[68] In this context, bureau efforts to secure the heteropatriarchal family as the primary way of organizing kin and other social relationships can be seen as an effort to produce and naturalize gender hierarchy within Black communities. Bureau officials required that freedmen exert power over freedwomen in order to fulfill the gendered obligations of citizenship, and they created political and economic structures that reinforced patriarchy within the home.

The bureau's emphasis on marriage sought to replace more collective understandings of freedom and social responsibility with reliance on the nuclear family. This construction of family was both economically a locus of privatization and culturally a site of intense public surveillance. A cornerstone in the definition of citizenship through a set of impossible gendered obligations, marriage worked to both delegitimize freedpeople's claims to even minimal material support from the state and criminalize those who did not or could not comply with heteropatriarchal norms. In practice, the gendered ideals of freedom espoused by bureau officials were both limiting and contradictory. Masculine independence functioned more as a constraint than as an expression of autonomy. Not only were the terms of independence predetermined for freedpeople, but the heavy emphasis on demonstrating one's independence through labor discipline and financial support for a family transformed independence into an obligation to be fulfilled rather than a basis for autonomy. Furthermore, one of the primary attributes of masculine independence was in fact continued dependence on white employers. In contrast, the discourse on feminine dependency curtailed freedwomen's access to political power. Freedwomen were expected to engage in wage labor and provide for children in many of the same ways as freedmen. However, the construct of female dependency functioned to devalue their labor and further limit their power in shaping the terms of their work. Both masculine and feminine citizenship were defined in contrast to the vagrant, who embodied the negative consequences of improper dependencies on charity or the state.[69] Bureau officials believed that enforcing gendered norms would make the formerly enslaved into men who conformed to liberal ideals of independence and women whose dependency was contained and controlled within the household, thereby cultivating the characteristics necessary for the proper exercise of freedom.

The contradictory ways in which gendered conceptions of citizenship were invoked in relation to freedpeople have significant implications for theorizations of racialized state power in the postemancipation moment. At first glance, marriage seems to mark a key moment in this transition from state power defined primarily by violence to state power that operates through the cultivation of particular forms of life. In promoting marriage, bureau officials sought to manage the health and character of a new population of citizens and in doing so linked individual performances of gendered citizenship to the well-being of the nation as a whole. However, freedpeople's relationship to norms of gendered citizenship was markedly different from that of white citizens. For white citizens, gendered citizenship, while still confining, became a vehicle for claims to privacy, individual rights, political power, and state resources. In contrast, for freedpeople, gendered citizenship became the basis for state surveillance, labor discipline, and austerity. In constituting the privatized family as the locus of responsibility for freedpeople's well-being, marriage in fact justified the neglect of freedpeople's material needs rather than underwriting an investment in the health of the population.

Drawing on Michel Foucault's understanding of the transition from sovereign power to biopower, it is tempting to see the Freedmen's Bureau's emphasis on gendered norms of citizenship as simply an extension of biopower and consequently a sign of the inclusion of freedpeople into the national population, even if at tremendous cost.[70] However, in this historical case, racism did not just delineate the proper exercise of sovereign power but also shaped the way the extension of these norms functioned.[71] Gendered citizenship was itself a racial construction, and as bureau officers sought to enforce particular constructs of masculinity and femininity, they were really demanding that freedpeople mimic the white ideals of civilization that had justified slavery in the first place.[72] This demand not only preserved the epistemological foundations of white supremacy but, in doing so, constituted freedpeople as perpetually behind at or unnatural to citizenship. To the extent that they could not shed their Blackness, freedpeople could never truly reach the gendered ideals of whiteness. Blackness continued to signify freedpeople's backwardness and formerly enslaved condition, and the most visible manifestations of this to bureau agents were deviant genders and sexualities. While bureau officials spoke extensively about the reform of freedpeople, the language of reform was less about the potential for integration and more about situating freedpeople's citizenship as contingent on education and surveillance. In this sense, Blackness marked a racial boundary within constructions of gendered citizenship. On one side of this boundary, gendered citizenship was characterized by rights, entitlements, and belonging, and on the other side, it was characterized by obligations, austerity, and contingency. The norms of masculine independence and feminine domesticity used to articulate these constructions were the same, but their effects varied greatly for differently racialized populations.

Civil War Pensions and the Construction of the Deserving Subject

The effects of these racially stratified constructions of gendered citizenship can be clearly seen in the Civil War pension system. As the image this chapter opened with suggests, military service and marriage were linked together as quintessential markers of the transition into citizenship. Nowhere is this more evident than in the ways that marriage and heteronormative ideas of the family emerged as the foundation for the first broad-scale system of federal welfare provision, Civil War pensions. In July 1862 the federal government expanded military pensions to include extended support for the families of Union soldiers killed in the war. Originally designed as a recruitment tool, the law addressed a significant barrier to enlistment for many men in the North, the fear that their families would be left destitute.[73] The new law made the widows and dependent children of deceased soldiers eligible for pensions from the federal government. The rationale behind this extension of the pension system was that it would stave off the economic threat that the war posed to Union families by having the state step in as a provider for women and children in the event a soldier was not able to play that role. In doing this, the law grounded the first extensive system of social welfare provision at the federal scale in maintaining the heteronormative family and the male-breadwinner ideal.[74] By making membership in a family the basis for claims to state support, the pension system linked the performance of gendered roles within the family to citizenship in a way that resonated strongly with the practices of the Freedmen's Bureau.

Within the pension system, the heteronormative family worked as the basis for constructing an individualized idea of deservingness as the measure of one's entitlement to state assistance. For widows especially, deservingness had both an administrative and a moral connotation. In the administrative sense, assessing a widow's deservingness entailed assessing whether a woman had actually been married to a soldier and whether she was in fact legally entitled to a pension. In the moral sense, a widow's deservingness was tied to how well she conformed to gendered ideals of citizenship as a wife and mother, the strongest measure of which was whether her sexuality was constrained within the boundaries of marriage. In practice, administrative and moral concerns overlapped a great deal. Administrative qualification was easily conflated with good character, while a lack of such qualification became read as evidence of poor morality.

The first administrative challenge many freedwomen faced in filing pension claims was establishing that their partner had in fact been a soldier in the war. Inconsistencies in the names used by freedmen in official records often complicated these claims. It was common practice for freedmen to take new surnames upon emancipation, and many had joined the military using one name and then changed that name after the war. In addition, men who had escaped slavery often enlisted under different names to minimize the possibility of recapture.[75] As in the case of marriage registration, names were key to establishing identity. When the names of freedpeople did not adhere to standardized conventions, pension officers often argued that there was insufficient proof that the claimant's husband had served in the war and therefore denied her pension.

The second administrative challenge freedwomen faced was verifying the legitimacy of their marriages. Because the practice of legally registering marriages was not yet widespread, many working-class white women also found this to be a challenge. However, pension officers' perceptions that Black women were more likely to make fraudulent claims meant that, for Black women, the absence of an official marriage record warranted a much more rigorous investigation.[76] In addition, the heteronormative kinship structure that pensions were grounded in and the standards of evidence required to claim pensions presented serious challenges for those who had previously been enslaved. Because kinship relationships under slavery were not legally recognized, it was difficult, if not impossible, for many freedwomen to provide the documentation required to establish their marriage to a soldier and legitimate their pension claim. An 1864 revision of the pension law attempted to address this problem by allowing freedwomen to collect pensions without a marriage certificate if they could prove that they had lived with a soldier as man and wife for at least two years before the soldier's enlistment through the testimony of credible witnesses. In lieu of a marriage certificate, freedwomen could provide affidavits from the person who had performed the marriage ceremony or from witnesses to the ceremony that verified the legitimacy of the marriage. However, freed-women still remained at a disadvantage because pension officers tended to view individual testimonies as less reliable and favored cases in which a claimant could provide official records as evidence.[77] When individual testimonies were the only proof available, pension officers preferred the testimonies of whites. Because the officers perceived the testimonies of other Black people to be unreliable, freedwomen were often put in the difficult position of having to secure testimonies from their former owners in order to make their claim.[78] To access pension benefits, freedwomen often had to endure processes that reiterated the racial hierarchies of slavery.

Despite these challenges, many freedwomen went to great lengths to prove the validity of their marriages. For example, Adeline Mozee filed for a pension in 1891 on behalf of herself and her five children as the widow of Washington Simms, a soldier to whom she had been married before emancipation and who had died in the war. Because Mozee was unable to provide a marriage certificate and the dates of birth of her children, who were born while she was enslaved, a special investigation into her claim was launched. As Mozee herself testified, she was unable to provide this evidence because "at the time of said marriage there was no record kept of marriage of colored persons" and "the person to whom I belonged kept no family records of said births."[79] The investigators interviewed numerous people in an effort to verify Mozee's claim, including her former owner, her former owner's daughter-in-law, and the son of the reverend who had performed their marriage ceremony nearly forty years earlier, as the reverend himself had passed away. While all of these individuals testified that Mozee had been Simms's wife and that Simms was the father of her children, the investigators still determined that there was insufficient evidence to substantiate Mozee's and her children's pension claim. Like Mozee, many freedwomen found the problem of demonstrating the legitimacy of their past relationships to be an insurmountable obstacle, even with supporting testimony.

In investigating claims, pension officers were empowered to define what constituted a legitimate marriage. Like the Freedmen's Bureau, the Pension Bureau employed a singular standard of marriage to assess a heterogeneous field of social relationships and, in doing so, not only normalized marriage but also linked federal assistance to a very specific narrative of what marital relationships should look like. Not only was marriage grounded in the gendered roles of an independent male breadwinner and a dependent wife, but the Pension Bureau's conception of marriage was linked to ideas of settlement, permanence, and exclusivity that had not necessarily been relevant or practicable within enslaved communities. Many freedwomen, while enslaved, had created families with men who went on to serve in the Union military. However, these kin relationships did not always look like the Pension Bureau's ideal of a marriage and therefore were regarded with a great deal of suspicion.[80] Freedwomen often struggled to demonstrate that their relationships met the requirements prescribed by the Pension Bureau. Designed to prevent fraud, these evidentiary requirements sought to secure the pension system from women claiming pensions for soldiers to whom they were not actually married, multiple women claiming pensions for the same soldiers, or pension claims for illegitimate children and children whom the soldier had not fathered, thereby grounding ideas of deservingness in the heteronormative family. Importantly, the heavy emphasis on assessing individual deservingness joined the prevention of fraud and the protection of the heteronormative family as twin objectives of the Pension Bureau.

The Pension Bureau's narrow understanding of kinship posed serious challenges for freedwomen. For example, one challenge emerged in cases where multiple women could lay claim to being a deceased soldier's wife. For example, the sisters Mary Boaz and Lucretia Boaz both filed a pension claim as the widow of John Boaz, a Black soldier who was killed during the war. Mary testified that John had been her husband when they were both enslaved and that they had lived together as husband and wife on the same plantation until John enlisted. About fifteen years later, in 1890, Mary's sister, Lucretia, also filed a claim. Lucretia's attorney argued that Lucretia had in fact been John's first wife and that it was only after Lucretia had been sold away from the plantation on which they lived that John married her sister, Mary. While both women had valid claims, the Pension Bureau's understanding of marriage as defined by the colonial dictates of monogamy, permanence, and settlement meant that only one woman could legitimately be entitled to a pension as John's widow. As a result, the Pension Bureau decided that Lucretia was not truly John's widow since he had later had a relationship with her sister, even though Lucretia and John had been forcibly separated. While the Pension Bureau recognized Mary as John's widow, her pension claim was also denied on the grounds that after John's death she had begun living with another man. In the end, neither woman was able to claim a pension—one was denied on the grounds that she had never legally been John's wife, and the other on the grounds that she had not lived up to the gendered expectations of widowhood. In both cases, the transiency of the Boaz sisters' relationships (as a result of force, death, and/or their own choices) made them undeserving of a pension in the eyes of the bureau.[81]

In a similar case, two women also filed for pensions as the widows of the soldier Joseph Valley. The first, Fannie Valley, had legally married Joseph Valley in 1870 and had lived with him until his death in 1897. Fannie and Joseph Valley's marriage had been legally registered, and, therefore, Fannie's claim seemed uncontestable. However, investigators found that Fannie had been living with another man since her husband's death and therefore denied her pension.[82] Eight years later, Harriet Valley also filed for a pension as the widow of Joseph Valley. Harriet testified:

> I was married under the American flag. I never was married until I married Joe Valley. . . . I lived with the soldier, Joseph Valley, near 20 years as his wife and was the mother of four of his children, all dead but one, Rosey Valley. She lives with me. The soldier Joseph Valley left me and went to live with this claimant, Fannie Valley. They claimed they were married, but I do not know whether or not they were married. I never was divorced from Joseph Valley, he just left me and went in the same house with this Fannie.[83]

According to Harriet, she had been deserted by her husband. While no official record existed of the marriage, investigators discovered that Harriet and Joseph Valley were most likely living together on December 1, 1869, when the Mississippi state constitution was adopted. In an effort to normalize freedpeople's relationships in law, Mississippi's constitution declared that "all persons who have not been married, but are now living together, cohabiting as husband and wife, shall be taken and held for all purposes in law as married, and their children, whether born before or after the ratification of this Constitution, shall be legitimate."[84] Under Mississippi law, Harriet and Joseph Valley would have been considered married. However, the Pension Bureau argued that the "Constitution of 1869 did not operate to 'sanctify the marital relation between a man and woman' simply because they happened on December 1, 1869, to be living together."[85] Rather, it was necessary to demonstrate an intent to be married, which they determined in this case to be absent because both parties had gone on to marry other people. Whereas the Freedmen's Bureau was quick to recognize cohabitation as marriage in cases of desertion, the Pension Bureau, when faced with a similar situation, decided that cohabitation did not constitute marriage for the purposes of pension allocation, even in a case when Mississippi state law would have recognized the individuals as married. While the Freedmen's Bureau strongly asserted that individual freedmen should be held financially responsible for their deserted wives and children, in this case the Pension Bureau decided that a deserted freedwoman was not entitled to government assistance because the fact of desertion invalidated her marriage. In contrast to the Freedmen's Bureau's efforts to secure marriage so as to hold men financially responsible for their families, those same families were often seen as illegitimate when the government might be asked to step into this same position of financial accountability.

In contrast, the Pension Bureau treated desertion quite differently in the case of Sally Christy. Having been married to the former Union soldier Samuel Christy, Sally filed an application for a pension after his death. After investigating Sally, the Pension Bureau denied her application for a pension because she had married Samuel without having received a divorce from her previous husband. Sally's attorney explained that she had believed her first husband, James Puckett, to be dead and that "James Puckett was a wild, quarrelsome and drinking man and that over twenty-five years ago said Puckett quit work, while on a spree, left home and that she has never since seen him or heard of him."[86] Comparing these cases reveals a great deal about how the bureau determined which marriages counted as legitimate and which did not among freedpeople. For Harriet Valley, the second marriages of both Joseph Valley and herself invalidated their first marriage and thereby also invalidated Harriet's claim to a pension. In contrast, Sally Christy's first marriage actually invalidated her second marriage, thereby also invalidating her claim to a pension. In the first case, the lack of a divorce was seen as irrelevant when it might have supported Harriet Valley's case, whereas, in Sally Christy's case, the lack of a divorce was the primary grounds for denial. In illustrating the inconsistencies that marked Pension Bureau's decisions, these examples suggest that rather than making determinations based on a consistent set of principles, the Pension Bureau used the ambiguity around what constituted a legitimate marriage to deny freedwomen's claims.

Another means of denying or terminating pension claims was through the 1882 revision to the pension statute that declared that "the open and notorious adulterous cohabitation of a widow who is a pensioner shall operate to terminate her pension from the commencement of such cohabitation."[87] Because widows lost their pensions upon remarriage, many feared that the pension system encouraged women to have sexual relationships with men without marrying them. By allowing widows a certain measure of economic independence from marriage, pensions potentially fostered sexual immorality. The "adulterous cohabitation" provision addressed this concern by linking pension receipt to the containment of women's sexuality within marriage. As in the cases of Mary Boaz and Fannie Valley, many Black women were denied pensions because they were found to be living with another man. For example, Anna Hayden's pension claim was denied on the grounds that she had lived with two men after the death of her husband. While Hayden maintained that she had simply served as a housekeeper for these two men, the Pension Bureau determined that she was guilty of "open and notorious adulterous cohabitation."[88] Similarly, Maria Bohannan testified that she lived with an elderly man in order to care for him in his old age and was not having a sexual relationship with him. However, the Pension Bureau again considered the fact that she was living with a man enough to deny her a pension.[89] These examples illustrate how far the Pension Bureau went to enforce the provision about cohabitation on freedwomen. The cohabitation law functioned much like an early version of the twentieth-century man-in-the-house rules that were used to deny women welfare assistance. Both linked the receipt of government assistance to the surveillance of women's intimate lives and were grounded in the belief that if a woman was having a sexual relationship with a man, he, not the government, should be providing for her financially.

As these examples illustrate, the concept of deservingness linked the performance of gendered norms of citizenship, particularly the containment of women's sexuality within marriage, to the allocation of federal benefits. Pension officers worked simultaneously as executors of the law and moral safeguards of national resources. The vigilant concern with morality reflected a belief that providing public assistance to undeserving women posed a threat to the nation because it potentially undermined the heteronormative family by providing women with the economic means to live outside of it. Therefore, in the transfer from economic dependence on a husband to dependence on the state, it was particularly important to ensure that the women receiving pensions would continue to properly act out normative femininity. This proved particularly challenging for Black claimants. Normative femininity was a white construction, and therefore it was far more difficult for Black women to convince pension officers of their good moral character. Black women's pension claims were haunted by the racialized perception that they lacked morality either owing to inherent racial characteristics or owing to their previous condition of enslavement. In addition, the Pension Bureau's singular definition of marriage often clashed with the more complex sexual and kinship relations that freedpeople had practiced both before and after slavery.[90] For these reasons, pension officers tended to hold Black women to a higher standard of evidence and were particularly rigorous in investigating whether Black claimants had taken up with another man after their husband's death.[91] These suspicions are also reflected in the files of Black applicants, who often went to extra lengths to demonstrate their respectability in their applications.[92]

Despite these obstacles, some freedwomen did successfully collect the pensions to which they were entitled, and these pensions undoubtedly played an important role in ameliorating some of the financial hardships they faced. However, the level of administrative and moral scrutiny that Black women were forced to undergo is significant in that it reveals the extent to which race and gender structured how marriage and domesticity were constituted for freedpeople. Black women who applied for pensions were treated in much the same way as welfare recipients who are assumed to be cheating the system are treated today. They were subject to special investigations and expected to reveal intimate details of their lives to state officials in exchange for the possibility of public benefits. Sometimes these investigations turned up affairs or other moral transgressions that were used as reasons to deny women pensions. However, even when they did not, these processes were still invasive and demeaning in that they tied collecting one's entitlement to a sacrifice of privacy and the scrutiny of pension officers. While some white women were also subject to these humiliating practices, adherence to the norms of white femininity offered a veil of protection that was never available to Black women.

Although Black women were not excluded from collecting pensions per se, the administration of pensions was structured through a racialized logic. At the root of pension officers' actions was a belief that while providing assistance to some individuals was in the national interest, providing assistance to others posed a threat to the nation. The line between valuable and dangerous investments of state resources might shift and change given the specific context of the case, but the underlying premise of the pension system was that there was a clear and determinable distinction between the two. This premise fundamentally tied federal social welfare provision to reinvented forms of state racism that articulated racialized forms of austerity to individualized constructions of deservingness.

The construct of deservingness was an inherently individualizing and privatizing rubric for the allocation of resources. Not only was deservingness a measure of one's individual behavior devoid of consideration of the context surrounding it, but deservingness as a construct rested on the same conception of the liberal individual that was used to define freedpeople's citizenship through the rubric of responsibility. The questions pension officers asked of freedwomen fixated on their individual behaviors, and this had the effect of mitigating freedwomen's entitlement to these benefits. In practice, freedwomen were presumed undeserving, and the burden of demonstrating their worth was placed on them. As opposed to a system of aid that might have emphasized redistribution or even reparation for the harms of slavery and war, the pension system reinforced the idea that rights were in fact contingent on the fulfillment of gendered responsibilities, particularly in the case of freedwomen because their capacity to fulfill those obligations was so suspect. Postemancipation, administrative decisions about legal and moral deservingness displaced more political questions about access to citizenship. In this way, the rubric of deservingness worked to embed social stratification within purportedly equalizing policies by shifting the scale of analysis from that of policy to that of individual behavior.

The policing of the boundary between who should receive support and who should be denied support also required expanded administrative record keeping that further grounded individual citizenship in a racialized conception of the heteronormative family. Stabilizing and standardizing names and family relationships was crucial to determining who was entitled to a pension. As Megan McClintock observes, the emergence of the pension system fueled efforts to do away with common-law marriage and promote greater state regulation of marriage.[93] Because the allocation of benefits depended on determining the veracity of a marriage, it was increasingly important to systematize and formalize marriage records so as to prevent fraud. The bureaucratic processes that developed for administering pensions necessitated the refinement of state record keeping of marital ties, excluding other kinship relations. In this way, the making of the heteropatriarchal family as the hegemonic structure of kinship was an important function of emergent state bureaucracies. Significantly, the expansion of social welfare provision rested on and reinforced the constitution of the domestic sphere as a primary means of organizing citizenship. Economically, while the pension system expanded federal responsibility for the economic well-being of some of its citizens, it did so in a way that shored up rather than contested the idea that, for freedpeople, economic self-sufficiency was the responsibility of families.

Despite these efforts to confine sexuality and reorganize kinship through the heteronormative family, many freedwomen remained skeptical of the heteropatriarchal family systems that were being pushed on them and exercised their agency in different ways. The pension application of a Louisiana woman by the name of Anne Ross illustrates the critical and complex approaches to marriage that many freedwomen took. Anne Ross (also known as Anne Madison) applied for a widow's pension after the death of her husband, the former soldier Jackson Ross, in 1902. The special investigation launched into Anne's claim focused on evaluating the legitimacy of her marriage and her moral character. The voyeuristic nature of Anne's pension file is striking. The investigation fixates on intimate details of Anne and Jackson Ross's private lives and, in doing so, places a great deal of weight on other people's interpretations of their behavior and relationships as the key evidence in determining her eligibility for a pension. The testimonies collected in the file are highly mediated accounts of Anne and Jackson Ross's lives. They not only reflect the perceptions and personal interests of the persons being interviewed but also are shaped both by the interviewer's preconceptions and by the ways individuals might have tailored their stories in response to an interviewer's expectations. While the special investigator in the case sought to piece together an incontrovertible truth about Anne's deservingness as a pension recipient from these testimonies, they actually reveal complexities and contradictions that challenge the very notion of deservingness that was at the heart of the investigation.

In her deposition Anne Ross gives her own personal history. Born Anne Williams, she was enslaved by a man named Charlie Percy in Louisiana until she was about ten years old. After emancipation, she took a boat south on the Mississippi River with her parents to Donaldsonville, Louisiana, where they settled and she continued to reside. At the age of sixteen, she married her first husband, Nathan Madison. While they never divorced, Nathan eventually left her and had passed away about twelve years before Anne's testimony in her pension case. While Anne had not married again until her marriage to Jackson Ross, she admitted to having a brief affair with Pier Butler, a married man from a nearby town. She began her relationship with Jackson Ross about a year and a half after Nathan Madison had left her and lived with him for approximately seventeen years. Anne and Jackson Ross had two children, both of whom died at a young age. Despite the length of their relationship, Anne and Jackson did not legally marry until the day of Jackson's death. Anne explained that while they had lived as man and wife for many years, she legally married him only to fulfill his dying wish.[94] When asked why she did not marry Jackson sooner, she responded:

Well, he had some very mean ways about him, and I had never decided to marry him until the day he died. I wanted to be free to leave him at any time in the event that he made it too disagreeable for me, and I would not have married him at all if he had not been on his death bed and begged me to do so. Yes, I always treated the soldier as a husband and recognized him as such—and he regarded me as his wife—and we were regarded as man and wife by the people generally. The soldier used to run around with other women a good deal after he and I began living together, and we used to have some words at times because of these other women and I would frequently tell him, "now Jack, I am not married to you, and if you don't stop running after these other women I will quit you."[95]

Anne Ross was not naive and had a clear understanding that her late husband had slept with many other women both before and while they were together. In response to the investigator's questions about her husband's sexual activities, she remarked, "I could not begin to tell you the number of women the soldier cohabited with after he began living with me—let alone those he lived with before he took up with me. It would take you six months to trace up all the women he ever lived with. He claimed to be 96 years old when he died—and he had many women during his time, or at least he had that reputation."[96] However, despite Jackson Ross's unfaithfulness, Anne consciously chose to remain living with him. At one point in the deposition, she explained this choice in terms of prioritizing her own sexual pleasure. She told the investigator quite directly, "I lived with the soldier because he could perform the sexual duties to suit me; if he had not been able to do that I would have quit him because he had bad habits that I did not like."[97] In his report the investigator cited this statement in particular as evidence of Anne's poor character and lack of "matrimonial intent."[98]

Anne Ross's approach to marriage was distinctly different from that of government officials. In contrast to an idealized narrative about marriage, Anne's understanding of marriage emerged from the material conditions that shaped her life. Like many freedpeople, both Anne and Jackson Ross had multiple relationships both inside and outside of marriage. While government agents regarded this as a sign of promiscuity and immorality, for freedpeople these kinds of relationships most likely resonated with the transiency that often characterized their own circumstances. Not only did people move around a great deal after emancipation, but illness, death, and economic hardship took a toll on relationships. Freedpeople moved between different relationships for a broad range of reasons that reflected the intersections of these circumstances and individual desires. Pension officers often judged or blamed freedwomen for having had multiple relationships, even when their relationships ended because of events beyond their control, such as the death or desertion of a partner. At the same time, freedwomen's actions were also informed by their own desires and an understanding of marriage that recognized it both as one of many kinds of relationships and as not necessarily a permanent relationship. Perhaps this understanding made it easier for them to act on and realize their desires even when they did not align neatly with hegemonic constructions of heteronormative marriage. While government officials read these actions as a sign of moral failure, freedwomen themselves did not seem to hold that having been with multiple partners diminished their personal or moral value or that of their partners. For example, Anne Ross is quite straightforward in her description of Jackson Ross's infidelities. While critical of the impact this had on her, she also does not appear to view his sexual activities as a source of shame or as reflecting poorly on her own character or capacities as a potential wife. Rather, given her decision to continue living with Jackson, it appears that she might have thought of his sexual transgressions as simply an element of his character (albeit a challenging one) rather than as a definitive sign of his moral failures as a partner.

Anne Ross's testimony contains a strong critique of the institution of marriage, one that was likely held by many freedwomen. Anne never talks about marriage in terms of heteronormative gender roles or the creation of economically self-sufficient independent families. In fact, the question of receiving financial support from her husband does not even surface in her discussion of her relationship. Anne never says that financial support factored into her decision to stay with Jackson, and she never attempts to occupy the position of dependent wife in her testimony. Rather, she states very clearly that she remained in the relationship to fulfill her own sexual desires. In the eyes of pension officers, this invalidated her marriage because sexual pleasure was not conceived as the proper basis for matrimonial commitment. A relationship grounded in sexual pleasure ran contrary to the emphasis on work, austerity, and permanence that state officials sought to cultivate through marriage. Pleasure was what needed to be contained through marriage, so it is not surprising that Anne and Jackson Ross's relationship would have been unintelligible as a marriage to state officials.

Anne Ross's testimony highlights the ways in which the ideas of settlement associated with the institution of marriage worked to her disadvantage.

Anne understood not getting married as a way to retain her power and agency in the relationship. As she says in her deposition, her primary reason for not marrying Jackson Ross earlier was that she wanted to be able to leave him if necessary. Her testimony implicitly acknowledges how marriage as an institution worked to undermine women and place them in a dependent position. However, Anne herself made choices that maximized her own independence. She recognized that the permanence of marriage was not in her self-interest and that keeping her relationship informal actually allowed her greater freedom. For her, the legally binding contract of marriage obligated women to stay in a relationship while offering few benefits or protections. Significantly, when Anne did choose to marry, it was at a moment in which it was evident that the marriage would end quickly and therefore would not compromise her independence.

From her testimony, it appears that Anne Ross chose pleasure and transiency over settlement and domesticity, recognizing that for women like her, marriage held few benefits and many sacrifices. However, even though she clearly did not meet the Pension Bureau's definition of a deserving widow, Anne still asserted her right to compensation. As Michelle Krowl notes, filing for a pension was an important way that Black women asserted their newfound claims to citizenship.[99] Anne endured a complicated application process and a long and degrading special investigation of her claim even though she clearly did not aspire to the standards of heteronormativity that the pension system was based on. Her sense that she should be entitled to a pension regardless of how well she conformed to the Pension Bureau's standards of deservingness reflects a vastly different understanding of what citizenship ought to have meant in the lives of freedwomen and foreshadows the claims welfare rights activists would make in the latter half of the twentieth century.

Pension officers went to great lengths to discredit Anne Ross's claim. In addition to arguing that her marriage was illegitimate because of her lack of matrimonial intent, disputes around key facts in the case, such as whether the name she used was Anne Ross or Anne Madison and the number of years she lived with Jackson Ross, were interpreted as evidence that Anne was a liar. The investigation also focused on discrediting Anne's moral character by highlighting her associations with sex workers. The special investigator's report stated that since Jackson's death, Anne had been keeping a house of prostitution and that even before the death of the soldier, she had run an assignation house under the guise of a restaurant.[100] In her deposition Anne explained that while she had sublet a room in her house to a prostitute who did do business in the house, she herself had never engaged in prostitution. She declared that she made her living by washing, ironing, and subletting the room in her house. While her tenant corroborated Anne's story, her neighbor, Annie Russell, portrayed the situation very differently. Russell told the investigator:

> I have been knowing the above named claimant since last February and ever since that time she has kept a house of prostitution here in this district. During all of said time she has kept a house right next to mine and has had as high as five women at one time whose business it was to entertain men for money by cohabiting with them. . . . I have seen the claimant talking and laughing with the girls and men in her house here and have seen the "drinks" carried into her house and have heard carousing and great noise there, but I don't know whether claimant was doing part of the carousing or not.[101]

The evidence collected in Anne Ross's pension file is open to many different interpretations. It is clear that constructing an association with prostitution was a key way of discrediting Anne and establishing that she was not deserving of state support. However, it is impossible to know with any certainty whether Anne engaged in sex work herself and what her relationship with the women she lived with was actually like. Pension officials constructed a story about Anne in which she was a conniving, deceitful, and immoral woman who had married a dying soldier solely to claim his pension. Another interpretation of the evidence might emphasize how the harsh financial circumstances that freedwomen faced and the lack of other viable economic options might have led Anne to engage in sex work. This version of Anne's story might conclude that the pension process actually contributed to the problem; had Anne received her pension, she might not have needed sex work, either directly or indirectly, as a source of income. In this way, policies that assumed that freedwomen were immoral produced the economic circumstances in which freedwomen were compelled to make choices that were deemed immoral. A third interpretation might foreground Anne's agency and the way in which her words and actions actively defied dominant norms around race and gender. This story might highlight the elements of a feminist consciousness that informed her choice to prioritize her own independence and claim ownership over her body and her sexuality.

All of these narratives offer explanations for Anne Ross's actions—some more plausible than others. They also make visible the ways in which, despite the range of interpretations available, the archive is structured to elicit a story that centers on Anne's motivations in order to evaluate her deservingness as an individual citizen subject. The very nature of the information collected by pension officers constituted Anne's relationship to the state in terms of this singular question. Devoid of a larger context of the aftermath of slavery, Anne's presence in the national archive is defined by the question of her deservingness as an individual subject. The prominence of this question displaces the consideration of her in any other terms. For example, how did she understand herself and her actions? What did she and other freedwomen want for their freedom? What role did pleasure play in these desires, and what circumstances would have made it possible for those visions of freedom to be actualized?

Within the narratives that the archive enables, it is striking that any sign of Black female pleasure must be either rationalized as evidence of undeservingness or recuperated as an expression of necessity or resistance. This tendency to explain pleasure in terms of something else speaks to its irreconcilability with racialized and gendered constructions of citizenship grounded in the liberal individual and the heteronormative family. For example, what if the scene that Annie Russell describes is simply a scene of pleasure or what Tera Hunter might call the enjoyment of one's freedom?[102] It appears that pleasure is the very thing that must be contained in the transition from slavery to citizenship, and it is the specter of pleasure that both undermines Anne Ross's claim and in the bigger picture motivates pension officers' scrutiny and regulation of widows' lives. Deservingness ultimately required a denial of the possibility of pleasure, thereby tying economic assistance to sexual austerity. Anne's refusal to subscribe to this vision of citizenship marks her as a queer figure within the archive. Because she lays claim to her right to pleasure and her entitlement as a citizen at the same time, her narrative points to an alternative vision of belonging, one that the bureaucratization of social welfare provision and expanded systems of surveillance sought to erase.

Conclusion

Marriage and the gendered ideas of citizenship it secured played a central role in the transition from slavery to racially stratified citizenship. While enslaved people had a broad range of kinship and sexual relationships, the denial of marriage rights in particular worked to constitute marriage as a primary sign of freedom. However, just as it held the promise of undoing the social death of slavery, participation in marriage simultaneously erased other possible ways of organizing kinship and reinforced racialized constructions of civilization that upheld binary gender as a key marker of racial progress. Marriage articulated family and nation to contractual ideas of freedom, thereby replacing the natal alienation of slavery with a conception of the liberal individual that was embedded in the alienating conditions of wage labor. In the aftermath of the Civil War, a primary charge of the Freedmen's Bureau was the "domestication" of freedpeople through the cultivation, registration, and enforcement of marriage. Bureau officials educated freedpeople about the virtues of marriage, issued marriage certificates, and criminalized behavior that did not conform to the gendered norms established by marriage, thereby constituting heteronormativity as a prerequisite to Black citizenship.

The marriage-promotion practices of the Freedmen's Bureau represent an important moment in the production of gender as a foundational element of citizenship and as a rubric through which racial difference was given meaning. While the tendency is to think of formerly enslaved men and women getting married upon emancipation, it was frequently the act of marriage that legally constituted the formerly enslaved as men and women. As the image described at the opening of this chapter depicts, for those who had legally been property, the act of entering into marriage was simultaneously the moment at which they were first recognized as persons in state records. The performance of normative gender and sexuality was key to the establishment of this personhood, and the Freedmen's Bureau compelled these performances through practices of marriage promotion, which stabilized formerly enslaved people's identities as clearly differentiated men and women who as citizens became obligated to exist in heteronormative relationships with each other. Sexual practices and forms of kinship that deviated from these norms were understood as a lingering cultural effect of slavery, as a failure to fully shed one's former condition and take up the responsibilities of liberal personhood. In this way, gender and sexuality were increasingly invoked as a means of reproducing racial hierarchy. The transgressive genders and sexualities of freedpeople became a sign of the threat that Blackness posed to the nation, and in an effort to contain that threat, bureau officials cultivated an idea of freedom rooted in settlement, domesticity, and wage labor.

The marriage-promotion practices of the Freedmen's Bureau and the ways in which the heteronormative family grounded the Civil War pension system offer important insights into the history of the U.S. welfare state. Feminist histories that locate the origins of welfare programs in the Progressive Era have correctly highlighted the role that gendered ideas of citizenship played in the production of a stratified system of benefits. However, in emphasizing the role that ideas of motherhood, domesticity, and feminine dependency, on the one hand and masculine independence and wage labor, on the other, played in the allocation of social benefits, they have been less attentive to the racialized contradictions that inhered within gendered constructions of citizenship. Situating Reconstruction as a key moment in the reconstruction of the heteropatriarchal family makes visible the central role that race played in defining gendered citizenship and the ways in which gender became a terrain on which the struggle to maintain racial inequality was waged. Marriage and the language of gendered citizenship that accompanied it developed a double meaning. On the one hand, it was the basis for both privacy and the exercise of rights in the public sphere. On the other hand, it could be used to privatize economic obligations in a way that tied people to wage labor, rationalized state austerity, and enabled surveillance within the home. While for whites the emphasis was clearly on the former, for freedpeople marriage was primarily seen as a vehicle for the latter. Even when racial equality was a formal principle of resource allocation, as in the case of Civil War pensions, these multiple meanings of marriage enabled racial stratification to continue. In this way, gendered citizenship became not only a vehicle for producing hierarchy between men and women but also a key language through which racial inequality could be secured within the welfare state.

Assessing individual deservingness emerged as a central function of nascent welfare bureaucracies such as the Freedmen's Bureau and the Pension Bureau. Deservingness as a construct was an effect of liberal constructions of personhood and reflected the contradictions that liberal ideas of freedom presented for freedpeople. Deservingness had both a legal and a moral connotation, and one had to fulfill the obligations of gendered citizenship to be considered deserving of state assistance. However, the ideals of gendered citizenship were defined in ways that were frequently unattainable for freedpeople. For freedwomen, the ideals of domesticity were incompatible with the economic mandate that they work outside the home. Even though this produced an impossible position for freedwomen, the rubric of deservingness focused exclusively on the individual, to the exclusion of the larger context that surrounded her. In this way, state austerity toward freedwomen was cast as the outcome of their own failure to become normative women. In particular, the idea of deservingness reflected state investments in containing Black women's pleasure, particularly sexual pleasure. Sexual pleasure became a sign of the dangers that indiscriminate state assistance posed to the nation, of what investment in the wrong people might unleash.

FOUR

Domestic Labor and the Politics of Reform

The virulently racist attack on the Freedmen's Bureau shown in figure 4.1 appeared during Hiester Clymer's 1866 bid to become governor of Pennsylvania. Clymer, who ran against and was eventually defeated by Republican candidate John Geary, played on the white public's antipathy toward the bureau to advance his white supremacist political platform. Emblematic of some of the most explicit examples of postemancipation racism in the visual culture of the era, this image presents a nightmarish vision of the implications of extending freedom to Black people. At the focal point of the poster, a racist caricature of a vagrant freedperson lounges beneath words attributed to him: "What is de use for me to work as long as dey make those appropriations," a reference to aid provided by the bureau. The image explicitly reframes public assistance to the formerly enslaved as creating the conditions in which freedpeople might indulgently live off the labor of white men. In a perverse erasure of slavery, the poster argues that while "the white man must work to keep his children and pay his taxes," freedpeople would simply reap the benefit of those tax dollars, offering nothing in return. The figures itemized on the right-hand side compare federal appropriations to Black and white citizens. At the top, the poster erroneously claims that Black veterans received substantially larger benefits than white veterans. At the bottom, it argues that while freedpeople received millions of dollars in assistance from the federal government through the bureau, the only allocations made to the white man were "heavy taxes, hard labor."

Monstrously large, the Black vagrant quite literally pushes white citizens to the periphery of the image: white men toil in the margins, and a concerned white woman and her child watch the scene in the distance.

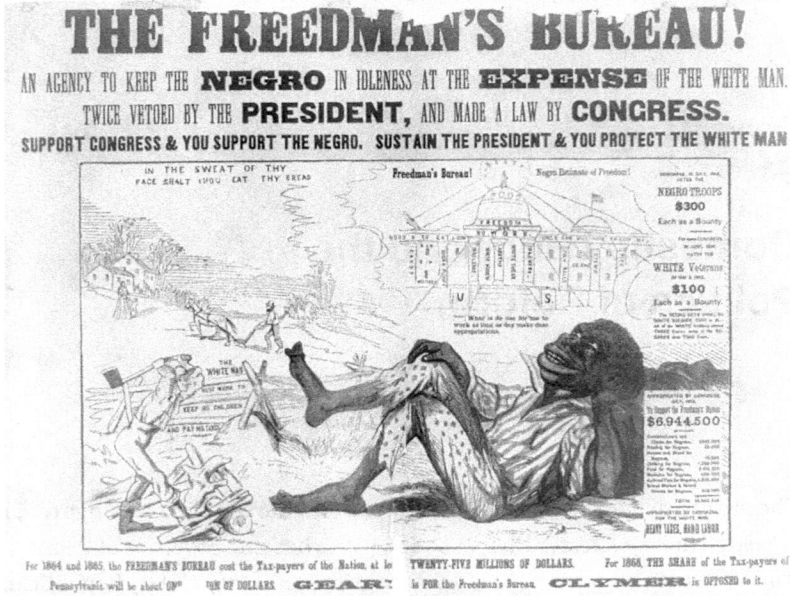

Figure 4.1 Poster from Hiester Clymer's Pennsylvania Gubernatorial Campaign in 1866. https://www.loc.gov/item/2008661698/.

Capitalizing on white anxieties about what the end of slavery would mean, the poster suggests that the ultimate threat of Black freedom was the enslavement of white citizens to freedpeople's uncontrolled desires. The background image of the capitol building reiterates this fear. The words "freedom and no work" sit at the crest of the building, with the statements "good to eat and drink" and "Uncle Sam will have to keep me" on either side. The writing on the pillars of the capitol forms a list of what the federal government is imagined to be giving away to freedmen, a list that includes everything from white sugar to white women. These words not only reveal underlying anxieties about miscegenation but also highlight the ways that white fears about the degeneration of the domestic space of the nation were intimately connected to fears about the degeneration of the domestic space of the familial home.

While the racism of this image is palpable, racialized representations of vagrancy such as this one also gained their meaning through constructions of gender and sexuality. The implicit danger the vagrant presented was to a gendered order of political and economic life. The marginalized white figures in the image properly embody heteronormative gender roles. The white men work to ensure the economic independence of their families, while the white woman properly fulfills her role as a dependent wife and mother. In contrast, a queer figure, the Black vagrant, defies the established boundaries of gender. While ostensibly male, the vagrant lies in a highly feminized position. His body lacks the virility of the other men in the frame; instead, with his legs crossed and his hand propping up his head, he seems to mimic the pose of a lady lounging luxuriously in the intimacy of the domestic sphere. Engaging in a seemingly private activity in public space, the vagrant threatens established boundaries that were central to how gendered political life was organized. The vagrant is seemingly single, and Black women and children are notably absent in Clymer's dystopic vision of the postemancipation future. Nothing compels the vagrant, who is not grounded in familial ties like the white men in the image, to take up the responsibilities of masculine citizenship. Citizenship appears instead as pure indulgence, as entitlement without obligation. The image presents the Black body in undisciplined pleasure as the threat that austerity must curb, not unlike the modern-day construction of the welfare queen.

Clymer's campaign defined the Freedmen's Bureau as "an agency to keep the Negro in idleness at the expense of the white man" and asserted that abolishing the bureau and the assistance it provided was necessary to restore order and send freedpeople back to work. Particularly ironic in the aftermath of slavery, the fear that public assistance might undermine the work ethic effectively reframed all potentially redistributive claims as government handouts that would turn freedpeople into a permanently dependent class. These kinds of attacks on the bureau were common and put the bureau in the position of constantly having to demonstrate its own legitimacy by reiterating its commitment to the heteronormative family and labor discipline. One way it did this was to minimize the amount of direct assistance it provided and instead insist that its mission was to transform freedpeople into self-sufficient wage laborers.

The idea of cultivating economic independence resonated strongly with hegemonic ideas of masculine citizenship. However, given the ways that feminine citizenship was understood through dependency, the bureau's relationship with freedwomen was more contradictory. While the bureau sought to cultivate the ideals of domesticity through the institution of marriage, the provision of material support so that freedwomen might realize those ideals came under intense scrutiny. The lack of a family wage and the diversity of freedpeople's families made dependence on a husband an impossible ideal for most freedwomen. Rather than supporting women who could not depend fully on a man, the bureau insisted that these women work for wages. While gendered constructions of citizenship rested on the idea that women were naturally dependent, the possibility that this might be mobilized toward claims for state support inspired great anxiety among both bureau officials and the general public. In contrast to the maternalist reformers of the Progressive Era, who were able to successfully lobby for financial support for single mothers on the grounds that women's place was in the home and their most valuable contribution lay in the raising of future citizens, public assistance to freedwomen and their children was very controversial. Much like the welfare reformers of the late twentieth century, the officers of the bureau ultimately expected that all freedpeople, women and children included, should be independent of government support.

Many scholars have documented the bureau's role in combating vagrancy and enforcing labor discipline. However, the vast majority of this scholarship has focused on freedmen. In contrast, this chapter centers the bureau's efforts to regulate freedwomen's labor and the contradictions between gendered constructions of citizenship and the mandate that freedwomen work outside the home that emerged in these efforts. Like freedmen, freedwomen were vulnerable to the charge of vagrancy. However, female vagrancy was understood differently from male vagrancy. Two figures dominated discussions of female vagrancy—the prostitute and the housewife who "played the lady." This chapter begins by examining these constructions and the ways in which the problems inherent in them laid the groundwork for the promotion of domestic work among freedwomen.

Next, the chapter turns to the specific role that labor contracts for domestic workers played in the Freedmen's Bureau's efforts to combat female vagrancy. Much scholarship has examined the role that the agricultural labor contracts promoted by the bureau played in reestablishing social relations that closely resembled slavery in the South. However, the bureau also certified contracts for domestic work, while on a much smaller scale, and often coerced freedpeople, especially women and children, into such work. Because of its association with women of color, domestic work has long been marginalized both in histories of the Freedmen's Bureau and in histories of the U.S. welfare state's efforts to regulate women. While histories of the bureau tend to emphasize the role it played in putting Black men to work, feminist histories of the welfare state have focused on efforts to keep white women within the home by defining women's citizenship through their roles as mothers. However, forcing freedwomen to take up domestic work both in the South and through coerced migration to work in northern homes was one strategy that the bureau employed to address concerns about freedwomen's potential vagrancy. While the bureau's efforts to channel freedwomen's labor into domestic work never operated at the scale of their efforts to return freedpeople to agricultural labor, they are significant because they reveal how state officials negotiated the conflicts that emerged between the ideologies of domesticity that defined women's citizenship in terms of their roles as wives and mothers and the mandate that all freedpeople be economically self-sufficient. A focus on domestic labor highlights the ways that struggles to define freedom in contractual terms produced and reproduced racially stratified constructions of public and private space. In the ways that they both assessed freedwomen's value in term of their roles as mothers while simultaneously directing their labor away from the care of their own families, the practices of the bureau resonate strongly with the late twentieth-century framing of workfare.

The last part of the chapter turns to bureau efforts to recruit and train freedwomen in Washington, D.C., to serve as domestic workers in northern cities. While marriage was put forward as a key mechanism for controlling women's sexuality, in practice the heteronormative family remained an elusive ideal. Freedpeople continued to choose other family formations, and, in a context in which a family wage and property ownership were largely unavailable to freedpeople, the heteronormative family was not an economically viable means of survival. The self-sufficient, independent family was an illusion that was possible only with extensive government support. Recognizing this, bureau officials often chose to push freedwomen into wage labor instead. Domestic work in particular offered an alternative to marriage as a mechanism for containing women's sexuality. Frequently contrasted with the vagrant prostitute, the domestic worker offered a different trope through which racially stratified gendered citizenship could be understood, one that has had continued significance in undermining claims to public assistance into the twentieth century.

This chapter argues that domestic labor's significance lies in the specific way that it linked the performance of gendered domesticity with wage labor in the Freedmen's Bureau's responses to freedwomen's material needs. While there was an economic imperative for putting women to work, the benefits of domestic work were viewed as not exclusively or even primarily monetary. Bureau officials and white reformers saw domestic work as offering a different pathway to domestication than marriage. While marriage contained women's sexuality within the heteronormative family and cultivated the values associated with gendered citizenship, domestic work subjected freedwomen to surveillance, regulation, and moral reform within the white domestic sphere. The possibility of continual white supervision coupled with the idea that freedwomen would acquire homemaking skills by working in white homes articulated ideals of domesticity and a civilizational mission to the mandate that freedwomen work. Extending rather than challenging the roles freedwomen had been confined to under slavery, domestic work redirected freedwomen's reproductive labor toward white families and away from their own.

Efforts to put freedwomen back to work in domestic labor were engaged in the process of reconstructing gendered citizenship so that it could accommodate and facilitate continued racial stratification. While it is tempting to read the evidence presented in this chapter as proof of the wholesale exclusion of Black women from citizenship, that interpretation rests on the assumption that citizenship is a singular, static construction that one is either given complete entry into or barred from entirely. In contrast, I am interested in the ways that citizenship functioned as a legal status whose meaning was constructed and reconstructed through changing discourses and day-to-day practices.[1] While freedpeople were clearly excluded from the privileges of citizenship granted to white people, their new legal status as citizens was employed to impose obligations and to justify surveillance, policing, and the use of forced labor in efforts to reform them. The dominant logic held that freedpeople had been granted a legal status they were not yet ready for, and so the first obligation, or burden in Saidiya Hartman's terms, of citizenship for freedpeople was to prove their deservingness.[2] The question of deservingness was fundamentally a question about freedpeople's gendered nature that, in its selective application, simultaneously reinforced the naturalized deservingness of white men and women. To be seen as deserving, freedpeople had to demonstrate that they could perform gendered citizenship properly, and so reform efforts focused on compelling this performance. However, while the bureau employed marriage promotion, the criminalization of vagrancy, limits on public assistance, and forced labor as mechanisms of producing properly gendered citizens, embodying the ideal of feminine citizenship was an impossible task for Black women given the lack of public investment in Black families and the racialized constructions of gender that conflated femininity with whiteness. In this way, efforts at reform actually reproduced the undeserving subjects they sought to remedy, as gender became a vehicle for maintaining racial hierarchies within constructions of citizenship that were ostensibly grounded in equality.

The Threat of Vagrancy and the Performance of Gendered Citizenship

In response to white anxieties that emancipation would result in an epidemic of vagrancy, the Freedmen's Bureau extended state vagrancy laws to apply to freedpeople, and in the years immediately following the Civil War, new vagrancy statutes emerged throughout the South as part of the elaborate system of Black Codes. Although the specific terms of these laws varied from state to state, any Black person who did not have a long-term labor contract with a white employer or did not adhere to the terms of that contract was generally considered vagrant. Those convicted of vagrancy could be both fined and imprisoned, and their punishment often included forced labor, as most states had provisions for hiring out vagrants and prisoners who could not pay their fines.[3] These practices literally reinstituted slavery as a "punishment for a crime," within the parameters of the Thirteenth Amendment.[4] A primary objective of vagrancy laws was to limit Black mobility and thereby stabilize labor relations in the South by quite literally keeping Black workers in their place. While freedom of movement was central to Black struggles to define freedom on their own terms, a major priority of both southern and northern whites after the Civil War was to transform a "'wandering' and 'strolling' people into sedentary agricultural laborers."[5] Controlling Black mobility was central to efforts to reassert white supremacy and became a fundamental aspect of the labor system that developed in the South during and after the Reconstruction era.[6] Freedpeople who went looking for family members whom they had been separated from during slavery or who simply chose to exercise their newfound freedom of mobility were frequently charged with vagrancy.[7]

As Linda Kerber argues, while vagrancy laws theoretically codified an obligation to work and be self-supporting, this obligation manifested itself primarily in the obligation to not appear idle. The meaning of idleness—a deeply raced, classed, and gendered construction—varied greatly across different populations. For example, while it was commonplace for white people of means not to work, the same behavior was defined as vagrancy for freedpeople. Similarly, wage labor was often seen as degrading to white womanhood and therefore as something from which white women needed protection. In contrast, freedwomen who were not engaged in wage labor were deemed idle and could be charged with vagrancy.[8] By criminalizing idleness, vagrancy laws ostensibly promoted economic independence and deterred people from seeking public assistance. In reality, however, vagrancy laws conflated economic independence with wage labor for white employers. Landownership and forms of work that allowed for economic independence from whites were central to freedpeople's own visions of freedom. Politically, freedpeople pushed for land redistribution as reparation for slavery and as the surest path to economic self-sufficiency for the newly emancipated. In addition, many freedpeople sought to define their own working conditions through self-employment, seasonal work, and odd jobs or to survive outside of the confines of plantation labor by using their knowledge of the land and its resources. However, bureau officials, local governments, and white citizens perceived these practices not as an exercise of freedom or efforts toward self-sufficiency but rather as evidence of laziness. As Kerber argues, it was not enough for freedpeople to work or to be economically independent. Vagrancy laws required that they engage in work that was "observable, contractual, and regular" as well as in the service of and under the surveillance of a white employer.[9] Given the nominal compensation and structural barriers to economic advancement, work as a kind of theater through which labor discipline might be exacted was far more significant than work as a vehicle for economic security. In this way, vagrancy laws reinforced the idea that freedom equaled participation in wage labor by criminalizing other options. In the aftermath of slavery, freedpeople's refusal to return to the kinds of work they had done when enslaved was read as a failure to embody the discipline that characterized the free subject.

As the image that opens this chapter illustrates, the construct of vagrancy linked a range of anxieties about social instability, public assistance, gender deviance, and sexual immorality. A lack of settlement and proper attachment to home and family made the vagrant, as a transient subject, particularly threatening. Without heteronormative domesticity as an anchor, the male vagrant operated with no compulsion to fulfill the kinds of obligations that the support of dependents required. As a result, the vagrant's unconstrained freedom was thought to be antithetical to true independence and sovereignty. Instead of the self-control and stability that masculine citizenship demanded, the vagrant tended toward dependency on charity or public assistance, transient sexuality, and wandering.[10] These anxieties can clearly be seen in the depiction of the Black vagrant as both sexually deviant and threatening to dominant constructions of masculinity in the image that opens this chapter. Bureau officers and other government officials often understood combating vagrancy as closely connected to efforts to make freedmen into proper men and organize freedpeople into self-sufficient, heteronormative households.

The male vagrant posed a threat precisely because his existence was antithetical to the stability, discipline, settlement, and attachment to a domestic sphere that characterized the liberal subject. However, it was not only freedmen who were charged with vagrancy. Freedwomen were subject to the same vagrancy laws as freedmen even though gendered constructions of citizenship precluded women from being free liberal subjects in the same ways as men. The meanings associated with female vagrancy were complex and contradictory, illustrating the fundamental problems that gendered constructions of citizenship presented for Black women. On the one hand, idealized feminine citizenship revolved around the home, and the dominant discourse of domesticity suggested that the natural and proper situation for women was dependency. On the other hand, the Freedmen's Bureau vehemently asserted that all freedpeople, regardless of gender, had to engage in wage labor to become economically independent. These contradictory expectations reflected the difficulties that freedwomen encountered in being recognized as part of a category of womanhood that was fundamentally defined through whiteness. While bureau officers posited that the transition to citizenship required freedwomen to take up domestic norms, when domesticity competed with wage labor for freedwomen's time, the bureau insisted that wage labor take precedence. This effectively rendered the ideals of womanhood unreachable without the privileges of whiteness. At the same time, the failure to live up to these ideals was read as evidence of cultural inferiority and a lack of the capacities required for citizenship.

While much of the scholarship on vagrancy in the Reconstruction era has focused on men, a closer examination of how freedwomen's vagrancy was constructed reveals the tensions between racial stratification and gendered constructions of citizenship. Unlike male vagrancy, female vagrancy involved both a failure to be independent and a failure to embody proper forms of female dependency. However, like male vagrancy, female vagrancy was figured as a specifically sexualized threat. In relation to women, the danger signified by vagrancy was female sexuality unconstrained by the domestic sphere. Often conflating vagrancy, prostitution, and any public display of Black female sexuality, efforts to combat vagrancy sought to regulate sexuality by criminalizing freedwomen's presence in public spaces. At the same time, however, what was distinctive about female vagrancy was that it could extend into the private sphere, as freedwomen were also often deemed vagrant for not working outside the home. The two key figures that animated bureau officers' anxieties about female vagrancy—the prostitute and the Black woman who "played the lady"—illustrate the ways that efforts to regulate vagrancy actively linked the processes of instilling labor discipline and cultivating normative sexuality. Closer examination of both of these figures highlights the contradictions that racialized and gendered discourses about dependency and domesticity presented for Black women and the ways in which discourses of vagrancy worked to constitute normative gender, and as a consequence full citizenship, as highly elusive.

Female vagrancy was frequently associated with illicit sexuality, especially prostitution. Bureau officials consistently viewed as vagrants Black women who engaged in prostitution or whom they assumed to be engaged in prostitution. Informed by a dichotomous construction of womanhood that divided women into good women who were idealized as morally and sexually pure wives and mothers and bad women who were vilified for transgressing domestic norms, beliefs about a freedwoman's character were often more significant than her actual behavior in determining whether she should be charged with vagrancy.[11] As Mary Farmer-Kaiser argues, freedwomen who were able to appeal to bureau officers' gendered sensibilities by using their marital status and moral standing within the community to demonstrate their status as deserving female subjects evaded being charged with vagrancy in some specific instances.[12] However, given the racialized construction of female sexuality, the idea of the deserving female subject more frequently worked against Black women.

Long-standing beliefs about Black women's sexual immorality and availability played a key role in the labeling of them as vagrants. Historically constructed in dichotomous opposition to white women's sexuality, Black women's sexuality was simultaneously "invisible, visible (exposed), hypervisible, and pathologized in dominant discourses."[13] Black women's bodies signified unrestrained sexuality in the dominant imaginary, often erasing Black women's own sexual subjectivities. In particular, Black women capitalizing on their own sexuality stood in stark contrast to the reproductive economy of slavery, which had constructed Black women's bodies as property perpetually available to white men. This construction rationalized sexual violence in that it refigured that violence as originating from the Black female body. Regardless of what Black women did or desired, their bodies were inscribed with an excess of sexuality that shaped how they were treated in public space. Whereas white women were seen to be in need of protection, the social order needed to be protected from Black women. In the context of vagrancy laws, this meant that Black women were highly vulnerable because their bodies were read as sexually deviant regardless of their behaviors. For many, their mere presence in public space was enough to mark them as prostitutes in the public eye.

The influx of freedpeople into cities after the Civil War was often associated with an increase in vagrancy and prostitution. A primary function of vagrancy laws was to keep freedpeople in one place so as to ensure a steady and reliable supply of Black labor. While freedmen who went in search of lost family or a different life were simply seen as idle, freedwomen who did the same were presumed to be prostitutes.[14] As one observer noted of the influx of freedpeople to the city of Houston, "A great number of negroes are daily making their appearance in our city. . . . They are almost all ragged and dirty, and ill fitted to stand the cold of winter. The women will of course provide for themselves by a life of prostitution, but the men will not work at anything, and can be seen any day squatted around the corners and lanes and back streets of the city."[15] This statement constructs as common sense the belief that without external regulation freedmen would fall back to a natural proclivity toward idleness, and freedwomen would resort to prostitution. The speaker frames his observations as self-evident, which speaks to a racial optics in which freedpeople's unregulated presence in public space automatically signified vagrancy regardless of what they might have actually been doing. These perceptions of vagrancy were also clearly gendered. While, for freedmen, a perceived failure to take on the role of male provider became evidence of racial inferiority, for freedwomen, sexuality untethered to the domestic sphere played a similar role. In both cases, vagrancy operated as a racial construction that criminalized improper performances of gender, and vagrancy laws connected the enforcing of labor discipline to the policing of racial and gender boundaries.

The association of growing numbers of freedwomen in southern cities with an increase in crime and prostitution reflected the belief that emancipation represented a specifically gendered and sexualized danger to the social order. Freedwomen's unchecked presence in public spaces was read as a sign that freedom for Black people would translate into sexual immorality. This was particularly perverse given that slavery as a system was founded on sexual violence against Black women, and the depiction of emancipation as demoralizing rested on the erasure of this fact. In addition, the positioning of Black women's bodies as a source of sexual deviance worked to reproduce their vulnerability to violence. The idea that Black women's presence in public space signaled sexual availability was a continued obstacle to recognizing Black women as victims of sexual assault.

Many of the freedwomen whom white residents and government officials observed to be prostitutes may not have been engaged in sex work at all. As Hannah Rosen notes, they "may well have been observing African American women liberated from the necessity of plantation labor by the wages of soldiers in the Union Army or other employed family or community members."[16] For those freedwomen who did engage in it, sex work likely provided greater opportunities for economic self-sufficiency and self-determination than agricultural or domestic work, the only other forms of wage labor readily available to Black women. However, even though it was work that offered the possibility of economic independence, sex work still constituted vagrancy in the eyes of white officials. Not only was sex work deemed immoral, but it also defied the principles of labor discipline in that it was not "observable, contractual, and regular" and did not require the supervision of a white employer.[17]

Freedwomen who were perceived to be prostitutes and charged with vagrancy were imprisoned and often hired out. One bureau officer described his investigation of a freedwoman named Hannah as follows:

> With regard to the case of the colored woman, Hannah. I beg leave to state that I have most fully investigated the case. . . . She was a common vagrant and prostitute and as such I committed her to jail, from which place she hired out. I am happy to state that I have cleansed the place of these characters and made them go to work on Plantations, instead of being a nuisance to the town as they formerly were.[18]

Bureau officers saw sending freedwomen back to the kinds of work they had done when enslaved as a way of correcting the perceived sexual and moral transgressions that freedom enabled. Forced labor in this context was a way of returning freedwomen to their proper place, both figuratively and literally. The implicit message in these practices was that, having inadequately internalized the surveillance and disciplinary mechanisms of slavery, vagrants needed to be returned to the plantation. In this context, the objective of reform was not to produce free liberal subjects but rather to produce subjects who continued to act as slaves in the absence of formal structures of slavery. Forced labor blurred the distinction between reform and punishment in ways that were central to the production of the meaning of Blackness. For freedwomen in particular, sex work and the public displays of sexuality that were being criminalized can also be understood as ways of claiming ownership and enjoyment of their own bodies and therefore as practices of freedom.[19] Forced labor attempted to sever these newfound relationships to the body by asserting that freedwomen's bodies were not really their own. As such, these punishments were racially specific, and putting white women to work in these ways would have been virtually unimaginable.

While, for men, to be vagrant meant failing to take up the responsibilities of independent citizenship and instead remaining in a state of dependency, proper citizenship for women was in fact defined by dependency. In the case of prostitution, it was women's potential economic and sexual independence that was threatening, and it was women's failure to embody proper forms of feminine dependency that rendered them vagrant. As a result, Farmer-Kaiser notes that marriage may have protected freedwomen from charges of vagrancy because it offered them the protections of normative femininity.[20] While married freedwomen were less likely to be categorized as prostitutes and therefore less likely to be formally charged with vagrancy, freedwomen who took on the role of housewives also inspired great ambivalence among bureau officials as this role directly contradicted the mandate that Black women work outside the home. Freedwomen who chose to withdraw their labor from the public sphere and redirect it toward their own families were often accused of "female loaferism" or "playing the lady."[21] As one official noted, "Most of the Freedwomen who have husbands are not at work, while they are as nearly idle as it is possible for them to be, pretending to spin—knit or something that really amounts to nothing."[22] Similarly, another observed of freedwomen who took on the role of housewives, "Are they not in some sort vagrants as they are living without employment?"[23]

These statements illustrate the contradictions that marked bureau officials' approach to freedwomen and to Black families more generally. As discussed in the previous chapter, the bureau's marriage-promotion efforts sought to organize freedpeople into privatized heteropatriarchal families that were defined by a gendered division of labor. However, when freedwomen attempted to take on the feminized roles heteropatriarchal families demanded, they were accused of idleness and vagrancy. Behaviors that would have been considered normative for white women were evidence of deviance in freedwomen. The idea that freedwomen were simply playing the lady when they engaged in femininized activities is particularly significant given the performative character of gender. While for white women doing femininity was central to the production of a gendered identity that appeared both real and natural, freedwomen who did the same were seen as simply engaged in play, imitating white norms that remained unnatural to them. Even though in other contexts bureau officials compelled freedwomen to act out white domesticity, these acts failed to have what Judith Butler would call a performative effect.[24] Imitation remained simply imitation and never produced the appearance of a natural femininity. Race operated as a persistent barrier to being recognized as truly women. Freedwomen could only play as ladies; they could never truly achieve that status, despite officials' insistence that they conform to gendered ideals of citizenship.

The idea that freedwomen who took on the role of housewives were vagrant also reveals bureau officers' contempt for reproductive labor done in the service of Black households. The belief that housework was "something that really amounts to nothing" erases reproductive labor as a form of work. Given the totalizing structures of slavery, in which Black familial connections were often violently disrupted and slaveholders controlled Black women's productive and reproductive labor, claiming the right to be housewives was an important expression of freedom for many freedwomen and a way of claiming their labor for themselves, their families, and their communities. As in the case of sex work, however, bureau officials failed to see work that was not done under the supervision of a white employer as work at all. While sex work provoked anxieties about too much sexual and economic independence for women, freedwomen's efforts to inhabit more traditional ideals of female dependency were also seen as threatening. Freedwomen's efforts to withdraw their labor from the public realm were read as laziness and perhaps even more significantly as a way of laying claim to privileges of womanhood to which they were not really entitled.

One way that bureau officers resolved the contradictions between their own idealization of domestic norms and their insistence that freedwomen work outside the home was by arguing that freedwomen's wage labor was necessary to the maintenance of the domestic sphere. For example, the subassistant commissioner James Devine in Huntsville, Texas, wrote:

> In Walker Co., the women are generally opposed to working in the field; being supported in this by the freed men. I have had considerable trouble

to point out the error of their course, have in every instance in making speeches to Freedpeople, explained the necessity of assisting in the support of their families, to be economical, labor diligently, and after acquiring sufficient knowledge of household duties to require their presence at all times at their houses then, and not until then to think of ceasing to labor.[25]

For Devine, the domestic sphere, rather than protecting freedwomen from work in the fields, required that labor. He argues that freedwomen's responsibility to their families is first and foremost to "labor diligently" to ensure their material support. A sharp contrast to the appeals for a family wage that would ground the formation of Progressive Era and New Deal welfare programs, the rhetoric about masculine independence was not accompanied by wages that reflected a belief that male heads of households should earn enough to support an entire family. Rather, in this context the heteropatriarchal family form required freedwomen's labor as a supplement to the family's income. Louisiana assistant commissioner John Brough reiterated this point:

> The laborer has the idea that his family should not work particularly the wife and grown up sons and daughters of the Freedman, which if, these should devote their time or at least a portion of it to labor would be of vast assistance and when the years labor closes, much more would have been earned, the family been supported and better feeling would have existed. The planter would also appreciate such and would (as in many cases they have) reward them for so doing. But alas, this as a general rule is not the case. Hence all that is earned must be taken to support his family who do little or nothing and when he closes his labor for the year, he has comparatively speaking little or nothing to show. Hence he thinks he is cheated and consequently is dissatisfied.[26]

The inadequacy of a freedman's wages to support an entire family is reframed in this statement as a problem of freedwomen and children refusing to work. Rather than forming the basis for a family wage for male heads of households, as was the case for white families, for freedpeople the construction of the family as a self-sufficient unit depended on all of its members being engaged in wage labor. In this way, freedwomen's work outside the home was seen as an essential supplement to freedmen's wages. The heteronormative household depended on women making up the difference between what was needed to survive and what the freedmen earned, just as it also exalted women's dependency on male earners.

Devine addresses this tension when he suggests that only when freed-women have acquired "sufficient knowledge" of domestic responsibilities to require their full attention should they consider withdrawing from work in the fields. In his eyes, freedwomen were not yet domesticated enough to warrant the protections of a private sphere. In a racialized evolutionary schema in which clearly differentiated gendered roles signified the apex of civilization, freedwomen still lagged behind and, in concordance with this position, could and should continue to engage in masculinized forms of work. This presented a paradox for freedwomen in that their participation in masculinized labor was also one of the primary signs of their lack of true femininity. Kerber notes that freedwomen who were convicted of vagrancy and put to work were often described in masculinized terms, such as "stout and muscular," and that "black women could not by their work enhance their identity *as women*" because to work as a laborer ran contrary to the definition of respectable womanhood.[27] While, for Devine, freedwomen's lack of preparation for domestic responsibilities warranted their continued engagement in fieldwork, as long as they continued to work in the field, they would never actually be seen as women who could take on the gendered responsibilities of domesticity.

In contrast to gendered ideals of citizenship that confined white women to the home, bureau officers saw Black women as innately suited to work outside the home. For example, in assessing the potential costs of Reconstruction activities, the Freedmen's Inquiry Commission wrote of freedpeople that, in contrast to white immigrants, "the women as well as the men—even girls of fifteen and upwards—are usually accustomed to plantation labor, and often, from force of habit, prefer it to any other."[28] This statement is particularly notable given that the commission had expressed great anxiety about the sexual practices and family forms of the formerly enslaved in the same report. While the commission advocated strongly for marriage, the cultural ideals of domesticity, and clearly differentiated gender roles in the context of moral reform, these same principles did not extend into the realm of labor relations. Alongside the promotion of marriage and domesticity, this belief in the inclination of Black women to work outside the home amounted to a form of gendered citizenship that was marked by all of the expectations of femininity and none of the protections. While discourses of domesticity positioned Black women as in need of cultural reform—particularly the adoption of heteropatriarchal family norms, entry into the institution of marriage, and sexual restraint—they did not offer Black women protection from entry into the labor force. Importantly, the logic of state austerity tied together expectations that Black women both work and conform to heteronormative domestic ideals, as both were safeguards against state dependency.

While, as Farmer-Kaiser argues, housewives were rarely formally charged with vagrancy, the perception of them as vagrant is particularly significant in that vagrancy is usually a crime that happens in public space. The idea that one could in fact be vagrant within the private sphere further demonstrates the contingency of the division between private and public space for freedpeople. While the privatized family could be deployed as a rationale for forcing women into wage labor, it did not carry with it an actual right to privacy within the home. Bureau officials instead tried to compel freedmen to force their wives into wage labor, arguing that freedmen needed to assert greater control over their families.[29] This practice reiterated gender hierarchy in the home while simultaneously denying men the prerogative that might come with being the head of a household, and women the potential protection from wage labor that domesticity might have offered. In addition, as freedmen and freedwomen often worked together to enable freedwomen to redirect their labor toward their own families, these efforts also sought to disrupt solidarities across gender within the family.

While distinctly different, the figures of the prostitute and the Black woman who played the lady embodied similar anxieties about female vagrancy. While vagrancy was frequently understood as idleness or unwillingness to work, both of these figures illustrate that efforts to control vagrancy were really efforts to reassert white control over Black women's bodies and time. Although bureau officers may not have recognized them as such, women engaged in sex work and housework were indeed working. In addition, sex work potentially offered women a pathway to economic independence, whereas housework signified the adoption of dominant gender norms, two ideals the bureau actively promoted in other contexts. What both these figures shared, however, was a desire to assert self-ownership outside of contractual labor relations and to engage in activities that were not easily surveyed and controlled by whites. The prostitute (or suspected prostitute) expressed female sexuality outside of the marriage contract and the confines of domestic space, while the housewife refused the labor contract, seeking refuge instead in domesticity. Both figures represent attempts by freedwomen to claim their bodies and time as their own by refusing the contracts that bureau officers believed to be emblematic of freedom. As such, they elicited anxieties about illicit sexuality, out-of-control bodies, indulgence, and wasted time. At the same time, these two figures also revealed a significant contradiction. While sexuality outside of marriage was criminalized in the figure of the prostitute, the housewife, the figure who most closely embodied proper sexuality confined to the domestic sphere, was also suspect. While bureau officials asserted that women should be confined to the domestic sphere, they also wanted them to work outside the home. A third figure, the domestic worker, emerged out of this contradiction, and within their efforts to promote contractual domestic labor among freedwomen, bureau officers sought to have it both ways, to confine women to the home and use them as a supply of low-wage labor.

Contracting Freedom

Just as vagrancy laws targeted deviance, Freedmen's Bureau officials employed the labor contract to induce normative ways of embodying freedom. A primary objective of the bureau was to secure a shift from slavery to contractual labor relations by compelling both white employers and freedpeople to enter into formal, long-term labor contracts and enforcing the terms of those contracts. In the fight against vagrancy, labor contracts worked to limit mobility and cultivate the attributes of citizenship associated with settlement. A defining aspect of liberal personhood, fidelity to contract became a measure through which freedpeople might demonstrate their deservingness of freedom. Although the vast majority of labor contracts the bureau oversaw were for agricultural workers, in many states the bureau also approved and enforced contracts for domestic workers. In this section I examine the role that contracts played in defining the boundaries of freedom, with particular attention to the contracts that secured freedwomen's employment as domestics. I argue that domestic workers' contracts are particularly significant in that they reveal many of the gendered contradictions inherent within contractual ideas of freedom. These contracts show how employers and federal officials navigated racialized and gendered concerns not just about women's work but also about fundamental tenets of liberalism like the definition of the independent subject and the division between public and private space. A precursor to the discourse about workfare that would emerge in the late twentieth century, domestic workers' contracts warrant particular attention in the way they link the performance of menial labor to a process of becoming gendered citizens.

Central to liberal definitions of freedom, the labor contract was what fundamentally distinguished the free worker from the slave.[30] Hence, emancipation was frequently equated with a newfound ability to enter into contracts. Contractual ideas of freedom rested on the belief that contracts were both consensual and reciprocal, even when contracts secured unequal or exploitative relationships (as in the case of both the marriage contract and the labor contract). At the heart of contractual ideas of freedom lay the presumption of a particular kind of self-owning subject that was incompatible with slavery. Employing market metaphors that extended a proprietary conception of the self, contract relations likened freedom to the ability to exchange oneself rather than be exchanged by others. Of course, despite the appearance of consent, the labor contract was implicitly rooted in coercion. While the contract ostensibly protected freedpeople from white employers by placing limits on their power and guaranteeing compensation, many freedpeople rightly feared that they might be enslaved yet again by the contract. Bureau officials tended to dismiss these fears as irrational. For example, the assistant commissioner for the state of Mississippi, Samuel Thomas, addressed freedpeople as follows:

> Some of you have the absurd notion that if you put your hands to a contract you will somehow be made slaves. This is all nonsense, made up by some foolish or wicked person. There is no danger of this kind to fear: nor will you be branded when you get on a plantation. Any white man treating you so would be punished. Your danger lies exactly in the other direction. If you do not have some occupation, you will be treated as vagrants and made to labor on public works.[31]

Thomas's statement lays bare the contradictions inherent in contractual ideas of freedom. Freedpeople were encouraged to see the labor contract as an expression of freedom, a kind of labor that did not carry the dangers of slavery. At the same time, if freedpeople did not choose to contract their labor, they could be reenslaved through the criminal justice system. In this way, the labor contract was simultaneously an extension and a contraction of freedom. While one was at least theoretically free to choose the terms of one's employment, choosing not to be employed in the specific manner prescribed by the bureau was grounds for revoking that freedom.

Despite the belief that contracts extended to the formerly enslaved the same freedoms that workers in the North enjoyed, the labor contracts promoted by the bureau were distinctly different from the more abstract idea of contract that governed labor relations in the North. Rather than an informal agreement negotiated between employee and employer, these labor contracts were formal written documents that were registered with and enforced by the federal government. Unlike northern workers, who despite having few mechanisms for holding employers accountable, still retained the power to leave a job, freedpeople's labor contracts bound them to their employers for long periods of time, most commonly a full year. While employers provided room and board, workers were not paid until the completion of a year's work, creating a system that looked more like debt peonage than free labor. Although written contracts were ostensibly instituted to protect freedpeople from being abused or taken advantage of by former slaveholders, in reality they worked to limit freedpeople's mobility and bargaining power. In conjunction with vagrancy laws that criminalized freedpeople who did not have contracts, long-term labor contracts tied freedom to continued employment for a white employer. In this way, labor contracts forced freedpeople to settle in one place and accept highly exploitative working conditions, often on the same plantations or under similar circumstances to those they had endured during slavery.

The ability to enter into a contract marked a subject as responsible, disciplined, rational, and able to subordinate their individual desires to obligations. In contrast to the vagrant, who symbolized the demoralizing effects of a lack of constraint, the capacity to enter into and fulfill contracts signified the self-possession and restraint that was necessary to truly practice freedom. For white subjects, this capacity was presumed to be innate. However, in the eyes of whites, Black subjects lacked this capacity either because of an inherent racial inferiority or as a result of the degrading effects of slavery. For bureau officials, who believed that the capacity for citizenship could be cultivated in freedpeople, the labor contract assumed a pedagogical function that extended beyond simply securing the exchange of labor. They believed that the obligations of contract would mediate the transition from slavery to freedom by disciplining freedpeople into the obligations of citizenship. They spoke frequently of labor contracts inculcating morality and self-control, traits that freedpeople were thought to lack. A direct response to freedpeople's efforts to express their freedom through mobility, nonconformity, and self-definition outside of the strictures of working for white people, the contract tied freedpeople to long-term employment and thereby cultivated settlement, obligation, and restraint as defining features of what it meant to be free. In addition, the contract solidified the notion that to be free was to be economically independent of the state, charity, or more communal efforts at subsistence. This notion of independence fundamentally obscured the dependency and subordination inherent within the employment relation.

The dominant discourse on contract both situated freedpeople in the unique position of having to prove their worthiness of freedom and framed contractual labor not simply as an economic necessity but rather as a performance by which one's worthiness of citizenship rights would be measured. Bureau officers viewed the contract as an opportunity for freedpeople to demonstrate that they were indeed ready for freedom.[32] By extension, they hoped that this performance would also demonstrate the legitimacy of the bureau itself to its political opponents. In contrast to the anxieties about Black freedom embodied in the image that opens this chapter, submitting to contract signified an ability to delay gratification and constrain one's own desires in favor of obedience, discipline, patience, and maintenance of the social order. As Samuel Thomas argued in his efforts to entice freedpeople into contracts, "But even if there be some things denied you as yet, which you wish to gain, you cannot get them by disobedience and idleness. You cannot make people treat you well by showing that you do not deserve it. If you wish for rights, do right yourselves. If you desire privileges, show that they may be safely entrusted to you. Such a course, with patience, will make you happy and prosperous."[33] According to Thomas, it was freedpeople's own responsibility to show that they were worthy of freedom, and if freedoms were denied them, they had to strive to improve their circumstances by better demonstrating their deservingness. Indeed, in a profound reversal of responsibility, the emphasis on contract displaced consideration of white accountability for the violence of slavery with a fixation on Black deservingness.

Although the vast majority of contracts the bureau oversaw were for agricultural workers, the bureau also certified and enforced contracts for a small number of domestic workers. Domestic workers' contracts differed significantly from agricultural workers' in several important ways. First, domestic workers' contracts tended to be much more personal in nature. While a large number of agricultural workers might sign a single contract with a plantation owner, contracts for domestic labor tended to be specifically crafted agreements between an employer and one worker or family. Much more intimate in nature, the contracts often explicitly stipulated requirements about character, behavior, and comportment that extended beyond the labor relation, thus making visible the ways in which labor contracts were about much more than work. Second, the vast majority of workers entering into these contracts were women or children. While the capacity to enter into a contract was theoretically a sign of a subject's independence, women and children were also understood to be dependents within the patriarchal familial structure. Not only do the contradictions between these two positions make visible the fiction of the independent contracting subject, but, for married freedwomen, the convergence of the marriage contract and the labor contract also often worked to further diminish their autonomy in labor relations. Finally, domestic workers' contracts were unique in that they were labor contracts that operated within the private sphere. While liberal political philosophy relied heavily on a strict gendered division between public and private, domestic workers' contracts illustrate the ways in which the ostensibly public realm of contract extended into the private sphere. Together with constructions of vagrancy that scrutinized freedwomen's activities in the supposed privacy of their own homes, these contracts illustrate the ways the bureau participated in the construction of dynamic boundaries between public and private space that enabled the racialized and gendered stratification of citizenship rights and obligations.

The bureau's practice of issuing contracts for domestic labor can be understood as a direct response to the specific anxieties around female vagrancy that both the prostitute and the housewife who played the lady elicited. On the one hand, anxieties about prostitution and sexual promiscuity necessitated the confinement of freedwomen's sexuality to the domestic sphere. On the other hand, officials feared that the domestic sphere offered freedwomen a shield from the discipline of wage labor. While for white women motherhood and domesticity were the primary vehicles through which feminine citizenship was defined, for freedwomen the cultural attributes of female domesticity were still coupled with the expectation of work outside the home. In the domestic workers' contracts certified by the bureau, the domestic worker emerged as a model of female citizenship who embodied the simultaneous confinement of women to the home and the compulsion to work under white surveillance. For this reason, while relatively small in number, domestic workers' contracts are an important subject of analysis. The model of citizenship they constructed extended well beyond the specific contracts issued in that it offered a way of making coherent the racialized and gendered contradictions that emerged with the inclusion of freedwomen in citizenship. Although contractual ideas of freedom rested on clear divisions between independent and dependent subjects and between the public and private realms, the expectations placed on freedwomen simultaneously undermined these divisions. As a liminal figure that straddles these divides, the domestic worker potentially

denaturalizes the foundational dichotomies that structure liberal constructions of citizenship.

The subordination required of domestic workers contrasted starkly with
the idea of the free and independent subject that was central to contract
freedom. Reiterating the social relations that had characterized slavery, domestic workers' contracts often created the appearance that freedpeople
were consensually entering into the same circumstances that they had
been forced into under slavery. For example, contracts contained stipulations limiting workers' mobility. The contract entered into by one domestic
worker stipulated that she must "work under the directions of the employer
and not leave the premises without his consent."[34] Another way contractual labor relations resembled slavery was in the amorphous terms through
which labor was defined. Labor contracts frequently used language like
"render true and faithful service" to describe the work that was expected
to be done. Some freedwomen's contracts included cooking, cleaning,
and agricultural work, essentially meaning that an employer could put
them to work in any way she or he saw fit. Contracts like these meant that
there were few boundaries around what workers were expected to do
and that workers had little or no negotiating power with regard to whether
or not they wanted to do a particular task. In this way, contract labor looked
remarkably like slavery even though the contract provided the facade of
consent and nominal compensation.

The idea of service blurred the line between free labor and servitude.
Good service included stipulations about behavior that went well beyond
the completion of particular tasks in exchange for compensation. For example, the contract between the freedwoman Lizzie Crofford and her employer, G. F. Smith, stipulated that Crofford "engages to deport herself at all
times in a becoming and obedient manner. Showing neither insolence to
the said G. F. Smith or his wife but to treat them at all times with the utmost
respect and obey implicitly all legitimate and proper orders from either."[35]
The emphasis on deportment, obedience, respect, and the curbing of insolence in this contract hearkens back to slavery. Ironically, while the labor
contract was theoretically a sign of one's free will, the very terms of their
contracts forced workers to give up their independence and agree to be-
have as they had been expected to when enslaved. Some contracts spelled
this out quite literally. For example, one freedwoman's contract stipulated
that she "render . . . true and faithful service obeying all his lawful com-
mands as she was in the habit of doing when a slave."[36] Other contracts

required that workers provide service "as in times past" in a blatant attempt to reproduce relations of slavery.[37] While what distinguished contract labor from slavery was its supposedly consensual nature, the working conditions it engendered were remarkably similar to slavery, as these contracts indicate. Work in this context had few boundaries, if any, and contracts such as these required that freedwomen not just sell a portion of their labor time but rather subordinate themselves completely to their employers' desires.

While the premise of contract freedom was independence, domestic workers' contracts often required freedwomen to enter into relationships characterized by dependency. Indeed, one of the legacies of slavery was the lingering idea that, as servants, domestic workers were dependents within their employers' home (i.e., part of the family) rather than independent subjects in their own right. The liminal status that domestic workers occupied between independent contracting subjects and dependents within the private sphere made it possible to both fulfill the mandates of wage labor and simultaneously perform constructions of feminine citizenship that were grounded in domesticity and containment within the home. In this context, the idea of "true and faithful service" or service "as in times past" takes on an added weight. To demonstrate one's deservingness of freedom, one had to show that one was willing to choose the same forms of subordination that one had been subjected to under slavery. To demonstrate one's independence, one had to enter into contractual relations that ensured one's continued dependency.

In the eyes of bureau officials, domestic work offered a positive alternative to the threat posed by the two figures of female vagrancy, the prostitute and the housewife who played the lady. Anxieties about prostitution focused specifically on the dangers of public displays of uncontrolled female sexuality. In contrast, domestic work contained freedwomen within the private sphere and subjected them to the surveillance of white employers. Domestic workers' contracts brought freedwomen into a structure in which they had relatively little control over their working conditions and were constantly subjected to an employer's oversight. In contrast, sex workers most likely had far more control over the conditions of their work precisely because they were not subject to long-term labor contracts or supervision by an employer. While sex workers' activities were heavily policed and they were subject to the same economic constraints other freedwomen faced, sex workers at least potentially enjoyed freedom of movement, control of their living conditions, and the ability to choose when to work, who their clients would be, and what the terms of their labor would be. In comparison, domestic workers had far less autonomy and were almost completely subject to the desires and whims of their employers.

Bureau officials often understood domestic employment as an antidote to the moral degradation associated with sex work in particular and the sexual promiscuity that was associated with Black women more generally. Bureau officials believed that containment within the white domestic sphere might have an uplifting effect on freedwomen. Domestic work potentially offered freedwomen exposure to and training in the norms of white civilization, and the surveillance of white employers was seen as a safeguard against immorality and a way of protecting women from sexual exposure. However, while bureau officers saw prostitution as sexually degrading to freedwomen, they were blind to the very real threats of sexual violence that Black domestic workers faced in the workplace. Grounded in the idea that as property Black women were always sexually accessible to white men, sexual violence had been a cornerstone of the reproductive economy of slavery. Under slavery, working within the intimacy of the white home was permeated with the risk of sexual violence. Postemancipation, labor contracts that required women to provide service "as in times past" implicitly evoked these sexually violent working conditions. The rigid terms of domestic workers' contracts undoubtedly exacerbated their vulnerability to sexual violence and made that violence difficult to contest when it happened. Within African American communities, even into the contemporary period, domestic work within white homes has a strong association with sexual assault, and in other historical contexts, it has been documented that Black women frequently chose sex work over domestic work because it offered them greater sexual and economic autonomy.[38]

Domestic work also addressed bureau officers' anxieties about the housewife who played the lady because it directed freedwomen's labor toward the maintenance of white families rather than their own. While bureau officials tended to see reproductive labor done by housewives as vagrancy, that same labor counted as legitimate and desirable work when done under white surveillance in the service of white families. In this way, domestic work encouraged freedwomen to take up feminized forms of work associated with domesticity but did so in ways that still enabled control by white employers. When this is viewed in relation to anxieties about sex work and housewives playing the lady, it becomes clear that the push toward domestic work articulated constructions of feminine citizenship to a particular form of labor discipline. While both sex workers and housewives worked, their work still constituted vagrancy because it was not contractual in nature and it was not controlled by whites. In contrast, domestic workers engaged in many of the same activities that housewives did, but because their activities were contractual obligations that were subject to white supervision, their labor was understood very differently.

Both domestic workers' contracts and marriage contracts sought to contain women's sexuality within the confines of the home, whether it be as wives or as workers. While both had specific and distinct mechanisms of regulating women, they also worked together to further exacerbate freedwomen's vulnerability to exploitation. While the labor contract was premised on the idea of self-ownership and independence, married freedwomen were still understood legally to be dependents on their husbands. Wives could not enter into labor contracts legally without their husbands' approval, and often men signed labor contracts guaranteeing their wives' labor. Men generally received the wages for the labor of their entire family, and the bureau's guidelines on wages recommended that freedwomen be paid less than freedmen by virtue of their sex.[39] Men were encouraged not only to work disciplinedly themselves but also to ensure that their wives did the same. The Freedmen's Bureau encouraged freedmen to control the labor of their wives and held men responsible when their wives were unwilling to work. As Farmer-Kaiser shows, rather than applying vagrancy laws to married women, bureau officials frequently chose to use the nuclear family as the preferred vehicle for enforcing labor discipline by demanding that freedmen exercise control over their wives, a practice that significantly blurred the distinctions between private and public spheres.[40] Rather than constituting a space of privacy, the heteropatriarchal family was used by bureau officials as another tool for exacting discipline in the workplace.

The following contract between an employer and a freedwoman's husband shows how labor contracts facilitated the trade in freedwomen's labor between husbands and employers:

> This indenture made and entered into between Mary Galbreth of Robeson Co. of the one part and Willis M Lauchlin of the other in behalf of his wife Martha and three children of said County witnesseth that for and in consideration of the sum of four bushels of corn to be paid by the said Mary Galbreth to the said Willis M Lauchlin in behalf of his wife Martha and her three children, He the said Willis agrees to let his wife remain on the prem-

ises of the said Mary Galbreth. She the said Mary Galbreth agreed to give the said Martha food, clothing, and ordinary medical attendance until the first day of January 1866. She the said Martha binds herself to serve truly and faithfully the said Mary Galbreth and obey all lawful orders that she may give as in times past.[41]

This contract highlights one of the primary contradictions of freedom for Black women. Entering into freedom as women, they were subject to the doctrine of coverture, in which their legal personhood was subsumed within that of their husband or father. Coverture was rooted in a belief that women's place was in the private sphere and that women were not fully independent political subjects but rather dependent on male heads of household. However, as Black people, freedwomen were also expected to work outside the home and were not entitled to the protection from wage labor that dependency potentially offered other women.[42]

The marriage contract and the domestic worker's contract were similar in that they subsumed freedwomen within the private sphere. However, if marriage seemed to secure the division between public and private, the domestic worker's contract troubled the perceived stability of that boundary in significant ways. While white domestic space was often equated with the private sphere, for freedpeople it was in fact a workplace that was publicly regulated by government-supervised contracts. At the same time, for domestic workers, social relations within the ostensibly public space of work were also intensely privatized. Domestic workers' contracts in fact secured the private power of employers to dictate working conditions within their own homes without much public or legal scrutiny. The simultaneous way in which white domestic space operated as both a workplace and a private sphere greatly increased the vulnerability of Black domestic workers to economic exploitation and violence.

The situation of domestic workers also made visible the fiction in the idea that citizenship entitled one to a private sphere. For example, most domestics (and most agricultural workers as well) were paid at least partially in room and board, creating conditions in which the home was quite literally an extension of the workplace. At the same time, as discussed in the previous chapter, freedpeople's homes were also the site of intense public surveillance. The quality of one's home life was often seen as the measure of one's preparedness for citizenship. Therefore, rather than a protected private space, freedpeople's homes became the subject of much national debate. Domestic workers, in particular, were entitled to few, if any, protections of privacy, as their contracts often stipulated that they be available whenever their employers needed them. In fact, one of the key struggles of Black women employed in domestic labor was to establish boundaries with their employers so that they could carve out time and space to have private lives.[43]

The contracts for domestic labor that were registered by the bureau reveal many of the central contradictions that animated contractual ideas of freedom and efforts to maintain control over freedwomen's labor. While the ability to enter into contracts was ostensibly a sign of a free and independent subject, freedpeople frequently entered contracts under coercion, and the terms of those contracts often produced working conditions that were remarkably similar to slavery, veiled under the illusion of consent. For domestic workers in particular, gendered ideas of citizenship and the mandate that all freedpeople work converged in ways that exacerbated their vulnerability to exploitation. From the perspective of bureau officials, domestic workers' contracts addressed the anxieties about female vagrancy embodied in the figures of the prostitute and the housewife who played the lady by simultaneously containing female sexuality and redirecting freedwomen's labor toward white families. However, for freedwomen, the contract secured the obligation to work under white supervision without securing the rights associated with liberal personhood. Freedwomen were seen as neither fully independent nor entitled to rights of privacy. In fact, these domestic workers' contracts demonstrate how the gendered dichotomies of independence/dependence and public/private that are foundational to liberal ideas of citizenship were constructed in racially specific ways. While, for white women, citizenship demanded confinement and dependency within the privacy of the domestic sphere, for Black women, citizenship also necessitated economic independence and constant surveillance by whites. Just as the homes of white women were the workplaces of freedwomen, domesticity took on a very different gendered meaning in the construction of citizenship for these two differently situated groups. These differences are even more apparent in the Freedmen's Bureau's efforts to encourage freedwomen to migrate north to work as domestic workers. These efforts linked domestic education and domestic labor as part of the effort to reform freedwomen and prepare them for citizenship. Effectively displacing the need for redistributive social welfare policy, these practices posited labor discipline rather than public assistance as the solution to deeply entrenched structural inequalities.

Domestic Labor and Migration North

In February 1865 the *Freedmen's Record* described the condition of the growing number of freedpeople in the District of Columbia as follows:

> Coming as they do, fresh from slavery; ragged; stripped of every thing; many of them sick; few accustomed to any other than agricultural labor; at the mercy of speculators,—the condition of newcomers, especially, is abject and miserable in the extreme. Their dwellings are described as "not so good as good pigsties." . . . Two rooms for a large family are rarities: the majority of these huts or hovels have only one room. No wonder that casual visitors—though the inmates of these dwelling think otherwise—ask, "How much better off are these than they were in slavery?"[44]

A publication of the New England Freedmen's Aid Society, the *Freedmen's Record* drew attention to the plight of freedpeople who had fled the South in an effort to elicit northern sympathies. In the aftermath of the Civil War, many freedpeople congregated in the District of Columbia. Formerly enslaved people who had escaped plantations and joined the Union army often chose to stay in D.C. after the war, and many others made their way from the rural South to Washington looking for safety, protection, assistance, and compensation from the federal government in a time of great uncertainty and economic hardship. In D.C., they found crowded conditions, harsh winters, illness, and insufficient food and housing. In highlighting the suffering faced by these migrants, this passage draws particular attention to the inadequacy of domestic circumstances. Using language that invoked the Freedmen's Inquiry Commission's descriptions of the backward conditions fostered by slavery, the *Freedmen's Record* portrayed freedpeople's housing as crowded, dirty "huts or hovels," likening them to the dwellings of animals. Implicitly invoking the white abolitionist trope that the greatest harm of slavery was that it had denied enslaved people the civilizing influences of heteronormative domesticity, the *Record* suggests that despite emancipation freedpeople continued to live as they had as slaves. Linking economic inequality and a lack of civilization, these parallels became the basis for questioning whether freedpeople were actually better off than they had been in slavery and signified the important role that the domestic scene played in dominant understandings of both slavery and freedom.

The question of what it would mean for these newly arrived freedpeople to be better off than they had been in slavery became a central preoccupation of the Freedmen's Bureau's D.C. offices; for them, the answer to this question was firmly attached to wage labor. The considerable growth in the district's Black population after the war caused great anxiety among bureau officials about how to manage the increasing population of freedpeople in the capital.[45] The demand for direct assistance was great, with many lacking adequate food and shelter, but bureau officers also feared that providing relief would sanction dependency on the government among freedpeople. In the face of this crisis, local superintendent William Spurgin wrote, "Work can be obtained for every man, woman, and child in the District. . . . They must sooner or later learn to depend upon themselves nothing can make them independent and respectable quicker or more thoroughly."[46] Spurgin's comments succinctly express the bureau's approach to managing freedpeople. Work, regardless of gender and age, was not just an economic necessity but a vehicle toward moral reform. Even women and children, whose dependency was deemed proper within the heteronormative family, were seen as in need of labor discipline. In contrast to gendered constructions of citizenship that confined women to the domestic sphere, the bureau pushed freedwomen to find economic self-sufficiency for themselves and their families in wage labor.

There were significant contradictions between the compulsion to work and the gendered constructions of women's citizenship that were simultaneously being enforced on freedwomen, and the domestic worker emerged as a trope of gendered citizenship that sutured these contradictions. As the bureau pushed freedwomen into domestic service, it linked wage labor to cultivating the performance of normative womanhood in the domestic sphere. The key difference was that freedwomen's work in white homes (rather than their own) was understood as a pathway to reform and civilization. While white women's citizenship was defined by their status as wives and mothers, freedwomen's citizenship was increasingly understood in terms of the specifically racialized form of gendered subordination that domestic service signified. In the ways she revealed the state's investments in the heteronormative family to be race and class specific rather than universal, the domestic worker appeared as a shadow to normative constructions of gendered citizenship in the practices of the bureau.

In this section I turn specifically to the Freedmen's Bureau's efforts to manage the influx of freedpeople into the nation's capital and to grapple with the economic hardship they faced. These efforts offer a useful case study in the role race and gender played in early social welfare provision. While there was a pressing economic need for immediate aid, because public assistance (even for women with children) became associated with vagrancy and the cultural characteristics of slavery, bureau officers were reluctant to provide direct relief. When they did provide assistance, it was attached to stringent tests of morality, particularly surveillance within the home. After analyzing these forms of surveillance, I turn to the D.C. Bureau's primary strategy for dealing with freedwomen's economic insecurity: coercing them into low-wage labor. Through industrial schools and the transportation of freedwomen to work as domestics in the North, the bureau sought not only to alleviate economic hardship but also to engage in moral reform. Further entrenching the racialized and gendered contradictions inherent within contractual ideas of freedom, these practices rested on a slippage between economic inequality and cultural deficiency that would come to characterize poverty knowledge of the twentieth century.[47] The practices of the bureau offer an important and much-neglected contrast to the mothers' pension programs of the Progressive Era. Unlike maternalist reformers, who saw motherhood and domesticity as the key to cultural reform, bureau officials believed that low-wage domestic labor in white homes could play a key role in the making of properly gendered citizens.[48]

While the D.C. office of the bureau did provide some forms of relief, the bureau saw this work as part of a larger project of reforming freedpeople that sought to mitigate the supposed cultural degradation of slavery and prepare freedpeople for citizenship. The home took center stage in these efforts, as transforming housekeeping, child-rearing, and sexual practices was seen as central to improving the respectability of freedpeople.[49] Bureau officers in the district placed particular emphasis on home visits in determining the allocation of aid. Visiting agents inspected the homes of those requesting and receiving assistance and, as they did so, also provided domestic instruction as a part of their moral-uplift efforts. Visiting agents often found unruly domestic scenes such as crowded living conditions and women and children who lived without a male head of household. One visiting agent described freedpeople in the district as living in "miserable little huts" with six to eight people crowded in two small, "smoky, dingy and dirty" rooms.[50] Another inspector complained about a boardinghouse that contained a large dance hall where people congregated at night. Officers linked these findings to disease and destitution, suggesting that poor family structure and inappropriate leisure activities were the cause of freedpeople's material condition.[51]

A primary job of visiting agents was to determine who was deserving of assistance and who was able to work. Although the bureau did provide direct assistance, it was plagued by anxieties that federal aid would sanction idleness, immorality, and sexual promiscuity. Bureau officials saw their primary purpose as cultivating self-sufficiency and were reluctant to provide relief to those who were seen as able-bodied. Distinguishing between those who could work and those who could not became an important part of the process of aid distribution, and agents rigorously investigated each case before providing direct assistance. While the vast majority of aid recipients were the elderly, the disabled, and widows with small children, bureau officers expressed fears that receiving direct assistance would make "paupers" of freedpeople by undermining their work ethic.[52] Therefore, even as they provided limited assistance to some freedpeople, they reiterated that the federal government had no obligation to support freedpeople and compelled them to find ways to support themselves.[53]

Freedwomen occupied an ambivalent position with respect to what Farmer-Kaiser describes as the bureau's "war on dependency."[54] Farmer-Kaiser argues that gendered ideologies that cast women as naturally dependent enabled freedwomen to more successfully claim federal assistance than freedmen. In particular, freedwomen who could demonstrate their deservingness by showing that their economic circumstances were no fault of their own and that they adhered to the standards of respectable femininity were sometimes able to leverage gendered discourses of dependency and domesticity to their benefit. Among freedwomen, the bureau was most likely to provide aid to widows, wives who had been abandoned, and mothers of small children.[55] However, even for these categories of women, assistance was not a given. Rather, bureau officials expressed great reluctance to provide aid even to the seemingly most deserving categories of women and children. Rather, much like policy makers in the late twentieth century, they sought instead to either relocate freedwomen's dependency within the home by cultivating marriage or put freedwomen to work.

One of bureau officers' primary concerns about providing material assistance to freedpeople was that it would support sexual deviance. In contrast to marriage, which contained sexuality and promoted labor discipline through the ideal of the self-supporting family, direct aid was seen as generating idleness, immorality, and promiscuity. Bureau officers believed that providing assistance to freedwomen would undermine efforts at marriage promotion by supporting freedwomen when freedmen failed in their responsibilities as husbands. Instead, they argued that the bureau should focus its efforts on enforcing freedmen's familial responsibilities. For example, local superintendent William Spurgin complained that many freedmen used new legal marriages to shield themselves from financial obligations to their former wives and children. He noted that freedmen with wives and children from unions made during slavery would simply legally contract marriage with another woman, thereby absolving themselves of any obligation to their former families. Spurgin saw curbing practices such as this as more important than relief in alleviating the economic hardships freedwomen faced.[56]

Similarly, in describing the Freedman's Village, a camp for freedpeople set up by the federal government in Arlington, bureau officials cited not only poverty and illness as major problems but also idleness and immorality. Residents of the village were provided with housing, educational services, health care, food, and clothing. However, many bureau officials believed that by allowing freedpeople to live in a continued state of dependency, the Freedman's Village compounded the problem. Official descriptions cite "too familiar intercourse between the sexes," "a disregard for lawful marriage," and women "raising children without husbands" as problems that plagued the village and therefore pushed strongly for residents to leave and take up employment elsewhere. Bureau officials were particularly concerned with the presence of women who could not work because they had small children to care for. In his 1866 report on the Freedman's Village, the officer A. H. Lawrence observed, "Among the dependents are many women with children; most of these women are able to work but are living here on a scanty ration in idleness and rags, because they cannot on account of their children and the scarcity of work get employment in this vicinity."[57] The following year, the officer H. N. Howard similarly observed, "There are able bodied women living in the village as dependents, rendered dependent by having young children whom the earnings of the mother at service could support."[58]

Bureau officers' concerns about idleness even extended to mothers with small children, evidence that, despite gendered ideologies that cast women as dependents, freedwomen were generally regarded as capable of working outside the home and were expected to become economically self-sufficient regardless of their marital situations. While some freedwomen may have been able to use gendered discourses of domesticity to their benefit, the bureau's policies toward freedwomen were defined not by a unilateral belief that freedwomen deserved the protections of womanhood but rather by a set of contradictory obligations that were both racialized and gendered. While, as noted in the previous chapter, bureau officers linked freedom to the performance of heteronormative gender roles, they also firmly believed that freedwomen, unlike white women, could and should work outside the home. Wage labor was far preferable to dependency on the state, and even married freedwomen were expected to contribute to the household income, with their wages supplementing the low wages paid to freedmen. While ideologically the bureau promoted domestic reform as the key to integration into the nation, it also denied freedpeople the economic basis for normative domesticity. Unlike the maternalist activists of the Progressive Era, who invoked gendered ideals of domesticity to make claims for a family wage and state support of single mothers, the bureau officers' normalizing efforts were divorced from material benefits. This left freedwomen in a paradoxical position. To demonstrate their deservingness of citizenship, they were compelled to perform gendered forms of domesticity. At the same time, the racial imperative that they continue to work outside the home consistently undermined that performance.

Given the bureau's reluctance to provide direct relief, its primary response to the economic hardships faced by freedpeople in D.C. was to look for ways to employ them. One approach to this was the establishment of industrial schools for freedwomen. In collaboration with northern freedmen's aid societies and white women reformers, the bureau supported the development of seven industrial schools for freedwomen in the D.C. area that taught women sewing, ironing, laundry, and other domestic skills in preparation for positions as domestic workers. Often run like small factories in which freedwomen worked in exchange for food, clothing, or a small wage, these schools brought together the beliefs that freedwomen needed education into citizenship and that they ought to work in exchange for assistance.[59] Run by white women who saw the uplift of freedwomen as an extension of their abolitionist and feminist politics, the industrial schools were intended not just to provide concrete employment skills but also to instill the discipline and character that citizenship and civilization required.[60] Susan Walker, who ran one of the schools in the district, explained that the purpose of her school was "to encourage in them [freedwomen] habits of industry, economy, cleanliness. To elevate them in character & condition generally. To inspire an ambition for self-improvement and an earnest desire to be faithful to their responsibilities as freedwomen."[61] In this articulation of the industrial school's mission, Walker linked labor discipline to the cultivation of good womanhood. For Walker, work did not simply provide a means to economic self-sufficiency; the act of engaging in disciplined labor reformed the character as well. According to discourses of domesticity, "industry, economy and cleanliness" were what women should strive for in the home. These values contrasted sharply with the image of freedpeople's homes as plagued by overcrowding, pauperism, and promiscuity, as painted by bureau officers. Reform of the home was as central to inclusion into citizenship. However, in this instance, domestic reform was to be cultivated through the discipline associated with wage labor. The value of work was not so much the material benefits it might provide but its power to replace dependency, unruliness, and unrestrained pleasure with self-sufficiency, hygiene, and sexual restraint.

In sharp contrast to Progressive Era reformers' view that work outside the home was degrading to womanhood, for freedwomen wage labor was understood as a pathway to those same gendered ideals. The relationship between white women reformers and freedwomen in this context highlights the way that race structured gendered ideas of citizenship. While the reformers may have imagined that as women they understood and shared freedwomen's experiences, work outside the home in fact meant very different things to these different women. For white women, participation in relief efforts like industrial schools offered a kind of financial independence and escape from the domestic sphere. In contrast, for freedwomen, the push toward wage labor was framed as a moral obligation of citizenship. While for both groups work was linked to ideas of freedom, reform work offered white women freedom as the possibility of expanded independence, whereas for freedwomen freedom became synonymous with an obligation to work. These differences are clearly evident in the kinds of work that white women reformers saw as appropriate for freedwomen. Extending the legacy of slavery, white women reformers focused on forcing freedwomen into domestic service, ensuring that they would remain subordinated to white instructors or employers.[62]

In addition to employing freedwomen in industrial schools within the District of Columbia, the bureau facilitated the transport of freedwomen to other regions where there was a high demand for domestic workers. After the particularly harsh winter of 1865–66, Charles Howard, the assistant commissioner for the bureau's D.C. offices, started an aggressive program to transport freedpeople to jobs in the North, West, and South.[63] While abolitionist critics likened this practice to the slave trade, bureau officers saw the concentration of freedpeople in the district as a primary obstacle to their employment.[64] Despite the bureau's efforts, many freedpeople were reluctant to leave D.C. The bureau officers suggested that freedpeople maintained unfounded fears of returning to rural areas and held irrational prejudices against the North that had been "sown in their mind as slaves."[65]

In contrast, freedpeople frequently complained about mistreatment at the hands of bureau agents and about the bureau's disregard for keeping families together, which indeed resembled the practices of slavery.[66]

The parallels critics drew to the slave trade raise important questions about the role coercion played in the bureau's efforts to put freedpeople to work. While technically participation was voluntary, and some freedpeople clearly chose to use the bureau's employment program to facilitate migration elsewhere, the refusal to provide assistance to able-bodied freedpeople who remained in the district also made relocation the only viable option for many. Freedpeople were forced to choose between labor migration and state neglect, revealing the ways that free labor as a construct was implicitly backed by coercion. Notably, while the bureau readily paid for migration facilitated through labor agents, it refused to pay for transportation costs when freedpeople sought assistance in leaving the city to reunite with their families in the South. In these instances, the bureau opted "not to recommend transportation but to secure work for them so that when they have accumulated sufficient means they can return to their homes should they still desire so to do," in an effort to dissuade freedpeople both from returning to the South, where they were likely to encounter economic hardship, and from making claims on the government.[67] In its willingness to fund transportation only for the purposes of wage labor, the bureau reiterated the prioritization of wage labor over all other potential needs. The primary intention behind transporting freedpeople to other locations was not simply to reduce their numbers in the district. It was to put them to work.

The perception of freedpeople as a specifically racialized threat amplified the coercive elements in the bureau's transportation policies. The failure to work was criminalized, and the threat of legal reprisals hung over those who remained in D.C. One officer declared, "If moral persuasion should fail to induce these people to leave the City, I would recommend that all who can not give a satisfactory account of their ability to provide for themselves be considered vagrants and forced to leave."[68] Freedwomen were a particular target of the bureau's efforts to move freedpeople north. As Janette Thomas Greenwood notes in her study of post–Civil War Black migration to Worcester, Massachusetts, while the migration of freedpeople through personal connections was overwhelmingly male, migration facilitated by the bureau was approximately 60 percent female, and the vast majority of these women worked in domestic service.[69] Indeed, the demand for domestic labor in the North offered a potential solution to the problem of destitution in the eyes of the bureau. Viewing freedwomen as a potential solution to the "servant problem," many people from the North wrote to the bureau requesting domestic servants. While domestic work in the North had previously been done by European immigrants (most notably the Irish), as those women began to move into other occupations, Black women were seen as potentially filling the void they left.[70]

In conjunction with private charities, the bureau established intelligence offices to facilitate the employment of freedpeople. Intelligence offices connected employers and unemployed freedpeople, often arranging for the migration of freedpeople to places where their labor was in demand. The bureau received numerous requests for servants from families up north, and northerners were encouraged to solicit domestic workers from the bureau as part of the effort to support the integration of freedpeople into the nation. In May 1865 the *Freedmen's Record* announced that the Union Freedmen's Aid Intelligence and Employment Agency had been established with the intention of finding employment and homes for freedpeople who had congregated in D.C. Appealing to northerners to submit their requests for workers to the agency, the announcement explained that the agency offered both a convenient supply of new labor and an opportunity to help freedpeople in a way "that shall encourage industry and prevent pauperism." The announcement made a particular plea for requests that could be filled by women and children, explaining that "few able-bodied men can be had, at present, and not many first-class, well-instructed house servants. There are many mothers, with children, who, if favorably situated, could be more than self-supporting; and many young women, girls, and boys, who, with proper and kindly training, will become most valuable domestics, farm-laborers, etc."[71] Such appeals not only highlighted the employability of women and children but also suggested that employers were performing a kind of charity by hiring freedpeople. In the context of domestic service, this exacerbated the racialized character of the work by reinforcing the idea that the employer's role was to educate and uplift freedpeople. In this framing, the employer was seen as doing a service for the employee rather than the other way around.

One important example of efforts to secure domestic employment for freedwomen in the North can be found in the work of Anna Lowell. A former nurse in the Civil War, Lowell worked with the bureau to establish the Howard Industrial School in Cambridge, Massachusetts. Lowell saw the school, modeled after the industrial-education efforts of General Samuel

Armstrong, as providing freedwomen with an opportunity for economic self-sufficiency and moral education. The school's defined purpose was "to provide a temporary home, food, clothing, instruction, and advice, and to secure permanent places for colored women and children."[72] Run as a private charity, the school was developed in collaboration with the bureau and received financial support from it. The bureau not only recruited women and children to make the trip north and provided for their transportation but also contributed money to help support the operations of the school.

The Howard Industrial School opened in November 1866, and during the approximately five years of its operation, it sponsored the migration of 818 freedwomen, the vast majority of whom came from the D.C. area or Hampton, Virginia, where General Armstrong's normal school was located.[73] According to both its own and the bureau's accounts, the school was very successful at placing women as domestic workers. Charles Howard, the assistant commissioner of the bureau for the District of Columbia, praised Lowell's work, arguing that "embracing instruction in all sorts of useful house-work, and the finding of good homes for the freedwomen, where they will be self-supporting . . . seems to me not only highly desirable, but almost a necessity laid upon such of our Christian people as can appreciate the need."[74] Howard viewed Lowell's school as providing an important and necessary service and as forming one of the most successful efforts to move freedwomen into domestic service positions in the North, with success measured primarily in terms of Lowell's ability to find placements for freedwomen. Putting freedwomen to work became understood as a Christian responsibility much like charity, and descriptions of Lowell's work often conflated the projects of economic and moral uplift. While her institution was called a school, the educational components focused primarily on vocational skills related to domestic work and were clearly secondary to placing freedwomen in jobs. Lowell herself noted that "on account of the general demand here for servants, and the eagerness of the women to earn money, very few of them have remained long enough in the school to receive much instruction."[75]

Lowell discovered that one of the most significant challenges to moving freedwomen into domestic labor was finding placements that would accommodate women with small children. In response to this challenge, the school allowed freedwomen to take up work and leave their children at the school, charging them a small amount for room and board.[76] Because the positions available to women were as live-in domestic workers and were often in rural locations a considerable distance from the school, for freed-women these arrangements would have meant extended separations from their children. The practice of separating freedwomen from their children so that they could work in other people's homes was not unusual. Other employment agents also advocated placing children in asylums or orphan-ages so that their mothers could take up positions as domestic workers, demonstrating that their efforts to help freedwomen prioritized wage labor over family unity. Some agents even patronizingly suggested requiring mothers to pay a portion of their wages to the institutions in which their children were housed so as to "keep alive the interest the mother should always feel in her offspring."[77] Statements such as this one reveal the con-tradictory relationship to motherhood embedded in efforts to put freed-women to work. On the one hand, bureau agents clearly felt that maternal instincts needed to be fostered among freedwomen. On the other hand, they actively encouraged the separation of freedwomen from their children when this would enable them to engage in wage labor.

The story of Rebecca Tolliver illustrates many of these contradictions. Tolliver's case was included in the school's report on operations as an ex-ample of the many successes fostered by the program. The report reads:

> Mrs. Tolliver had given up her four children to the Trustees of the Colored Orphans Home in Washington where they had been for several months when she wanted them back. They refused to give them back to be brought up in Washington; but consented on condition she would come North with them to our school. She did so, and is now living in a family in the country with two of them and writes as follows for the others to be sent to her. "am very much pleased with my place; the children are going to school, the doc-tor's family are very kind, good, religious people, and treat us very nicely indeed. Jimmy has marks and three cards of merit already . . . give my best love to my daughters and tell them to be good girls, and love the Lord for he is good."[78]

While ostensibly presented as an example of the benefits the school pro-vided, this description also highlights the coercive power of the Howard School and the losses that freedwomen must have endured in making the trip north. For Tolliver, moving north was the only means of getting her children back, and she writes of the success of her placement in an effort to reunite with her two daughters who still remain in D.C. Most likely, Tolliver had "given up" her children because of economic hardship, and the orphanage refused to return them to her because she was seen as an unfit mother owing to her lack of both a husband and employment.[79] Only through employment in a good white home could Tolliver be recognized as a worthy mother who deserved to have her children returned. This represents an important inversion of maternalist discourses that used women's practices of mothering within the private sphere as the basis on which to secure women's place in the public sphere.

While Lowell and the bureau saw themselves as providing freedwomen with a valuable service through the school, the structure they created to facilitate migration north often resulted in isolation and hardship for freedwomen. Not only were freedwomen often required to leave their children either at the school or in orphanages in order to take positions as domestics, but Lowell also strove to create an exclusively female environment at the school. This decision was most likely motivated by a desire to provide freedwomen with a refuge from the sexual violence that had characterized slavery.[80] However, it effectively required freedwomen's separation from male family members. In addition, the school often placed freedwomen as live-in domestics in white homes in isolated rural locations where there were few, if any, other Black people. These positions often mirrored the structure of the plantation household in that freedwomen had little autonomy and were under constant surveillance by white families. Their isolation and dependence on their employers would have left freedwomen extremely vulnerable to workplace abuses, particularly sexual harassment. As a result, those who migrated to Massachusetts through the bureau were far less likely to stay than those who had initiated their own migration through personal or military connections.[81]

These practices illustrate a fundamental tension between the ideals of domesticity and self-sufficiency that animated efforts to move freedwomen into domestic labor. On the one hand, there was a strong discursive emphasis on the idea that inclusion into citizenship could be facilitated only through cultivating heteronormative families and gender roles. On the other hand, in contrast to dominant ideals that linked womanhood to dependency and motherhood, freedwomen were compelled to find work even when it meant separation from their own children. Notably, within this context, self-sufficiency did not mean economic independence as much as it meant taking on a position of subordination within white households. The language of finding "homes" for freedwomen that was used throughout the period demonstrates the ways that employment and domesticity were conflated.

Conclusion

Anxieties about vagrancy cast a long shadow over the work of the Freedmen's Bureau. The belief that directing any federal resources toward freedpeople was a direct assault on white citizens and a threat to the moral fabric of the nation led the bureau to prioritize labor discipline over meeting the immediate economic needs of freedpeople. Given that the national resources in question had been acquired in no small part through the stolen labor of enslaved people, the bureau's persistent vigilance against Black vagrancy is particularly notable. In the aftermath of a system that had extracted Black people's labor under intensely violent conditions to produce white wealth, the primary question that animated bureau practices was how to put freedpeople back to work. Anxieties about vagrancy reproduced slavery's racial logic in that they suggested that without white supervision Black people would be incapable of the restraint necessary for the proper practice of freedom. While vagrancy laws were framed as an incitement to work, they in fact criminalized not the failure to work but the failure to work under contract with a white employer. Bureau officials or the white public often deemed Black people's efforts to exercise their freedom as laziness and a sign of racial inferiority, effectively limiting freedom's scope.

The heteronormative family played a central role in anxieties about vagrancy. The family was constructed as the fundamental unit of economic self-sufficiency, and it was believed that attachment to the family would promote settlement and wage labor. In conjunction with a lack of labor discipline, figures of vagrancy also embodied nonnormative genders and sexualities. While male vagrancy connoted the absence of the familial attachments that promoted healthy masculinity, female vagrancy was a more complex construction. Two key figures animated bureau officers' anxieties about vagrancy among freedwomen. The first, the prostitute, represented female sexuality uncontained within the domestic sphere, and the second, the housewife who played the lady, represented a false claim to femininity and the protections of the domestic sphere. Together, these representations demonstrate the contradictions that characterized efforts to make freedwomen into gendered citizens. While both sex workers and housewives worked, their labor was not under the direct control and supervision of white employers and so was not regarded as legitimate labor. On the one hand, sex workers defied gendered norms of citizenship that sought to confine women and their sexuality within the home. On the other hand, when freedwomen attempted to occupy the position of the housewife, they were vulnerable to charges of vagrancy within the private sphere. The idea that one could be found vagrant within the private space of one's own home illustrates the contingency of the boundaries between private and public space for freedpeople. While liberalism ostensibly guaranteed a realm beyond state interference, the domestic sphere remained a site of surveillance and criminalization for freedpeople.

If the liberal right to privacy eluded freedpeople, the obligation to enter into contracts was omnipresent. Contract marked the difference between the free worker who consensually entered into labor relations and the slave who was legally incapable of consent. However, while entrance into contracts was a key marker of emancipation, it simultaneously signified a narrowing of the possible meanings of freedom. Although contracts were understood to be consensual arrangements, vagrancy laws effectively criminalized freedpeople who did not enter into labor contracts. In addition, because the free subject was understood as synonymous with the contracting subject, a failure to enter into contracts was understood as a failure to transcend slavery. In this context, bureau officials believed that the labor contract could have a pedagogical function by encouraging freedpeople to shed the characteristics of slaves and adopt the norms of citizenship, such as economic independence, settlement, and the fulfillment of one's obligations. Given the controversies surrounding public assistance, bureau officials also believed that fulfilling the terms of labor contracts was a means by which freedpeople could demonstrate to the rest of the nation their deservingness of freedom.

The labor contracts of domestic workers highlight the racialized and gendered fictions inherent within liberal conceptions of contracts. Contractual ideas of freedom were premised on the independence of the contracting subject and a belief that contracts governed relationships between individuals within the public sphere. Domestic workers, however, occupied a liminal position as both fully independent and dependent subjects, yet also neither. The expectation that all freedpeople regardless of gender be economically independent fueled the push toward domestic work, and bureau officials sought to use compulsory labor contracts as a means of preventing potential dependency on public assistance. However, the terms of domestic workers' contracts reiterated the kinds of dependencies that had characterized slavery. Contracts often required total subordination, allowing domestic workers few, if any, boundaries around their time and person. In fact, any expression of independence could easily be construed as a violation of the contract. The marriage contract often worked to exacerbate the dependencies produced by the labor contract in that it allowed freedmen to contract the labor of their wives. In this way, contract relations made freedwomen doubly vulnerable owing to their dependencies on both their husbands and their employers. A dubious instrument of freedom, the contract in fact enabled the exchange of freedwomen's labor between men.

That these contracts governed labor relations within the ostensibly private sphere exacerbated the exploitative nature of the contracts and reveals the situational character of liberalism's division between public and private space. While liberal discourse naturalized the separation of spheres, in practice the division between public and private has operated differently for differently situated subjects. The bureau's domestic worker contracts were federally supervised contracts that governed labor relations in an area where government jurisdiction was questionable. Because the workplace was also the employer's private home, employers enjoyed a shield against government intervention that domestic workers did not. At the same time, given that freedwomen's efforts to exercise privacy by withdrawing their labor from white surveillance were seen as vagrancy, the push toward domestic labor can be understood as part of a larger project to constitute Black subjects as subjects who were not entitled to privacy. In this context, the domestic worker emerged as an important alternative to the mother as a figure of racialized, gendered citizenship in that she performed all of the labors of domesticity with none of its privileges and protections.

In its efforts to deal with overcrowding and urban poverty among freedpeople in the District of Columbia, the bureau began to use domestic labor as a more systematic substitute for public assistance in ways that resonate strongly with more recent efforts to move women from welfare to work. Within national discourse, public assistance for freedpeople elicited strong anxieties about cultural degeneration. These anxieties tended to conflate dependence on state assistance with a failure to become a free and independent liberal subject and to exercise the self-restraint and discipline associated with that subjectivity. The economic devastation freedpeople experienced after the Civil War was interpreted not as inequality that centuries of racial violence and exploitation had necessarily produced but rather as a problem of culture. In other words, the harm of slavery was that it had kept the enslaved trapped in a degenerate culture of dependency, one that public assistance threatened to prolong. To facilitate the transition to freedom, the bureau was pressured to curtail public assistance and instead cultivate economic self-sufficiency. Therefore, eligibility for aid was strictly limited to those whose dependency could be justified, and it was accompanied by strict surveillance. For freedwomen, claims to assistance were fraught with contradictions. While gendered norms of citizenship cast women as naturally dependent, bureau officials were still reluctant to provide assistance to all but the most destitute and deserving of women. Rather, they first sought to cultivate marriage as a solution to freedwomen's economic needs. In the many cases where this was not a possibility, they focused instead on forcing freedwomen into wage labor through industrial schools, job-placement services, and transportation to work as domestics in the North.

The belief that the value of work was not just economic but rather lay in its capacity to cultivate the characteristics of good citizens was central to the bureau's labor programs. For freedwomen, this took on a particularly gendered cast. Industrial schools sought to inculcate freedwomen with feminine virtues but linked these ideals to wage labor. In contrast to the mothers' pension programs that would emerge in the Progressive Era, which sought to produce better citizens by keeping women out of wage labor, the D.C. bureau actively pushed freedwomen into wage labor. While bureau officials believed that cultivating the ideals of domesticity was essential, they thought this could be achieved through gendered forms of labor discipline. This belief speaks to the centrality of white surveillance to dominant constructions of what constituted freedom for Black people. Domestic labor, when performed in the privacy of one's own home and in the service of one's own family, was seen as idleness or vagrancy. However, that same labor, when performed under the watchful eye of a white employer and in the service of white domesticity, was seen as a pathway to moral uplift. This contrast demonstrates how the bureau's policies toward freedpeople often compelled them to perform their deservingness of freedom for a white national audience, often eclipsing freedpeople's efforts to actually practice freedom.

Juxtaposing these labor policies with the bureau's efforts to promote marriage makes apparent the racialized and gendered contradictions inherent in state efforts to remake Black kinship in the form of the heteronormative family. The bureau exalted marriage as the cornerstone of citizenship. Marriage ostensibly held together the heteronormative family as a unit of economic self-sufficiency and, in doing so, cultivated gendered roles that were essential to the moral execution of citizenship. However, without state support and material redistribution, the ideal of the self-sufficient family was an impossible myth. Unlike New Deal–era programs, which stabilized the white working class by distributing resources through the heteronormative family, bureau policies held freedpeople to the ideals of the family without the simultaneous investment of resources. As a result, without access to benefits like a family wage, income security, or housing assistance, the economically independent household was an unobtainable ideal. Frequently, it fell on freedwomen to bridge the substantial difference between the reality that freedpeople confronted and the expectations of self-sufficiency through wage labor. When families failed to achieve economic independence, freedwomen's labor was seen as a necessary supplement. When marriage itself proved to be an elusive, unrealistic, or undesirable option, unmarried women were expected to take on the role of breadwinner on their own. In this way, bureau policies glorified the sanctity of the domestic sphere and violated it simultaneously.

While bureau officers saw themselves as helping freedpeople rise out of poverty, their practices of pushing women into domestic work often had highly detrimental effects. First, domestic workers' contracts left freedwomen in highly exploitable circumstances. There were few, if any, boundaries around the workers' time, and freedwomen were often forced into employment relationships that mimicked slavery. The emphasis on moral rather than economic uplift meant that little consideration was given to how freedwomen might improve their long-term economic prospects. Ironically, while bureau officers pushed freedpeople into wage labor as a way of combating the cultural vestiges of slavery, the circumstances of domestic work were often contrary to the goal of cultivating independent free subjects. In many ways, the "vagrant" housewives and sex workers whom bureau officers feared exercised far more independence than domestic workers did. Not only were domestic workers highly dependent on their employers, but their isolation often left them vulnerable to sexual violence and abuse. Second, domestic labor effectively consigned freedwomen to the labors of domesticity while providing none of the privileges of the private sphere. Domestic workers not only experienced little privacy around their person or time as employees within white households but were also forced to endure separation from their own children. In prioritizing labor discipline over all other concerns, bureau officers argued that engaging in reproductive labor for white families would make freedwomen better mothers just as this labor took them away from their children. In this way, the bureau prioritized ensuring that one's children were not dependent on state assistance over investing time and care in familial relationships in their definition of what constituted good motherhood for freedwomen. This ran contrary to freedwomen's own assertions that the protection of their relationship to their children was one of the most important aspects of freedom. Finally, while the bureau constituted marriage and the hetero-normative family as the basis of citizenship, it also consistently violated that family form in the interest of promoting labor discipline. The bureau did not recognize how this made gendered norms of citizenship impossible for freedwomen to meet; instead, freedwomen's failure to achieve these norms was taken as a sign of their undeservingness of basic rights and their perpetual need for reform. This structure would lay the foundation for the material and discursive conditions out of which the narrative of the welfare queen that was so central to the restructuring of the welfare state in the late twentieth century would emerge.

FIVE

The Chains of Welfare

We have a welfare system here in the United States that has paid people not to work, has paid people not to get married, has paid people to stay where they are in a life of poverty and not to succeed. By changing this system we have an opportunity to give these people a new lease on life, and to help them take control of their future and enjoy a new freedom that many of them have not enjoyed because they have been enslaved with the chains of welfare in this country.
—**U.S. Representative E. Clay Shaw** (1995)

Representative E. Clay Shaw's remarks at the congressional hearings on welfare reform in 1995 demonstrate that by the end of the twentieth century, AFDC (Aid to Families with Dependent Children) was viewed as the greatest of social ills rather than as a valuable form of social support.[1] Shaw vividly describes welfare as a set of chains that kept recipients enslaved in poverty and restrained them from becoming free and independent subjects. The invocation of slavery in this context is striking in that it both situates welfare as slavery's reincarnation and rewrites what slavery was in ways that foster its afterlife.

Here slavery appears not as a violent and dehumanizing white supremacist structure but rather as a reflection of the cultural deficiencies of the enslaved themselves. In Shaw's imagination, slaves lived indulgently off their masters, not the other way around. Slaves were dependents, while masters bore the burden of their upkeep. This supposed dependency discursively links welfare receipt with slavery and constructs them both as the antithesis of the properly free subject. Simultaneously erasing the violence of slavery and the violence of poverty, Shaw focuses instead on the failure of welfare recipients to take responsibility and perform independence. Like the Reconstruction-era vagrant, the welfare recipient is backward, irresponsible, undeserving, out of control, and lacking in the discipline necessary for the proper exercise of agency.

Shaw positions welfare reform as facilitating emancipation, in much the same way as the Freedmen's Bureau was positioned. Strikingly, more than 125 years after the demise of the bureau, the simultaneous emphasis on marriage promotion and forced labor that had defined the state's treatment of freedwomen during Reconstruction resurfaced in efforts to restructure the U.S. welfare state. Much as in the Reconstruction era, public assistance was defined as antithetical to true freedom, and this belief spurred the late twentieth-century project of welfare reform. Echoing nineteenth-century anxieties about vagrancy, opponents argued that welfare rewarded idleness, sexual promiscuity, and a lack of achievement, trapping recipients in a state of unfreedom. For Shaw and others like him, welfare was the quintessential example of the federal government's overreach, and it and the bad behaviors it supposedly cultivated posed a threat to both nation and family that needed to be curbed.

Part of the Republican Party's larger effort to dismantle big government and restore the nation's family values in their "Contract with America," the attack on welfare culminated with the passage of PRWORA (the Personal Responsibility and Work Opportunity Reconciliation Act) in 1996. Many years in the making, this law represented a bipartisan compromise that restructured AFDC into TANF (Temporary Assistance to Needy Families), a program organized around the principles of state flexibility, stricter limits on eligibility, marriage promotion, stronger child support enforcement, and a work requirement. Heralded by Bill Clinton as "the end of welfare as we know it," the law turned to the heteronormative family and low-wage work as the solution to women's poverty.[2] While these changes aligned with the goals of structural adjustment and austerity that dominated capitalist states at the end of the twentieth century, the problematics of slavery and emancipation that animated the Reconstruction era haunted the public discourse about welfare reform.[3] This can be seen in the way that Shaw frames welfare reform as a moment of emancipation. In suggesting that welfare recipients had been "enslaved" by the very system that ought to support them, Shaw positioned proposed reforms that promoted both work and marriage as part of the making of free subjects in ways that hearkened back to the practices of the Freedmen's Bureau.

Shaw's remarks are but one example of how language and imagery associated with slavery and freedom appeared in late twentieth-century debates about welfare reform. Within public discourse of this period, welfare recipients were frequently referred to as trapped, bonded, imprisoned, or unable to escape the grips of the welfare system, and moving people off welfare was repeatedly equated with freeing them from the culture of poverty and dependency that the system supposedly fostered. The language of slavery created an inaccurate image of AFDC as a program that primarily served Black single mothers, signaling the deeper historical concerns that animated welfare reform. In contrast to early twentieth-century efforts that built the program around the figure of the deserving white widow, proponents of welfare reform portrayed AFDC recipients as unsympathetic "welfare queens" who lived large at taxpayers' expense. In Shaw's description, the contemporary welfare recipient did not work, did not marry, and did not contribute to her own advancement or to that of the nation. In other words, she embodied the same white anxieties that Hiester Clymer's campaign had sought to capitalize on in 1866. Much like the vagrant of the nineteenth century, the welfare queen linked fears of undisciplined Black labor and nonnormative genders and sexualities through the construction of both as part of a pathological dependency that threatened the nation. Also, as in the nineteenth century, the federal government emerged as the primary culprit, with federal public assistance being reframed as economic support for bad behaviors.

This chapter theorizes how twentieth-century welfare history was embedded in and produced by the continuing afterlife of slavery by rereading feminist welfare history and public discourse about welfare reform in relation to the practices of the Freedmen's Bureau. Drawing on Saidiya Hartman's conception of the afterlife of slavery as "a racial calculus and a political arithmetic" that devalues and imperils Black lives, I argue that twentieth-century welfare politics elaborated and promulgated the logics and practices developed during Reconstruction to curtail Black freedom.[4] I examine the historical development of the welfare state in the twentieth century as haunted by the Freedmen's Bureau's approach to the regulation of Black labor, gender, and sexuality. Looking at the different ways ideas of family were deployed in different historical moments, I argue that the shifting emphasis between the family as a source of rights and the family as a vehicle for enforcing responsibilities enabled the creation of a racially stratified welfare state that was organized through gender hierarchy. Many scholars have shown how racial exclusion and gendered constructions of citizenship were constitutive elements of the development of the U.S. welfare state. My analysis, however, emphasizes the way that constructions of the family linked race, gender, and class interests in the construction of a welfare state that mitigated some forms of inequality while exacerbating others. During the Reconstruction era, any support of Black families was met with hostility. In contrast, in the early twentieth century, maternalist activists and the white working class successfully built a federal welfare state by arguing that social supports for white families were crucial to the health of the nation. In later years, as welfare rights activists broke down barriers that maintained racial exclusion in welfare programs, however, public perceptions of those programs swiftly changed. As Black women gained access to programs like AFDC, the family yet again became a site for imposing responsibility rather than distributing entitlements.

The second section of this chapter explores the backlash against welfare programs that emerged in the post–civil rights era and was consolidated in the figure of the welfare queen. Situating the welfare queen as a reinvention of the nineteenth-century vagrant, this section makes visible similarities in the ways the two figures brought together a range of anxieties about gender deviance, labor discipline, and national belonging. Finally, the chapter turns to the policies enacted in response to these anxieties, specifically the increasing emphasis on marriage promotion and forced labor. While many scholars have understood PRWORA as either an effort to make a low-wage workforce available to an increasingly globalized economy or an effort to punish women who step outside of heteropatriarchal gender norms, I highlight how these two goals became linked in the figure of the workfare worker. Much like the domestic worker in the Reconstruction era, the workfare worker reconciled contradictions between domesticity and low-wage work, as women were engaged in feminized forms of labor under the surveillance of the state. In this way, workfare programs forced women to engage in public forms of reproductive labor as a reform project while simultaneously devaluing their reproductive labor when done on behalf of their own families.

Investing in White Families

While the life of the Freedmen's Bureau itself was short, the ideas about race, gender, and public assistance that it disseminated troubled social welfare policy long after its institutions were dismantled. During the twentieth century, the federal welfare state expanded tremendously and became a central terrain on which race, gender, class, and sexuality were articulated and struggled over. Various competing interests shaped welfare institutions, but the family continued to play a particularly important role in how these interests were articulated and how these institutions developed. On the one hand, expanded forms of state support for the white working class reinforced the heteropatriarchal family as the naturalized basis for organizing gender, sexuality, and kinship. On the other hand, demands that the state protect the seemingly natural family from unnatural threats legitimized an expanded welfare state. With the family's capacity to signify "hierarchy within unity," the discursive construction of the family was central to the construction of a welfare state stratified based on race and gender.[5] The unresolved problematics of emancipation that animated the Freedmen's Bureau's efforts to promote marriage and work haunted efforts to construct a more expansive welfare state in the twentieth century, and the flexible boundaries between state and family offered an alibi for constructing a welfare state that would simultaneously support white families and demand self-support from Black families. The welfare rights movement systematically challenged these inequalities in the 1960s and 1970s, ending the formal racial exclusions that had characterized AFDC and putting forward a vision of welfare receipt grounded in Black women's work. However, their successes were met with a powerful backlash that made culture the primary culprit for racial and economic inequality in a way that resonated deeply with the discourse of the Reconstruction era. By the late twentieth century, programs that had been necessary supports for white families became seen as "chains" of dependency as welfare recipients were increasingly imagined to be Black women. This section lays out the context for this transition by briefly sketching the history that shaped welfare policy toward single mothers, from the demise of the Freedmen's Bureau to welfare reform.

Maternalist Politics and the Early Welfare State

In the early twentieth century, maternalist reformers laid the groundwork for the growth of contemporary welfare bureaucracies. Responding to the conditions of industrial capitalism and the growing numbers of women in the workforce, maternalist activists were concerned about the impact of wage labor on gender roles, the family, and the nation. Maternalist ideology simultaneously reified and challenged the public-private divide by exalting the virtues of domesticity in order to forge a pathway into the state for women. Maternalists held that women's primary contribution to the nation was as mothers of a future generation of citizens and grounded their politics in gendered ideas that linked domesticity to the preservation of morality and culture. As women themselves, maternalist reformers believed they were uniquely positioned to advocate for social reform. They fought for public policy that would protect the traditional family by protecting women and children, thereby reshaping the boundaries between the state and the family.[6]

Maternalists' most significant successes were in the creation of protective labor laws for women workers and mothers' pension programs, both of which left important legacies for the welfare bureaucracies that would develop with the New Deal. Protective labor legislation was a response to the increasing entry of white women into the industrial labor force in the post–Civil War era and the heightened anxieties about gender roles this produced. Reformers believed that work outside the home jeopardized women's morality, distracted them from the more vital responsibilities associated with marriage and motherhood, and threatened the nation by destabilizing patriarchal family structures. As a result of maternalist advocacy and following on the heels of the Supreme Court ruling in *Muller v. Oregon*, which instituted a ten-hour workday for women, most states enacted laws to protect women in the workforce. Among other things, these laws "limited night work, restricted the number of pounds women could lift on the job, and required employers to provide seats to women workers and clerks in department stores."[7] Legislation like this sought to mitigate the potentially degrading features of wage labor by treating women as a protected class.

During the same period, maternalists also advocated for the creation of mothers' pension programs to provide material support to single mothers so that they could remain at home to raise their children. Mothers' pensions were founded on the belief that keeping mothers in the home was best for children and therefore best for the future of the nation. For this reason, these programs linked financial support to the cultivation of particular forms of mothering that would contribute to the creation of well-assimilated future citizens. As Gwendolyn Mink shows, anxieties about immigration figured prominently in the development of mothers' pensions, and financial assistance was used as a tool to promote Americanization. Mothers' pensions transformed the relationship between state and family; financial support "established the state's interests in the home, specifically the quality of home conditions maintained by recipients."[8] Because the primary beneficiaries were children rather than the mothers themselves, mothers' pensions became a vehicle for regulating motherhood and promoting assimilation. In addition, to ensure that mothers' pensions shored up rather

than undermined the heteropatriarchal family, strict eligibility requirements generally made assistance available only to widows or women who
had been deserted through no fault of their own. Even these women had to
demonstrate high moral character in order to receive aid, and divorced or
unmarried women were largely ineligible for any kind of assistance.[9]

The principles institutionalized by protective labor laws and mothers'
pension programs had several lasting impacts on the federal welfare bureaucracies that would develop later in the twentieth century. First, both
policies relied on a fundamental separation between the identities of
women and workers. While protective labor laws for women workers were
the earliest successful efforts to regulate working conditions under capitalism, they did so by creating a division between women and other workers.
These laws protected women workers on the basis of their gender, thereby
creating a legal structure in which women workers appeared as women first
and workers secondarily. Mothers' pension programs further entrenched
this division by linking public assistance to the gendered responsibilities
of motherhood. Through this politics, mothers and workers came to be
understood as distinct categories, laying the foundation for what Linda
Gordon has termed a "two tier welfare state" in which programs for men
were seen as entitlements for independent workers, and programs for
women were seen as charity for dependent mothers.[10] At the same time,
the separation of the categories of mothers and workers left individuals
who occupied both positions simultaneously in a tenuous relationship to
the welfare state.

Second, mothers' pensions relied on distinguishing between those
who deserved assistance and those who did not in order to support single
mothers without sanctioning childbirth outside of marriage. By supporting
only widows and deserted women who could not be faulted for their circumstances, mothers' pensions ensured that public assistance would reinforce
rather than threaten the heteropatriarchal family. As a result, assessing recipients' moral worth became a central activity of these and future welfare
programs. Finally, the morality and deservingness of recipients were closely
connected to ideas about cultural reform and assimilation. Maternalists
saw public assistance as an entryway into the home and used mothers' pensions as a tool to promote hegemonic ideals of domesticity.[11] This not only
had the effect of framing poverty as a problem of cultural assimilation but
also excluded racialized populations who were seen as outside the realm
of assimilation, barring them from receiving assistance. For Black women,
this meant an almost categorical exclusion from assistance in that they

were consistently seen as undeserving and incapable of reform. This exclusion persisted into the federal programs created through the New Deal.

The New Deal and the (White) Family Wage

The New Deal institutionalized mothers' pensions at the federal level with the creation of the Aid to Dependent Children (ADC) program. Alongside programs like unemployment and old-age insurance, ADC was a key piece of a new Keynesian welfare state that sought to mitigate the effects of capitalist crisis. However, while the New Deal intervened in class conflict, the shape this intervention took was fundamentally gendered and racialized. Building on the gendered ideas of citizenship that were central to maternalist politics, the family wage emerged as the scaffolding on which New Deal programs were anchored. Whether it be through work programs, collective bargaining rights, or social insurance, the New Deal treated men as breadwinners and heads of households, while women who received assistance were treated primarily as wives and mothers. The New Deal sought to organize the working class into stable, settled heteronormative families.[12] However, racial exclusion was also central, and most of these efforts extended only to whites. Shaped by the competing demands of the white urban working class and southern planters, New Deal programs brokered a compromise that gave the white working class a larger piece of the social wage while leaving undisturbed the social and economic relations in the South, which depended on a highly exploitable Black workforce.[13] While federal social insurance programs and the Fair Labor Standards Act both excluded domestic and agricultural work (occupations where Black workers were concentrated), ADC effected racial exclusion through its institutional structure, which allocated federal funds to support programs run by state and local governments.

As Robert Lieberman argues, ADC was a "doubly discretionary" program. First, because there was no uniform federal standard, states had considerable flexibility in the kinds of programs and eligibility requirements that they instituted. Second, while state laws set standards for eligibility, these standards were largely based on subjective determinations, which allowed for considerable variation in who actually received assistance both across and even within counties.[14] This level of discretion frequently worked to exclude Black women, especially in the South but also in other parts of the country. In addition, because there was no federal standard, local welfare authorities used their own discretion in determining what individual benefits would be. Even when Black families received assistance, authorities tended to see them as needing less than white families, and as a result, their benefit levels were set lower.[15]

The financial structure of ADC also made the cost of the program an overwhelming concern. Because ADC was a noncontributory program, each additional recipient was understood as an additional cost that would be financed by taxpayers. According to Lieberman, this combination of "weak fiscal capacity and weak national supervision" institutionalized a logic of constraint that fueled the exclusion of Black women.[16] This dynamic was exacerbated by the addition of federal survivors' benefits for the spouses and children of qualified workers in 1939. This expansion created a division between the widows of qualified workers, who received a social security entitlement that was not means tested and that did not subject women to state regulation within the home, and other women who received ADC. As a result, the "worthy widows" who had initially been the deserving recipients within ADC received survivors' benefits, leaving ADC to serve "an increasingly suspect group of women who were defined not by their misfortune but by their behavior."[17]

While on the surface ADC sought to promote cultural reform through domesticity and defined women's citizenship through motherhood, in practice these goals tended not to apply to Black women. The twin mandates of promoting work and marriage that structured the Freedmen's Bureau's activities were significant elements of how Black women were treated in ADC from early on, and it was local discretion within the program that enabled this. Within ADC, eligible children were defined as those who lacked the financial support of a father due to death, absence from the home, or disability. While financial support for children had originally been conflated with a father's income, over time some mothers were expected to take on both wage earning and caretaking. In 1943 Louisiana adopted the first "employable mother" rule, which denied assistance to mothers when agricultural work was available, and by the 1950s eighteen states had adopted similar rules.[18] "Employable mother" rules largely targeted Black and, in some regions of the country, Mexican women, who were seen as well suited to agricultural and domestic work regardless of whether they had small children. Local discretion enabled welfare authorities to both support white women in their work as mothers and deny those same supports to Black women on the grounds that they were employable. This reflected both the racialized perception that Black women should be working and an economic dependence on Black women's labor, particularly within agriculture in the South.[19]

Local discretion also emerged as a mechanism of policing sexuality within ADC. "Suitable home" rules enabled welfare officials to deny assistance to a child whose home was deemed unsuitable. Frequently, "unsuitable homes" were those in which mothers were unmarried or seen as sexually promiscuous, and many states denied assistance to "illegitimate" children outright, either through specific laws or in everyday practice. The exclusion of children born outside of marriage was disproportionately applied to Black women, and illegitimacy was seen as a sign of Black cultural inferiority that should not be supported by public assistance programs, an association that would deepen in the late twentieth century and beyond.[20] At the same time, welfare authorities also frowned on ADC mothers who had any relationships with men. Man-in-the-house rules coupled with strict surveillance of recipients frequently resulted in women losing their benefits when evidence of a man's presence surfaced. Rules like these explicitly policed sexuality outside of marriage and reinforced marriage as the normative way of organizing families. At the same time, they implicitly suggested that marriage offered a way of shifting dependence on ADC to dependence on a man. When women were denied assistance because of their relationships with men, the rationale was that these men, instead of the government, should be supporting the children involved. Similarly, the denial of assistance to illegitimate children also carried with it a sense that these children's fathers should be held financially responsible for the needs of their children.[21]

Despite the very high levels of need among Black women, these discretionary practices meant that initially ADC recipients were overwhelmingly white. While many maternalist activists contested the exclusion of Black women from ADC, they were largely unsuccessful in these efforts, perhaps because the cultural constructs of motherhood that their politics rested on were so difficult to apply to Black women.[22] However, over time, the number of Black women receiving ADC did grow. By 1948, 30 percent of ADC recipients were nonwhite, and by the 1950s ADC was increasingly seen by politicians and the public as serving women who were unmarried, divorced, and/or Black.[23] This shifting perception coincided with changing ideas about the purpose of the program. More and more, ADC was described as a program that served "broken" families. Whereas New Deal programs were guided by a belief that relief to poor families was necessary owing to external economic problems, in the postwar era poverty was increasingly understood as a problem with individuals. While early mothers' pensions had sought to promote proper dependency for women, by the 1950s economic dependence on public assistance was thought to be damaging to the family and a source of cultural and psychological harm. Dependency as an individualized social condition became the problem to be solved, and the emphasis of ADC began to shift from moral uplift through domesticity to rehabilitation through work. In contrast to work programs for male workers, which sought to address a lack of jobs, work through ADC was designed to address individual dependency by cultivating the skills and characteristics needed to be more independent.[24] The growing emphasis on work can, in part, be seen as a reflection of changing norms around women and work outside the home during this time. However, it might be more accurately understood as the result of ADC becoming increasingly associated with women who had a long history of working outside the home. In many ways, the turn toward rehabilitation rewrote in the more modern discourse of social psychology the earlier Reconstruction-era belief that disciplined labor was key to making Black women into gendered citizens. In doing so, it laid a foundation for work requirements that would proliferate in the decades to come.

The Welfare Rights Movement

The growing number of Black women gaining access to ADC, which was renamed Aid to Families with Dependent Children (AFDC) in 1962, was a key factor in the development of welfare rights organizing. Local welfare rights groups began to emerge in the early 1960s and came together to form the National Welfare Rights Organization (NWRO) in 1966. At its height in 1969, the NWRO included more than twenty-two thousand families and had local chapters in nearly every state and major city.[25] Ninety percent of the NWRO's members were Black women, and the critiques the organization launched connected issues of racism, poverty, and the recognition of women's work as mothers. In response to the stigma associated with AFDC receipt, the activists of the NWRO sought to reframe AFDC as an entitlement on par with other forms of state assistance. Drawing parallels between AFDC and financial aid for college, tax exemptions for married couples and homeowners, farm subsidies, and social security, welfare rights activists highlighted and contested AFDC's secondary status within the welfare state.[26]

The NWRO's political strategy directly challenged the "doubly discretionary" character of the AFDC program by using the federal courts to invalidate many of the procedures individual states had used to exclude Black women from AFDC. For example, in 1961 the federal government invalidated

Louisiana's "suitable home" regulations, which defined as unsuitable any home in which an illegitimate child was born to a woman receiving welfare.[27] In 1968 the Supreme Court ruled in *Goldberg v. Kelly* that the summary termination of benefits was a violation of the Fourteenth Amendment's guarantee of due process. In 1969, in *King v. Smith*, the Supreme Court unanimously struck down Alabama's substitute-father rule and prohibited states from denying aid to children on the basis of a mother's moral character. This reinforced the idea that a state could not deny aid to mothers and children eligible based on need unless the federal government authorized them to do so.[28] Following the *King* ruling, the Supreme Court also overturned Connecticut's residency requirement, California's man-in-the-house regulation, and New Jersey's rule that limited AFDC benefits to legally married parents. These decisions curtailed individual states' ability to deny assistance based on subjective categories of morality and behavior.[29] Through these legislative challenges, AFDC and other welfare programs became increasingly accessible to Black women and other women of color. This, in turn, contributed to dramatic changes in both the racial composition of the population who received welfare and the public perception of AFDC.

While welfare rights organizers successfully overturned many of the most racist state-level eligibility requirements, they were much less successful in the challenges they mounted against work requirements. The courts repeatedly ruled that states had the right to both force women to accept available employment and also make assistance contingent on forms of forced labor. In 1966 Black welfare recipients from Georgia organized to challenge the state's "employable mother" rule. Despite arguments that the rule violated their constitutional rights, enabled racial discrimination, devalued their work as mothers, and was used to guarantee a low-wage agricultural labor force, the fifth circuit court of appeals found the statute to be constitutional on the grounds that "there is no federally protected right of [a] mother to refuse employment while receiving assistance and remaining at home with her children."[30] Similarly, in 1973 the Supreme Court upheld New York state's AFDC work requirements on the basis that individual states had the right to enforce work policies in order to manage welfare costs and that states should be afforded flexibility in how they implemented welfare programs. These two rulings set the tone for future developments in welfare policy by advancing the idea that there was no right to subsidized motherhood (or no right for mothers not to engage in labor outside the home) and by making fiscal concerns a justification for work requirements. Just as

AFDC was becoming increasingly accessible to Black women, the character of the program shifted toward emphasizing work to combat public perceptions that the program was a drain on government resources.[31]

The women of the NWRO were aware of the ways in which the AFDC program was designed to regulate their labor as both wage workers and mothers. In response, they articulated a complex vision of what they wanted in relation to these two work roles. The NWRO activists insisted that mothering and housework constituted labor that should be compensated, and they consistently challenged the perception that women on welfare did not work by pointing out how much work they in fact did to care for their children and maintain their households. However, unlike Progressive Era maternalists, who likewise emphasized the value of women's work as mothers, NWRO activists also challenged the idea that welfare receipt should be contingent on their behavior or their perceived adequacy as mothers in the eyes of the state. In challenging "suitable home" laws, home visits by caseworkers, and forced paternity identification, welfare rights activists also contested the two-parent family norm. They insisted that there was nothing morally wrong with single mothers and that the real injustice was in the way that women's work as mothers continued to be unrecognized.[32] However, at the same time, NWRO activists also believed that a "woman should be able to *choose* whether to work outside her home or in it, to choose whether she wants to care for her own children all the time or part-time."[33] They were aware that welfare recipients and those denied welfare constituted a supply of cheap labor for the nation, and their concept of choice was linked to the need to make dignified work that paid a living wage a reality for low-income women.

Though not always framed this way and not always successful, the NWRO's efforts constituted a challenge to the way that racialized heteropatriarchy functioned as an organizing principle of the AFDC program. The NWRO confronted institutional racism within the welfare system by contesting the assumptions about gender and sexuality that underwrote it.[34] In claiming rights of motherhood for its largely Black membership, opposing the two-parent family ideal, and dismantling stereotypes about welfare recipients, the women of the NWRO argued for compensation for women's work as mothers while challenging the construct of the family wage that had been an organizing principle of the New Deal.

One of the most lasting contributions of welfare rights activism was the dismantling of many of the legal and institutional barriers that had kept Black women from receiving AFDC. By challenging the way that welfare receipt had been conditioned on the proper performance of femininity and the regulation of women's sexuality, welfare rights activism in many ways changed the face of welfare receipt. The original mothers' pension programs and to a lesser degree the New Deal's ADC program had been imagined as programs that served deserving white women or that linked welfare receipt to cultural reform so as to produce gendered citizens who were well assimilated to nationalist constructions of the heteropatriarchal family. In contrast, welfare rights activists envisioned AFDC as an entitlement, as compensation for their work as mothers that should not be contingent on their perceived morality or behavior. They imagined and attempted to use AFDC as an instrument through which the welfare recipient could expand her options and improve her living situation on her own terms, rather than as an instrument for the state to make well-assimilated gendered citizens. In expanding the welfare rolls to include greater numbers of Black women, welfare rights activists asserted their own humanity and implicitly argued that that humanity was not contingent on how well they adhered to the dominant norms of femininity. For example, NWRO leader Johnnie Tillmon noted that the welfare system punished women for their inability to perform normative gender roles. She observed that "an A.F.D.C. mother learns that being a 'real woman' means being all the things she isn't and having all the things she can't have."[35] In contrast to earlier movements, welfare rights activists did not believe that welfare recipients should have to conform to dominant ideals of "real womanhood" to be included as full and equal citizens; rather, they challenged these ideals and sought state recognition as they were.[36] However, as the welfare rights movement receded and the civil rights, Black Power, and feminist movements that buoyed it were transformed through police repression and state co-optation, this vision became more and more marginalized within welfare politics.[37] What remained, however, was a new association of AFDC receipt with Black women. Even though Black women had been largely excluded from receiving assistance for most of the program's history, in the aftermath of the welfare rights struggle AFDC quickly became represented as a program that primarily served the Black urban poor. This association of AFDC with Black women sparked a reemergence of Reconstruction-era discourses about vagrancy that ultimately delegitimized an already contentious program.

Race and the Emergence of Antiwelfare Politics

The shift in perceptions of AFDC from a program that primarily served white women to a program that primarily served Black women incited a discursive and legislative backlash against the program that was framed in two different but interconnected ways. The first strain of antiwelfare discourse that emerged in response to growing numbers of Black women receiving AFDC assistance was the emerging idea that welfare bred a culture of poverty. This discourse was strikingly different from earlier interpretations of the function of AFDC. While aid to single mothers had initially been viewed as a vehicle for cultural reform, within the culture-of-poverty discourse welfare assistance was reframed as promoting cultural degeneracy. The second strand of antiwelfare discourse that emerged in immediate response to welfare rights activism was the mounting belief that women on welfare should be forced to work. Although neither of these discourses facilitated large-scale changes in the welfare system in the 1960s and 1970s, they significantly transformed how welfare recipients were imagined and laid the groundwork for the dismantling of AFDC in 1996.

Perhaps the most influential iteration of the culture-of-poverty discourse was Daniel Patrick Moynihan's 1965 report *The Negro Family: The Case for National Action*.[38] Written in the aftermath of civil rights victories in an effort to develop a government strategy to deal with racial unrest, the Moynihan report sought to explain the persistence of Black economic inequality in the United States. In contrast to the structural explanations that were being put forth by the Black Power movement at the time, Moynihan located the problem of Black urban poverty in African American family structures. He argued that the persistence of Black inequality in the United States was a direct product of the failure of Black people to adhere to heteronormative, patriarchal ideals. Tracing the origins of Black matriarchy to the emasculation of Black men under slavery, Moynihan argued that the dominance of Black women within Black families produced a "culture of poverty." Although Moynihan saw the injustices of slavery as the original cause of the problem, he argued that the culture of poverty had by this point been transferred from generation to generation in a cycle of poverty perpetuated by Black women. According to Moynihan, Black matriarchy produced social disorder. It not only led to illegitimate births, female-headed households, and sexual promiscuity but also produced alienation and low achievement among Black men, leading them to turn to crime and violence. In essence, the Moynihan report explained racial inequality as a result of Black women's failure to do gender properly. By extension, Moynihan believed that the excesses of Black women—excessive sexuality and excessive power within the family—needed to be curbed. The solution to racial inequality, for Moynihan, was restoring patriarchal family structures in Black communities, primarily through increased participation of Black men in employment programs and in the military. In yet another version of racial liberalism, the key to assimilation into the nation was the cultural reform of families, and the state's obligation was to facilitate that reform.

While Moynihan's arguments were highly influential in setting the tone for debates about welfare reform, the report offered little that was new. In fact, its power lay not so much in what it said as in the political moment in which it said it. The association of certain cultural practices with poverty was nothing new. Both the Freedmen's Bureau and the Progressive Era maternalists had emphasized cultural reform in their approaches to poverty. In addition, American sociologists and anthropologists had begun to put increasing emphasis on culture and more specifically on family structure in their explanations for poverty both in the United States and abroad during the period after World War II. Moynihan himself drew extensively on the work of E. Franklin Frasier and borrowed the terminology of a "culture of poverty" from Oscar Lewis's work on Puerto Rico and Mexico.[39] What was unique about the Moynihan report was that it brought these ideas together in a historical moment in which the dominant language of race was in crisis. Michael Omi and Howard Winant argue that the passage of civil rights laws in the mid-1960s signaled a major transformation in racial politics in the United States. This transition away from what Omi and Winant call a racial dictatorship, or a racial order defined by the political and social exclusion of people of color, and toward racial hegemony, defined by struggles over the meaning of racial equality, was marked by the formal legal and political incorporation of people of color, as evidenced in the passage of civil rights legislation, the transformation of immigration laws, and a changing language around race and racism.[40] In this context, the Moynihan report and the language of a culture of poverty offered a new discursive vehicle for talking about race through the language of gender and sexuality. Prefiguring the image of the welfare queen, Moynihan's figure of the Black matriarch remained a vivid presence within welfare debates in the decades to come.

In conjunction with the belief that welfare fostered a culture of poverty, a second strain of antiwelfare discourse was developing that focused on requiring welfare recipients to work. While this discourse built on the idea that welfare produced cultural degeneracy by breeding dependency and ir-responsibility, in contrast to the independence and employment that work fostered, it also deviated from the work of early culture-of-poverty theo-rists. Instead of positing the restoration of heteropatriarchal family norms as the solution to the problem of dependency and gender deviance, this second strain of antiwelfare discourse suggested that the state should culti-vate independence among women on welfare through forcing AFDC recipi-ents to work outside the home, either by ending the program altogether or by instituting mandatory work requirements. As noted earlier, while the NWRO successfully challenged racist eligibility requirements, federal courts consistently let state work requirements stand. This set the tone for the increasing emphasis on work outside the home within AFDC, a trend that culminated in the passage of PRWORA. Up until the late 1960s, the AFDC program had encouraged some women to engage in wage labor by deny-ing them assistance through racist provisions like the "employable mother" rule. However, as these provisions were overturned and as Black women increasingly gained access to AFDC, efforts to reform welfare increasingly stressed making work requirements a precondition for welfare receipt and moving recipients from welfare to work. Therefore, while not entirely new, the idea that AFDC recipients should work outside the home assumed a new centrality as the AFDC program became increasingly associated with Black women. These early efforts at reform provided the laboratory in which both new policy alternatives and the new language of workfare would be invented.

The first of these legislative efforts was the Work Incentives Program (WIN). Created in 1967, WIN established a comprehensive plan to provide job training and employment for AFDC recipients. In its initial implemen-tation, WIN prioritized providing employment-related services for un-employed fathers and children over the age of sixteen, but the Talmadge Amendments of 1971 tightened the work requirements and broadened the scope of WIN to include single mothers of school-aged children.[41] The first workfare program, the Community Work Experience Program, was also developed at this time. It required women to work outside of the home in exchange for welfare. Although implemented in only a few states, these programs served as precursors to the proliferation of such programs under the Reagan administration.[42]

The next major legislative changes to AFDC came in the 1980s during the Reagan administration. In 1981 the Omnibus Budget Reconciliation Act restricted eligibility for AFDC to families with gross incomes less than

150 percent of the state poverty level. In addition, the law cut welfare payments and offered incentives for states to develop welfare-to-work programs. The act was also significant in the ways it revived the demand that women on welfare work and redeployed the language of workfare.[43] The passage of the Family Support Act (FSA) of 1988 marked an important transition in debates about the welfare system. The FSA struck a balance between conservative beliefs that people on welfare should be forced into the workforce and liberal beliefs that people on welfare wanted to work but needed help realizing that desire. The FSA emphasized education, training, and childcare services while at the same time creating the Job Opportunities and Basic Skills program, which required states to have 20 percent of AFDC recipients in workfare programs by 1995. The program conditioned welfare eligibility on participation in work or education programs, and while the childcare services made available through the FSA were often seen as a way of supporting welfare mothers, they also "codified the assumption that single mothers should work outside the home."[44] According to Mink, the "FSA transformed welfare from an income maintenance program for poor families into a temporary substitute for wages" and with its child support and paternity-establishment provisions "anchored the self-sufficiency of families in a paternal home."[45] At the time, Senator Moynihan noted that the FSA "links welfare and work irretrievably."[46] With the passage of the FSA, workfare, rather than being a question of moral and political principle, became a technocratic question of implementation. The shift toward discussions of program implementation and away from the question of whether work should be required at all reflected the acceptance of the racialized and gendered interpretation of the problem as "welfare dependency" rather than as poverty itself.[47]

Welfare rights activism had a lasting impact in making AFDC more accessible and available to women of color. However, these victories were contentious, and the backlash that emerged in response to them would become a powerful force in reshaping the welfare system in the late twentieth century. As Jill Quadagno argues, the association of welfare rights and the War on Poverty with civil rights struggles fueled a racial backlash against these programs.[48] In particular, the increasing association of AFDC with Black women led to changing public opinion about an already marginalized program. While originally AFDC had been designed to uphold the heteronormative family and support mothers in raising future citizens, by the end of the twentieth century the program was increasingly seen as a primary culprit in the decline of the family and a host of other social problems. This changing perception can be traced directly to the specific anxieties provoked by providing assistance to Black women, anxieties that congealed in the frequently cited figure of the welfare queen.

Welfare Queens and the New Vagrancy

By the late twentieth century, a new figure dominated public discourse about welfare, one that combined anxieties about a culture of poverty with the desire to push welfare recipients into the low-wage workforce. The welfare queen entered the scene in the aftermath of the welfare rights movement, and by the 1980s AFDC had become virtually synonymous in the public imagination with unruly and undeserving Black women who had too many children and too much sex, lived too large, and refused to work. The narrative of the welfare queen was rooted in a series of myths, all of which directly contradicted the empirical evidence available at the time. First, despite the racial diversity of welfare recipients, the welfare queen was consistently portrayed as Black. Not only did media representations of welfare receipt disproportionately feature Black women, but the welfare queen was also described in racially coded language even when her race was not revealed.[49] However, while the percentage of AFDC recipients who were Black had risen steadily since the program's creation, this percentage peaked at 45 percent in 1969 and declined in the subsequent decades leading up to welfare reform. In 1995, on the eve of PRWORA, just 36 percent of AFDC recipients were Black, roughly equivalent to the percentage of recipients who were white.[50] In contrast, media representations suggested that AFDC primarily or even exclusively served an urban Black population, simultaneously hypervisibilizing Black women and erasing white women as recipients of public assistance.

A second myth that dominated public discourse about welfare held that AFDC recipients were simply lazy and chose not to work. This belief not only erased the reproductive labor that recipients did for their own families but also ignored the well-documented fact that most AFDC recipients had extensive histories of work outside the home and struggled to piece together enough to support their families through a combination of public assistance, low-wage work, and other sources of income. As Kathryn Edin and Laura Lein documented, the nature of the low-wage labor market often necessitated that single mothers cycle between welfare and work, and the inability to make a living wage, rather than a failure to work, was at the root of the economic obstacles that single mothers faced.[51]

Finally, the image of the welfare queen fixated on the sexual and reproductive behaviors of welfare recipients, arguing that AFDC encouraged sexual immorality at a direct cost to taxpayers. In the 1980s and 1990s, much of antiwelfare discourse linked AFDC to a supposed crisis of teenage pregnancy by suggesting that AFDC financially supported "children having children." Similarly, antiwelfare discourse reiterated a belief that welfare recipients had additional children simply to receive a larger welfare check. However, as Kristin Luker demonstrated, the crisis in teenage pregnancy was largely manufactured, and only a very small portion of AFDC recipients were under the age of eighteen.[52] In addition to the ludicrousness of believing that women would have children for negligible increases in benefits, Dorothy Roberts notes that most welfare recipients had only one or two children and that families receiving welfare tended to be slightly smaller than those that did not.[53]

These myths surrounding welfare receipt persisted in the public imagination even though they were not true. A remarkable figure, the welfare queen did not fit any individual woman's personal experience with welfare receipt, but every Black woman was potentially read through the narrative she enabled. The stories told about her belied empirical evidence and everyday experiences of poverty. Regardless, they were an unrivaled political force in shaping the restructuring of the welfare state in the late twentieth century. As Wahneema Lubiano writes, the welfare queen operated as "the synecdoche, the shortest possible shorthand, for the pathology of poor, urban, black culture."[54] A weapon in what Lubiano calls an "ideological war by narrative means," she was a fiction that enabled a particular way of understanding social problems, one that obscured structural forces and instead placed responsibility for racial and economic inequality squarely on the shoulders of Black women.[55]

The welfare queen invaded the public consciousness and provoked a national crisis, transforming a comparatively small federal expenditure into the primary focus of critiques of big government. The narrative that surrounded her became evidence of its own truth, easily assimilating any potential confirmation while dispelling alternatives. The public saw the welfare queen everywhere, and each individual sighting reinforced the larger plotline. Her narrative was superimposed onto Black women and became a dominant way of reading their actions and motivations.[56] As Ange-Marie

Hancock notes, this projection produced a "politics of disgust" in which perceptions and moral judgments about welfare recipients distorted democratic decision-making and precluded welfare recipients from political participation. While welfare rights organizing had a tremendous impact in making welfare programs more equitable, the construct of the welfare queen undermined future political contributions by welfare recipients, situating them as subjects to be reformed rather than as potential political actors.[57] Perhaps what is most striking about the welfare queen is how a representation that was so clearly false could have such a wide impact. Irrespective of evidence, key words in her story, like *fraud, illegitimacy, laziness, dependency,* and *cultural deviance,* dominated the wider discourse on public assistance. These same key words had defined discourse about vagrancy during the Reconstruction era.

The connections between the nineteenth-century vagrant and the welfare queen are striking, and despite their very different contexts, the family resemblance between the two is uncanny. Both emerged as a response to significant expansions in citizenship rights for Black people and transformed the question of who deserved public assistance into a mechanism for debating who belonged in the nation. Both the welfare queen and the vagrant were regarded as threats to the family and were deployed in ways that called into question the legitimacy of very visible (though not particularly costly) federal programs. Both linked a host of anxieties about labor discipline, a failure to comply with norms of settlement, and sexual and gender deviance, and both suggested that the best way to shore up the heteronormative family was not through state investment but rather through regulation and retrenchment.

Comparison between the welfare queen and the Reconstruction-era vagrant makes visible how both figures were an effect of the contradictions that gendered conceptions of citizenship organized through ideas of independence and dependence fostered in relation to race and class. Nancy Fraser and Linda Gordon have pointed to the ways that *dependency* emerged as a key word in U.S. welfare politics. They show that dependency is an overdetermined concept whose meaning has shifted and changed in different historical contexts. With the development of industrial capitalism, the free worker came to be understood as independent in contrast to three "icons of dependency": the pauper, who did not work and whose character was degraded by a reliance on charity; enslaved and Native peoples, whose "natural" dependence was a sign of racial inferiority and worked to rationalize slavery and colonization; and the housewife, who relied on a husband's wage rather than receiving one herself. Fraser and Gordon argue that each of these three icons of dependency constituted an other against which the free and independent worker was defined. Both the nineteenth-century vagrant and the twentieth-century welfare queen effectively brought these icons together into a singular threat. Fraser and Gordon also point to the ways that dependency has multiple registers of meaning, including the economic, sociolegal, political, and moral/psychological. This understanding of the multiple valences of meaning in the term is particularly useful in explaining how a single figure can link a whole range of different anxieties.[58]

While Gordon and Fraser's analysis is particularly useful in unpacking the ways that dependency gets deployed in the discourse on welfare, in comparing representations of the Reconstruction-era vagrant and the welfare queen, I am particularly interested in the ways these two figures blur the boundaries between independent and dependent subjects. As discussed in chapter 2, proper intimacy within the home was seen as necessary for the constitution of proper political and economic subjects in the public sphere. Proper intimacy linked independent male subjects to female dependents through heteronormative sexuality within the settler household.[59] Juxtaposing the nineteenth-century vagrant and the late twentieth-century welfare queen makes visible the ways these figures were threatening in the public imagination not just because they implied dependency but also because they destabilized the ways that independence and dependence were mapped onto both familial and political relationships. Vagrants and welfare queens were often both too dependent in some registers of meaning and simultaneously too independent in others. This flexible capacity enabled these representations to link a broad range of political interests, thereby consolidating opposition to forms of public assistance that were seen as primarily benefiting Black people.

Both the vagrant and the welfare queen were defined in contrast to the taxpayer, who was imagined to be both hardworking and white. Much like the white men, women, and children who were pushed to the periphery in Hiester Clymer's campaign advertisement, antiwelfare discourse repeatedly invoked the plight of the taxpayer, who was often situated as the real victim of welfare dependency. For example, in Representative Shaw's opening remarks to a 1995 congressional hearing on welfare reform, he defined the goals of welfare reform as to both "protect the needy" and "protect the taxpayer." He went on to identify the flaws in the welfare system, demanding, "Is it any wonder that taxpayers are asking if all the money they have spent on welfare has done any good?"[60] These ubiquitous references to taxpayers in public discourse about welfare function to situate the taxpayer as an injured party. Creating a narrative in which people who work hard to be economically independent end up supporting those who simply choose dependency, the emphasis on the taxpayer inverts structural inequalities.

Notably, the figures of the vagrant and the welfare queen both emerged in response to a crisis in the racial order and demands for redistribution of resources toward Black communities. Emancipation and civil rights victories provoked white anxieties about what the legal inclusion of Black people into institutions of citizenship that had been defined through racial exclusion would mean. In both instances, the taxpayer surfaced as a subject of state protection that enabled the construction of boundaries between deserving and undeserving citizens along racial lines. Just as Reconstruction-era discourse about vagrancy erased the labor Black people had performed while enslaved, the idea of welfare dependency made invisible recipients' contributions as both mothers and workers. These constructs mapped racial hierarchies onto family roles, positioning white citizens as independent adults and Black people as the dependent children they supported. This mapping produced a racial division within citizenship as decision-making power was increasingly seen as the province of contributors while welfare recipients were infantilized as unprepared for citizenship. This replicated Reconstruction-era beliefs that freedpeople were also like children who needed to demonstrate their deservingness and capacity for citizenship before they could be fully included.

References to injured taxpayers rested on a belief that welfare recipients and taxpayers were mutually exclusive categories. Deployed to suggest that the federal government took from the deserving to support the undeserving, the construction of the taxpayer erased the plethora of ways that the welfare state also supported white, middle-class families. Instead, appealing to the taxpayer suggested that one group of individuals only contributed while the other only sought to benefit. Situating certain citizens as more deserving than others, the injured taxpayer reframed prioritizing particular interests as responsible fiscal conservatism. As Sidney Plotkin and William Scheuerman note, "balanced-budget conservatism elevates protecting taxpayer interests to the highest priority of government, [and] stigmatizes poorer, property-less people as somehow less than fully citizens."[61] Importantly, the taxpayer also operated as a structure of identification that brought people who might stand to benefit from expanded public assistance into antiwelfare discourse. While a diverse range of people received benefits from the welfare state, antiwelfare discourse interpellated most people as taxpayers, thereby emphasizing the potential harms of welfare over its benefits.

In contrast to the hardworking taxpayer, welfare receipt was increasingly characterized by forms of fraud and criminality that connoted Blackness. Politicians and the media frequently told outrageous stories about welfare fraud and the women who perpetrated it. Seemingly grounded in fact, these stories created a larger-than-life image of welfare criminality that became synonymous with AFDC receipt. For example, during his 1976 presidential campaign, Ronald Reagan popularized the construction of the welfare queen through frequent retellings of the story of a Chicago woman who exemplified the problems with the welfare system. He described her as follows: "She used 80 names, 30 addresses, 15 telephone numbers to collect food stamps, Social Security, veterans' benefits for four nonexistent deceased veteran husbands, as well as welfare. Her tax-free cash income alone has been running $150,000 a year."[62] Reagan's description invokes many of the same anxieties that animated Reconstruction discourse about vagrancy. She not only made a living through crime but also lived a life of luxury and ease while others worked to support her. The refusal of settlement and a singular identity enabled her, like the vagrant, to shirk the responsibilities of work and citizenship.

Interestingly, Reagan's welfare queen was loosely based on the story of the con artist Linda Taylor. Not only did Reagan exaggerate Taylor's crimes, but the treatment of a truly exceptional case as the norm also led to a gross overestimation of the prevalence of welfare fraud. In addition, several elements in how the story circulated were notable. The construction of Taylor as a symbol ignored the potentially more harmful crimes she had committed, such as kidnapping, theft, and possibly even murder, suggesting that welfare fraud was indeed one of the most significant criminal threats facing the country.[63] In addition, by most accounts, Taylor was a white woman who sometimes passed as Black, Latina, or Filipina in her scams. However, as the story of the welfare queen circulated, the imagery and language used to portray her increasingly connoted Blackness. For example, the welfare queen was frequently described as driving a Cadillac and as residing in largely Black urban centers. She was associated with a culture of poverty, a lack of achievement, deviant family structure, and criminality, which were all part of the vocabulary that social science had developed to talk about Black communities. Visually, in the political cartoons or media images of the period, she was almost exclusively depicted as Black. Even though Reagan's inspiration was a white woman, the way her story was mobilized to criminalize welfare recipients and produce a sense of injury among innocent, hardworking citizens necessarily turned her Black and her victims white.[64]

By the 1990s, the racist construction of the welfare queen had expanded to include immigrant women of color, whose dependency was seen as equally threatening to the white taxpayer.[65] Fueled by the post-1965 growth in immigration from Latin America, Asia, and the Caribbean, the linking of anti-immigrant racism with antiwelfare discourse was a powerful tool in the dismantling of AFDC. For example, in debates about the final version of the PRWORA in 1996, Representative Lamar Smith of Texas argued:

> Welfare has harmed our children, families, and taxpayers. It has created a culture of dependency that saps people's desire to better their lives. And welfare has undermined America's longstanding immigration policy. America has always welcomed new citizens with the energy and commitment to come to our shores to build a better future. We've always ensured that immigrants are self-reliant—not dependent on American taxpayers for support. . . . Welfare undermines this policy and harms immigrants. Rather than promoting hard work, welfare tempts immigrants to come to America and live off the American taxpayer.[66]

Constructing American children, families, and taxpayers as the real victims of a welfare system overrun with immigrants, these remarks perform an inversion of suffering. Those who suffer as a result of immigration are not the immigrants themselves but rather citizens whose way of life is threatened by immigration. For Smith, immigration offers immigrants the possibility of a better life in which they live off welfare while creating a tax burden for citizens and undermining national values of independence and hard work, an ironic statement given the role that immigrant workers play in the U.S. economy. Smith distinguishes between past immigrants, who were forced to be self-reliant contributors to the nation, and contemporary immigrants, who because of the current welfare system remain dependent on the state. This is largely a racial distinction between earlier waves of immigrants from Europe, who were viewed as assimilable to U.S. national culture, and contemporary immigrants of color, who are viewed as perpetual welfare dependents.

The welfare queen reiterated elements of both of the figures of female vagrancy discussed in chapter 4. Like the Reconstruction-era prostitute, her illicit sexuality posed a threat to the family, which continued to be understood as the cornerstone of the political order. Critics of welfare argued that AFDC undermined the family by encouraging women to have children outside of marriage. For example, Charles Murray famously declared in 1993 that "illegitimacy is the single most important social problem of our time" and argued that AFDC be eliminated as a means of curbing out-of-wedlock births.[67] Representations of welfare recipients tended to conflate single motherhood, teenage pregnancy, and sexual immorality, and the young, Black, single mother became a sign of the cultural degeneracy welfare supposedly promoted. These representations overstated the problem of teenage pregnancy and relied on a nostalgia for family values that was also inaccurate.[68] However, the idea that welfare posed a real threat to the family was one of the most effective accusations lodged against it.

While framed quite differently from constructions of female vagrancy that centered prostitution, the focus on welfare receipt as a threat to the family reflected many of the same anxieties about women having too much independence from the heteronormative family. While the prostitute used sex work to support herself outside of the family, the welfare recipient relied on public assistance. Critics of AFDC went so far as to argue that welfare provided an incentive for having children outside of marriage. While this was not sex work per se, the widespread misbelief that welfare recipients had additional children to increase their benefits manufactured a different way that welfare recipients used illicit sexuality for material gain. Much as had been the case during the Reconstruction era, these beliefs were grounded not in evidence but in hypersexualized representations of Black women. In addition, illegitimacy and teenage pregnancy, like prostitution, were framed as epidemics of immorality and cultural degeneracy that needed to be contained before they spread to other sectors of society. These racist perceptions played an important role in shaping policy outcomes. Most notably, PRWORA included the state option for a "family cap" that prohibited collecting benefits for any child born while a mother was receiving TANF as a direct effort to curb the excesses of sexuality and reproduction that welfare supposedly fueled.[69]

Just as opponents of welfare sought to push recipients back into the heteronormative family, they also faulted single mothers for not working. Some of the most frequent complaints about welfare recipients were that they were lazy and that they were enjoying benefits they had not earned. These sentiments hearkened back to the sentiment that Black women who withdrew their labor from the public sphere were vagrants who "played the lady." Although norms around women's work had shifted considerably since the nineteenth century, welfare recipients were still seen as indulgent for trying to have what was expected of white middle-class women. The resurgence of family-values discourse was accompanied by a nostalgia for a past in which women's roles in the domestic sphere were primary. Conservatives expressed great anxiety about white women's growing role in the workforce, often pressuring them to return to the home and center their roles as mothers. At the same time, they vociferously opposed social supports that might enable low-income women to make the same choices. The idea that welfare recipients were playing the lady can also be seen in representations of the welfare queen as living beyond her means or enjoying luxuries to which she was not entitled. For example, she was often depicted as driving a Cadillac or financing other expensive items through welfare fraud. All of these representations relied on a belief that she was playing at being something she was not.

Like the housewife, the welfare queen was deemed vagrant in the private sphere. While vagrancy is a public crime, and privacy ostensibly shielded the family from state intervention, both freedpeople and welfare recipients encountered tremendous state surveillance in their homes. Within the discourses on vagrancy and welfare, the domestic sphere was a site of public debate and speculation rather than a sanctuary. In the Reconstruction era, the idea that freedpeople had been given freedom required that they demonstrate their deservingness of it both inside and outside of the home. Similarly, the trade-off for welfare receipt was often the policing of private behaviors within the home. In both cases, a proper performance of gender, industrious labor, and assimilatory desires were central to demonstrating that one was a deserving subject. However, gendered constructions that located women's citizenship within the domestic sphere and the racial imperative that Black women work outside their homes put Black women in a position in which it was virtually impossible to succeed at being deserving.

Finally, both the vagrant and the welfare queen were regarded as a sign of unfreedom and a threat to the stability of the family and the political order. The Reconstruction-era vagrant was out of sync with liberal conceptions of freedom. Vagrants did not use their time in the ways prescribed for liberal, independent subjects and hence were seen as stuck in the past of slavery. Constructs of vagrancy denied freedpeople's agency, a fundamental aspect of liberal personhood. Actions that did not align with liberal goals were understood as a lingering residue of slavery rather than as choices about how to practice one's own freedom. The construction of the welfare queen functioned similarly. The culture-of-poverty discourse to which the welfare queen was linked framed sexual and gender deviance as a legacy of slavery rather than as expressions of agency or alternate ways of being in the world. The welfare queen was understood as culturally backward, not having fully assimilated to American culture or liberal ideals. She was driven by her dependence on welfare and unable to act on her own. As Representative Shaw argued, she was "enslaved with the chains of welfare." Freedom required that she become a better liberal subject. As in the case of Reconstruction-era vagrancy, marriage and forced labor paved the way toward that goal.

Family Values and Forced Labor

The figure of the welfare queen played a central role in consolidating support for welfare reform. As with the nineteenth-century vagrant before her, the moral, cultural, and economic crisis embodied in the welfare queen was key to arguments for replacing AFDC with a program that emphasized cultivating heteropatriarchal families and labor discipline. By the mid-1990s, the idea that welfare produced dependency and undermined the family had become common sense, and forcing women on welfare to work or marry was widely understood as a solution to these problems. The last vestiges of the founding belief that the purpose of AFDC was to enable single mothers to stay at home and perform the national service of caring for their children had been swept away. The NWRO's vision of AFDC as an entitlement and as just compensation for women's reproductive labor was also overshadowed. Instead, there was a resurgence of the discourses about public assistance that had dominated Reconstruction-era policy toward freedpeople with its unwavering belief in the redemptive powers of work and marriage.

In this section I look at the policies instituted by PRWORA in relation to the history of the Freedmen's Bureau presented in earlier chapters. While the context surrounding these two projects and the reach of their efforts are quite different, the similarity in the ways that both sought to address economic deprivation by pushing women into low-wage work and marriage is striking. Welfare reform reproduced articulations of race, gender, and citizenship that were developed during Reconstruction to secure continuities between slavery and emancipation in a new political and economic context. In both cases, marriage and forced labor operated as vehicles toward racialized and gendered forms of state austerity, profound structural inequalities were rewritten as problems of individual behavior, forced labor was cast as a pathway to freedom, and the family functioned as a vehicle for the privatization of responsibility rather than as a basis for fundamental rights. In both moments, efforts to reconstruct the heteropatriarchal family and to secure state legitimacy were intimately connected, and the contradictions that emerged from the state's multiple investments in structures of domination were displaced onto the bodies of Black women.

Rhetorically, PRWORA defined the primary goal of welfare reform as the need to restore family values and reinstitute a naturalized vision of heteronormative patriarchy among a welfare-dependent underclass. The preamble to PRWORA began with the declaration that "marriage is the foundation of a successful society" and continued by cataloging the ills of absent fathers, out-of-wedlock births, and teenage pregnancy, supposedly fostered by AFDC. Listing poverty, intergenerational welfare use, low levels of educational achievement, and crime as outcomes of single motherhood and teenage pregnancy, the law proclaimed out-of-wedlock births a "crisis in our Nation" that had to be addressed by transforming the welfare system. Notably, the preamble focused on the risks that out-of-wedlock births posed to children as well as the potential costs to society, painting a picture of a disordered culture of poverty that threatened the nation and its children's future. The law argued that AFDC needed to be dismantled because it trapped welfare recipients in this culture and perpetuated a cycle of poverty and dependency by sanctioning teenage sex and sex outside of marriage. Citing increasing numbers of out-of-wedlock births, the preamble argued that the threat AFDC posed to marriage was an epidemic that needed to be curbed.[70] In this configuration, the welfare recipient was figured as both lacking in agency (she was powerless to resist the lure of even minimal cash assistance) and having too much agency (her out-of-control sexuality threatened the very fabric of the nation). Marriage was a necessary response that would enforce gendered norms of citizenship grounded in the heteropatriarchal family, thereby ensuring both paternal responsibility and the containment of women's sexuality.

There are many notable similarities between the ways that marriage was used as a civilizing force in relation to freedpeople and the emphasis on marriage promotion within PRWORA.[71] First, the resonances between the discourse on vagrancy and the construction of the welfare queen effectively coded welfare recipients as Black even though the majority were not. Culture-of-poverty discourse as applied to Black communities in the United States emphasized the role of slavery in undermining Black men's patriarchal authority and empowering Black women. Reiterating Reconstruction-era discourse that sought to eradicate gender and sexual deviance among formerly enslaved people through the promotion of marriage, the emphasis on out-of-wedlock births and teenage pregnancy in antiwelfare discourse connoted Blackness in the public imagination. In this way, the emphasis on deviant gender and sexuality stood in for racial difference in antiwelfare discourse, operating as a way to talk about race without ever naming it. Promoting heteronormativity was a way of targeting Black communities specifically as Blackness was equated with gender nonconformity and sexual excess in public discourse. Second, in both cases, concerns about cultural reform and individual behavior displaced consideration of actual structural inequalities. While in the Reconstruction context the emphasis on freedpeople demonstrating their deservingness of citizenship through participation in marriage overshadowed the need to repair the violence and inequality that was a legacy of slavery, in the 1990s the idea that the roots of poverty were cultural and behavioral marginalized economic inequality as a problem to be solved. Third, as Angela Onwuachi-Willig notes in both the Reconstruction era and the case of welfare reform, the purpose of marriage was to minimize economic dependence on the government.[72] While self-sufficient families were framed as a moral obligation and a prerequisite for citizenship, the actual goal was to curtail state support of Black families. The many ways in which white heteropatriarchal families received state support through New Deal programs remained outside of the conversation about welfare reform, erasing how seemingly self-sufficient white middle-class families were in fact deeply reliant on state assistance. Finally, in both contexts, remaking the family functioned as a vehicle for remaking state power. Promoting marriage legitimized the activities of the Freedmen's Bureau in much the same way that protecting family values manufactured consent for dismantling social welfare programs. The push toward marriage under PRWORA was a reassertion of patriarchal power, in the face of representations of the federal government as weak, ineffective, and unable to discipline the women who were taking advantage of programs like AFDC. The law not only sought to reorganize families but also reasserted heteropatriarchal hierarchies and settler colonial sexualities as the basis of state authority.

The law created marriage-promotion programs, abstinence education, fatherhood programs, family caps, incentives to reduce births outside of marriage, mandatory paternity identification, and the requirement that TANF recipients assist in the collection of child support for their children. In doing so, welfare reform required "poor single mothers to conform to a one-size-fits-all heteropatriarchal model of kinship relations" through a combination of incentives and punishments.[73] While the array of programs designed to encourage marriage and punish single motherhood is remarkable, the child support enforcement and paternity-identification provisions in PRWORA were some of the most significant systemic changes in the regulation of low-income families. Anna Marie Smith argues that these requirements, which she calls *paternafare*, sought to shift support for low-income children from the state to their fathers. Framed in the language of cultivating male responsibility, these provisions actually undermined welfare recipients' privacy, autonomy, safety, and long-term economic well-being.

Smith argues that paternafare "symbolically constructs poverty as the fruit of immoral and pathological behavior on the part of deviant heterosexual women rather than the product of the structural conditions, and it exemplifies and legitimates the neoliberal transfer of the obligation to support the poor from the State to the private patriarchal household."[74] In this, paternafare bears a striking resemblance to the efforts of the Freedmen's Bureau to promote marriage and privatize responsibility for economic inequality. As demonstrated in chapter 3, the criminalization of fathers who failed to support their children was one way the bureau shifted responsibility for economic inequality back onto Black communities. In contrast to welfare programs that had primarily served white people, marriage and the heteronormative nuclear family became mechanisms of imposing responsibility and rationalizing austerity.

Similar to the case of the Freedmen's Bureau, child support enforcement policies assumed that fathers would have access to a family wage without putting in place the structural changes that would guarantee that possibility. The idea of paternal responsibility held particular appeal given the proliferation of representations of deadbeat dads as the cause of hardship for single mothers and their children. However, this framing of the problem did not account for the ways that structural inequality often created barriers to fathers economically supporting their children. As Dorothy Roberts points out "making black men symbols of fatherlessness . . . offers a convenient explanation for Black people's problems" while denying that "racism or the unequal distribution of wealth" is the root cause of inequality.[75] Because most fathers of children on TANF also struggle with joblessness and low incomes, child support enforcement policies rarely alleviate poverty and frequently have the effect of deepening economic instability. Low wages, job instability, and high unemployment rates, particularly among Black men, can make it difficult for fathers to make child support payments, and they often become saddled with debt that threatens their long-term financial stability and the economic prospects of their families as a result. In addition, punitive forms of child support enforcement often interfere with a father's ability to be a presence in a child's life. As child support enforcement has become increasingly intertwined with the criminal justice system, a failure to pay can result in incarceration, which then becomes another economic and social hardship that a family must bear.[76]

In practice, paternafare was a deliberate effort to reduce government support for single mothers. Because the law allowed child support payments to TANF recipients to be used to reimburse the government for the cost of TANF payments, paternafare sought to reduce government expenditures rather than to increase household incomes. As a 2014 study notes, as a result "thirty percent of the national unpaid child support debt is owed to state and federal governments—not to children."[77] Even if child support was used to subsidize TANF assistance, time limits and other restrictions on aid remained in place despite the reduction in government costs.[78] As a result, paternafare offered little economic benefit to low-income single mothers and instead simply punished low-income fathers. At the same time, paternafare provisions and other efforts to promote heteronormativity often created obstacles that deterred women from seeking TANF. Many women were unable or unwilling to comply with paternity identification and child support rules and therefore were potentially excluded from TANF assistance. Paternafare not only potentially endangered survivors of domestic violence but also fundamentally infringed on women's autonomy and right to determine for themselves what kind of relationship with the father of their children would be best for their own and their children's economic and emotional well-being.

While the law directed resources toward marriage-promotion programs and stronger child support enforcement, it also rested on the premise that women on welfare should work outside the home. In contrast to AFDC's original objective of preserving the institution of motherhood by protecting women from the degrading character of wage labor, forcing mothers to work outside the home was oddly inconsistent with a policy that promised a return to family values. Nevertheless, PRWORA institutionalized an array of practices designed to force recipients to transition from welfare receipt to wage labor. These practices included workfare programs that require recipients to work at state-specified tasks for a certain number of hours a week in exchange for their benefits and a renewed emphasis on training welfare recipients for jobs and on finding, and creating jobs for them. In addition, provisions of the law such as time limits on assistance and the creation of populations who can be excluded from welfare eligibility altogether pushed women into the low-wage labor market involuntarily. The law created a five-year lifetime limit on TANF assistance and gave states the option of shortening this limit. Additionally, PRWORA allowed states to exclude certain groups from receiving TANF, such as legal immigrants, unwed teenage mothers who did not live with their parents, and women convicted of felony drug crimes. Time limits functioned to drive welfare recipients back into the labor market after a set amount of time, and the creation of excludable populations functioned much like the "employable mother" and "suitable home" laws, deeming some women as completely undeserving of assistance.

These efforts to force welfare recipients into work bear a striking resemblance to vagrancy laws and other forms of forced labor that emerged after the Civil War. In chapter 4 I argued that for freedpeople the obligation to work was in fact an obligation to engage in labor that was "observable, contractual, and regular" and that benefited and could be surveilled by white employers.[79] Similarly, the push to move welfare recipients from welfare to work negated the work that welfare recipients were already doing both as mothers and as participants in informal economies by employing a narrow contractual definition of what counted as work. While the specter of vagrancy was used to put freedpeople back to work in southern agriculture or domestic service, by the late twentieth century the work welfare recipients were being pushed to take up was quite different. Deindustrialization and economic restructuring had produced a growing service sector in the U.S. economy, one in which the labor of women of color was in high demand. As Evelyn Nakano Glenn argues, the restructuring of reproductive labor in the late twentieth century has meant that whereas in earlier periods women of color were expected to perform reproductive labor for white families as domestic workers within white homes, by the late twentieth century they were increasingly compelled to do more public forms of reproductive labor within the service sector.[80] The idea that welfare recipients needed to be put back to work aligned neatly with this demand. Welfare recipients were often pushed to perform labor such as street cleaning, childcare, or food preparation that was "measurable, observable, and contractual" in the public sphere, unlike similar forms of work they may have done in their own homes. Given the contingent and poorly compensated character of much of this work, the transition from welfare to work was not so much designed to increase economic independence as to increase dependence on the low-wage labor market.

Like the case of the Freedmen's Bureau, ideas of contract played an important role in welfare-to-work activities. In PRWORA, welfare receipt was delineated as part of a contractual obligation to engage in work-related activities, and in implementing the law, state and local programs required that each individual sign a contract that detailed what these activities would be. As Sandra Morgen, Joan Acker, and Jill Weigt note in their study of TANF programs in Oregon, despite the prevailing idea that a contract would be negotiated between a caseworker and a TANF client, in practice there was no space for negotiation. Rather, caseworkers subjected recipients to a harsh intake process, drew up an employment plan, and informed TANF recipients that future aid was contingent on their compliance with the plan.[81] These plans frequently required TANF recipients to participate in work-readiness activities that many regarded as irrelevant, infantilizing, and demeaning and to take any job that became available regardless of their own career aspirations or long-term financial interests. Alejandra Marchevsky and Jeanne Theoharis describe a similar phenomenon in the case of the Los Angeles Greater Avenues for Independence (GAIN) program. Upon entry into the program, GAIN participants were required to sign a contract, which was a legally binding agreement with the state of California. This contract obligated them to "accept a job if you get an offer unless you have a good reason not to." However, it was up to the GAIN worker to determine what constituted a good reason for not accepting a job, and GAIN workers generally sought to push recipients into work.[82]

The pedagogical functions of the welfare-to-work contract are important to note. As in the case of the Freedmen's Bureau, the contract was conceptualized as a tool in the making of disciplined workers and liberal subjects. Whereas in the Reconstruction era the contract was seen as a remedy to the dependency and degeneracy fostered by slavery, within welfare-to-work programs the contract was a mechanism for pulling people out of the dependency and degeneracy fostered by a culture of poverty. Central to liberal constructions of the free subject, participation in a contract signified independence, responsibility, rationality, self-ownership, and self-control and was a mechanism for behavioral reform that might curb the supposed excesses and cultural deficiencies of welfare recipients. Enforcing a contractual relationship within TANF programs taught recipients how to abide by the rules of contracts in the workforce and was framed as an opportunity to demonstrate their deservingness as workers and contributing members of society. However, as illustrated in the preceding examples, the welfare-to-work contract was actually grounded in coercion and used to produce subordination. Those who failed to sign the contract or comply with its terms would be sanctioned, meaning that all or part of their benefits would be withheld. The time that a recipient was sanctioned for continued to count toward the lifetime limit on welfare receipt, so sanctions represented a significant loss to the overall benefits a recipient could receive. Sharon Hays reports that sanctionable offenses included "failure to make job contacts, attend a scheduled meeting with a welfare caseworker, go to all your job readiness classes, arrive at your workfare placement on time, or cooperate with child support enforcement, or quitting a job without good cause or getting fired from a job because of some mistake."[83] In other words, sanctions punished behaviors that were regarded as disobedient or out of line with the goal of moving from welfare to work. Ironically, while the contract was supposedly about cultivating independent and free subjects, it required subordination on the part of the TANF participant. Hays notes the contradictions between "demanding individual autonomy and exercising social control" that characterized these relations. Discursively, the language of welfare-to-work suggests that "reform will overcome welfare dependence by training clients in 'personal responsibility,' yet the routines and procedures of the welfare office systematically require of recipients obedience, deference, and passive compliance."[84]

Under PRWORA, behavioral reform was placed at the center of the welfare-to-work project. Rather than focusing on structural barriers to economic security, the law emphasized the need to transform deficient individuals. Marchevsky and Theoharis note the centrality of the language of empowerment and self-help in the GAIN program and the emphasis on personality as both "the cause and cure of all social ills."[85] Participation in GAIN required adherence to rules designed to discipline the individual into becoming a self-governing subject. The rules ranged from adhering to dress codes and being punctual to participating in mandatory job-search activities and demonstrating a willingness to work. The GAIN workers used the rules as the basis for surveillance and sanctioning of GAIN participants with the goal that the participants would internalize the rules and govern themselves. However, while designed to exact a performance of labor discipline, the GAIN rules simultaneously had the effect of distinguishing the participants from other workers. The women in Marchevsky and Theoharis's study noted that dress codes and mandatory job-search activities stigmatized them in relation to other job applicants and that the requirement that they accept any job reduced their negotiating power and made them more vulnerable participants in the labor market. Rather than empowering them to become self-sufficient workers, "GAIN turns asking for a job into a public spectacle."[86]

This element of public spectacle can also be seen in media depictions of welfare-to-work programs. For example, a *Newsweek* article entitled "The School of Hard Knocks" describes one such program in Milwaukee as a "kind of boot camp aimed at pushing some of the area's toughest welfare clients out of poverty."[87] The article begins by describing a scene of conflict at a meeting between case managers and welfare recipients at the Transitional Living Center, a federally funded welfare-to-work program that was administered by a local nonprofit organization. As described in the article, the meeting resembles a classroom in which a teacher disciplines unruly children:

> Soon the resentment comes pouring out: the unrelenting pressure to obey the rules is oppressive, the caseworkers are riding them too hard. The mood turns defiant. Some women admit they've been smoking pot, which violates the behavior contracts they signed when they entered. "I'm bored, I'm lonely, I got four kids!" one woman shouts. "So kick me out! I don't care!" . . . Wright and Green [the caseworkers] try to ease the tensions. Without conceding an inch to the mutineers' complaints, they contrive to end the meeting on a more positive note. "You're all doing a lot of wonderful new things," Wright tells them. "But we want to see more!"[88]

Following the session described, the staff of the program explains the incident as follows: "I let them attack me—and then I let them have it. . . . I told them, 'You need to be more serious about your futures and about your kids' futures. You need to get GEDs and get jobs. This isn't a free ride.'"[89] The director of the program adds, "Our clients come from families who spent generations on AFDC. . . . They don't have skills, or educations, or values of working hard, because their own parents couldn't teach them."[90]

This description of the program—conceptualized as a kind of "tough love"—defines one of the key goals of welfare-to-work programs as disciplining welfare recipients in much the same way that schools discipline children. The welfare recipients themselves are represented as childlike in that they are unruly, unable to control their emotions, and unable to delay gratification; they throw unreasonable tantrums and need to be placated. Breaking the cycle of poverty by parenting them in ways that their parents could not, welfare-to-work staff are constructed in this narrative as both the educators and the disciplinarians of the infantilized welfare recipients. The equation of poverty with immaturity and a lack of knowledge about how to act properly in the world is a theme that surfaced repeatedly in debates about welfare reform. Through these representations, preparation for work became defined as growing up and growing out of dependency.

In a similar article entitled "Dressed for Success," from *Time* magazine, welfare recipients' inability to act like good workers is again figured as the problem to be solved. This article begins with the story of Yvette Johnson. The article reads:

> Yvette Johnson was the kind of job applicant who makes employers dread hiring off the welfare rolls. She has been on welfare for six years. Jobs like cleaning hospital rooms and cutting vegetables ended with her quitting or being fired. And she had four kids who had to be shuttled to day care and babysitting. When Kimberly Randolph, an operations supervisor for the Sprint phone company in Kansas City, Mo, met Johnson at a job fair, she pegged Johnson as "a job hopper with a bad attitude."[91]

The article goes on to tell how Johnson managed to work her way to success through a Sprint experiment in hiring workers from welfare. Emphasizing the role that discipline played in Johnson's and other recipients' success, this article argues that the key to successful job training is not so much teaching job skills as instilling the behaviors associated with work. The article notes:

> The focus now is on "soft skills," basics like showing up on time, dressing appropriately and not fighting with co-workers. "Employers are saying, 'Give us people with the right attitude and job readiness, and we'll take care of the rest,'" says Eli Segal, president of the nonprofit Welfare to Work Partnership.[92]

Cultivating job readiness, or the ability to perform the desire to work, surfaced repeatedly as a primary goal of welfare-to-work programs. These practices demonstrate the way that welfare-to-work programs served as a kind of moral education for recipients that compelled them not just to do a certain kind of labor but to be a certain kind of person.

In these stories, state-enforced forced labor is conceptualized as a disciplinary prerequisite to free labor. In other words, mothers on welfare need to be forced to labor so that they will eventually labor freely. Within the two articles cited here, personal responsibility and self-sufficiency are defined in the negative as not making excuses for one's situation, not blaming external factors for one's poverty, and not receiving government assistance. Learning to act responsibly is equated with internalizing blame for one's own structural location, and learning to act more self-sufficiently is defined as no longer being dependent on government assistance. The concepts of personal responsibility and self-sufficiency have little or nothing to do with the overall quality of people's lives or even with ameliorating economic hardship. Rather, they were a means of redefining gendered citizenship for welfare recipients through the language of work. These pedagogical techniques of cultural reform that continue to be employed in welfare-to-work programs today are much like the efforts of the Freedmen's Bureau to channel freedwomen into domestic labor. The language of personal responsibility and self-sufficiency speaks to the individualizing effects of welfare-to-work programs. Not only does this language render individuals solely responsible for their own fate and displace any analysis of structural inequality, but the purpose of moving from welfare to work is defined as making welfare recipients into individuals who bear the burdens of their own individuality. In this discursive framework, for welfare recipients, being a self-sufficient, responsible individual is constructed as an obligation to the nation-state.

Welfare-to-work programs have instructed women "to compromise material gains like wages and health insurance for more elusive therapeutic benefits like improved self-esteem and happier family lives."[93] Nowhere is this more apparent than in the kinds of work that participants have been pushed to engage in. In the context of deindustrialization, welfare-to-work programs are geared toward meeting the labor demands of an expanding low-wage service sector. Overwhelmingly, job-training programs focus on clerical skills, food service, childcare work, and other kinds of public reproductive labor.[94] These professions not only tend to be feminized, unstable, low paid, and lacking in benefits but are "extensions of Black women's historical occupational roles" in fields like domestic service.[95] Welfare-to-work programs push participants to take any job regardless of whether it aligns with their career aspirations, offers them financial stability, or is feasible in relation to health and childcare needs. As a result, participants are often forced to endure tremendous hardship for little economic return.[96] In contrast, PRWORA created financial incentives for companies to hire TANF recipients, and local welfare offices often developed partnerships with companies to supply them with low-wage workers.[97] Indeed, Marchevsky and Theoharis describe GAIN as a kind of "state-subsidized temp agency" that provides employers with a steady stream of easily accessible and compliant low-wage workers.[98] Employers not only benefit from the training and prescreening of workers provided by GAIN but also receive significant tax breaks for each employee they hire from TANF. Despite these substantial benefits, employers have been lauded as helping in the effort to fight welfare dependency rather than as exploiting vulnerable workers.

In addition to producing a supply of highly exploitable low-wage workers, welfare-to-work programs have been deliberately used to undermine union labor. For example, New York City's Work Experience Program (WEP), the nation's largest and perhaps most controversial workfare program, quickly came under fire for replacing city workers with workfare workers in the late 1990s. Despite a New York state law that barred the replacement of civil servants with workfare workers, in 1998, 34,100 WEP workers were doing much of the work that had previously been done by the 20,000 city workers that Mayor Rudy Giuliani had laid off under the rubric of budget cuts.[99] Among these WEP workers, the case of Hattie Hargrove stood out as an example of the perils that workfare presented for civil servants. Hargrove was laid off from the Department of Social Services in Mineola in 1992. In 1997 she went back to work there as a WEP worker. She found herself doing the same work and reporting to the same supervisor but now in exchange for a $53.50 welfare check and $263 in food stamps instead of a wage.[100] The abuses of the WEP program were so appalling that even Stanley Hill, the executive director of New York's largest municipal workers' union and longtime supporter of the Giuliani administration, likened the program to a form of slavery.[101] These practices demonstrate the ways that the transition to welfare-to-work supported work while undermining wages and economic security.

While all TANF recipients have been impacted by the work provisions of PRWORA, studies show that Black and Latina women have experienced a stronger push toward work. In her study of how Black women who were survivors of violence experienced welfare reform in New York state, Dána-Ain Davis observed significant racial disparities in the ways that white and Black women were treated in TANF programs. While caseworkers were often friendly and eager to help white women, they enforced regulations much more harshly with Black women. Black women were required to work any job they could find almost immediately, regardless of pay, while white women were given more space and time to pursue opportunities that interested them and that had more long-term financial viability.[102] Similarly, Marchevsky and Theoharis found that Latina immigrant women were more likely to be pushed into part-time, temporary, low-wage work, while other TANF recipients were given priority in other kinds of education and job-training programs.[103] Rooted in a belief that Black and Latina TANF recipients are particularly undeserving, these practices mirror the local forms of discrimination that were key to maintaining segregation within AFDC.

The intensity of efforts to push TANF recipients into the low-wage labor market begs the question of how these policies could be reconciled with an emphasis on cultivating traditional heteropatriarchal family values. While some scholars have argued that work requirements and time limits represent yet another way of punishing single mothers for being unmarried, comparison to the practices of the Freedmen's Bureau illuminates the ways in which the meanings of domesticity, good motherhood, and good citizenship were rearticulated in relation to TANF recipients in this moment.[104] The workfare worker can be seen as an extension of the logic that produced the domestic worker as an alternate trope of women's citizenship during the Reconstruction era. Promoting domestic labor within white households offered a mechanism for inculcating domestic norms in freedwomen while continuing to direct their reproductive labor toward white families and away from their own children. Similarly, the welfare-to-work programs that were developed in the late twentieth century and that continue today have attempted to make welfare recipients into good mothers by pushing them to engage in forms of gendered reproductive labor outside of their own homes. These forms of work are predicated on behavior modification and often require gendered performances of subordination that are framed as necessary to move welfare recipients from a culture of poverty to self-sufficiency. However, because low-wage reproductive work does not offer economic stability, and the stringent requirements of welfare-to-work programs often interfere with women's ability to care for their own children, PRWORA produced a situation in which the actual mothering of their own children has become increasingly untenable for low-income single mothers, especially those who are Black and Latina.

This book opened with President Clinton's narration of the story of Lillie Harden, a participant in a welfare-to-work demonstration project who proclaimed that the transition to work had made her a better mother because she could be a role model to her children. In closing my discussion of workfare, I would like to contrast Clinton's description of Harden's story with a different representation of the relationship between motherhood and forced labor. The 2001 film *Eating Welfare*, produced by the Southeast Asian Youth Leadership Project of the Committee against Anti-Asian Violence, depicts the experiences of Southeast Asian youth in the Bronx organizing to oppose the treatment of their mothers in welfare-to-work programs. A particularly powerful scene depicts what the organizers jokingly refer to as "take-your-daughter-to-workfare day," a play on the ostensibly feminist practice of take-your-daughter-to-work day, which is designed to facilitate young women's entrance into the workforce and upward economic mobility. One of the youth organizers follows her mother through her day at a workfare assignment picking up trash in public spaces. The film shows the way the mothers' working conditions are physically taxing, socially isolating, and stigmatizing, firmly dislodging workfare from the discourse of opportunity and responsibility that it is so often embedded in. Rather, the scene reframes workfare as a kind of punishment that is incapable of producing intergenerational economic mobility. Through the daughter's eyes, the viewer sees the lack of value placed on her mother's time and labor and by extension the devaluation of the daughter's own life and future as worthy subjects of care. The scene forces a consideration of how, from the perspective of state power, picking up trash in a public spectacle becomes seen as more valuable labor than caring for one's own children. The uncomfortable truth in "take-your-daughter-to-workfare day" or in the belief that compulsory low-wage service work makes mothers into role models for their children is that these ideas rest on the premise that the children of welfare recipients will be confined to the same circumstances as their mothers.[105] While maternalist activists framed social supports for single mothers as an investment in children as the future of the nation, proponents of welfare reform saw the children of welfare recipients as at best the future of low-wage work.

Conclusion

While welfare reform was heralded as a success, its economic consequences for low-income women have been harrowing. Although PRWORA "successfully" reduced the number of people receiving welfare assistance, it did so by leaving low-income women to fend for themselves in a context where their labor outside the home was devalued and their labor within it unsupported.[106] Much like freedwomen in the Reconstruction era, these women found themselves trapped between efforts to promote heteronormativity and efforts to push them into low-wage work. Neither of these efforts addressed the structural forces that marginalized Black women economically. Instead, their focus on character, morality, and discipline reproduced the idea that Black women were themselves responsible for the inequalities they faced. While welfare reform resurrected Reconstruction-era efforts to push freedwomen into work and marriage, it was distinctly different from the programs that had developed in the early twentieth century to support white families. These programs also held citizens to heteronormative ideals but simultaneously invested resources in helping white families achieve those ideals. Through the family wage and the idealization of white motherhood, New Deal programs shaped white working-class families into heteronormative units that received a great deal of state support. In contrast, both the Freedmen's Bureau and welfare reform used the family as a way of imposing responsibility. The expectation that Black families be self-sufficient rationalized state austerity and facilitated the privatization of economic inequalities.

There are many parallels in how the workfare worker and the domestic worker operated to suture ideas of gendered citizenship to economic structures that relied on women of color's labor. Most notably, while the organization of reproductive labor had changed vastly between Reconstruction and the late twentieth century, in both periods Black women were put to work as paid reproductive workers. In both these scenarios, the primary benefits of work were moral rather than economic. Engaging in gendered forms of work under the surveillance of white employers in the nineteenth century and of welfare officials in the twentieth century offered the possibility of transforming delinquent subjects into disciplined workers. In contrast to maternalist projects that exalted motherhood, these efforts positioned reproductive labor done in the service of a presumably white public as a central mechanism of cultivating gendered citizenship. This had the effect of both undermining freedwomen's and welfare recipients' efforts to care for their own families and also reconfiguring good mothering as modeling disciplined labor for one's children.

Conclusion

In turning to both the Reconstruction era and the late twentieth century, this book has attempted to reimagine feminist histories of the welfare state from a perspective that centers the regulation of Black women's sexualities and labor. Throughout my analysis I have been less interested in constructing a linear history and more concerned with exploring how the afterlife of slavery structures these two historical moments. The striking similarities between these two moments are hard to miss. In both, similar depictions of vagrancy were employed to undermine various forms of public assistance. The vagrant and the welfare queen linked anxieties about racial inclusion, gender deviance, labor discipline, and the potentially unsettling effects of life outside the heteronormative family in similar ways. In both periods, these anxieties elicited similar responses in the promotion of both marriage and forced labor as mechanisms for reforming Black women. These two strategies were often in contradiction with each other, with one pushing women into the home and the other forcing them out of it. In the Reconstruction era, pushing freedwomen into domestic labor emerged as a way of resolving this contradiction by positioning reproductive labor in the service of white families as a better pathway to gendered citizenship than reproductive labor in the service of freedwomen's own families. In the late twentieth century, the workfare worker played a similar role, as good motherhood was linked to the performance of low-wage service work under the surveillance of the state. While the economic context was different, in both cases the moral benefits of work were emphasized, rather than the economic benefits, thereby reframing intense economic exploitation as a form of racialized and gendered belonging in the nation.

My purpose in drawing attention to these resonances is not to argue that history is doomed to repeat itself or to suggest that these two moments reflect an unchanging terrain of anti-Black racism in the United States. Rather, I want to highlight similarities in the way that linkages among race, gender, sexuality, and labor exploitation were forged in these two moments of political, economic, and cultural crisis. While the vast majority of feminist work on the welfare state begins with white women's experiences in the Progressive Era, locating the Freedmen's Bureau as a different point of reference makes visible the long-standing centrality of forced labor in U.S. welfare policy. In addition, three key themes emerge from reading late twentieth-century welfare policy through the history of the Freedmen's Bureau that I hope will be useful in future theoretical and political engagements with the U.S. welfare state.

First, over the course of the book, I have argued that state power and the heteronormative family are mutually constitutive and reinforcing in a broad range of ways. The comparisons made in this book show that the family has been a key vehicle for maintaining racial inequality, with white families being treated as a site of state investment while self-sufficiency has been demanded of Black families. The New Deal created a federal welfare state that guaranteed working-class white families a family wage, increased access to homeownership and a private domestic sphere, and gave them the ability to accumulate some wealth and enjoy a piece (albeit small) of the profits of capitalism. In contrast, in the case of both the Freedmen's Bureau and welfare reform, when beneficiaries were Black or were imagined to be Black, the state demanded self-sufficiency and privatized responsibility for economic inequality onto the heteronormative nuclear family. But without the social supports made available to white families, it was impossible to meet heteronormative ideals. In addition, without the incentives that white families received, it was often more desirable to organize kinship and sexuality in other ways. Black families were frequently pathologized for these choices, further reinforcing the belief that it was gender deviance rather than racial inequality that explained the economic precarity of Black communities.

This consideration of the way that race, gender, and sexuality are intertwined in constructions of deserving families raises questions about what it means to seek recognition and rights on the basis of family. In more recent years, issues ranging from gay marriage to stopping of deportations have been framed as a question of recognizing and protecting marginalized families. In light of the history presented here, these struggles raise important questions about when families are deemed worthy and to what extent the claim that some families deserve protection reinforces the belief that other families are undeserving unless they can demonstrate self-sufficiency. What would it mean to move away from constructions of deservingness and undeservingness in the ways we define kinship, sexuality, and belonging? The history of Reconstruction shows that Black people entered into freedom with an understanding of kinship, gender, and sexuality that exceeded the heteronormative family. If marriage recognition was central to narrowing the parameters of freedom, how might we begin to open up those parameters once again? Given that the naturalization of the heteronormative family has also worked to naturalize state power, how might changing the way we think about the family as a basis for rights and responsibilities also change the ways we think about the state?

Second, this project has highlighted the Reconstruction-era vagrant and late twentieth-century welfare queen as queer figures in that they both destabilize heteronormative constructions of the family and are marginalized by heteropatriarchal forms of state power. In doing so, I have tried to stress the ways that heteropatriarchy organizes not just gender and sexuality but race, class, and settler colonial relations as well. I have argued that the heteropatriarchal family plays such a powerful role in political discourse because of its capacity to articulate race, gender, sexuality, and class in a settler colonial context. As queer figures, the vagrant and the welfare queen destabilize these articulations by making visible their contradictions and suggesting alternate desires. In thinking about these two figures as queer, my point is not so much to situate them as resistant as it is to highlight their strangeness to liberal constructions of personhood. Both the vagrant and the welfare queen lacked the self-possession of the liberal subject, failed to embody proper forms of independence and dependence, and became signs of excess and irresponsible pleasure. The Freedmen's Bureau and welfare reformers defined these characteristics as antithetical to freedom and employed marriage and forced labor in an effort to channel divergent forms of agency into the contractual relations that defined the liberal subject. As much as these figures were projections of white anxieties about the inclusion of Black people into citizenship, they are also windows into the queer horizons of the past.[1] Through them, it is possible to glimpse what has to be continually excised in order for liberal conceptions of freedom to prevail.

Finally, when considered in relation to the Freedmen's Bureau, the history of welfare reform illustrates both the specificity and the expansiveness of anti-Black racism. Emancipation elicited a very specific crisis about what it would mean to include Black people into institutions of citizenship that had been defined against Blackness. Echoes of that crisis continued in the development of welfare institutions throughout the twentieth century, and the comparisons drawn in this book show that gendered forms of anti-Black racism have played a defining role in the development of the U.S. welfare state. Antiwelfare discourse specifically imagined the welfare queen as Black, drawing on a long history of racialized and sexualized imagery that has been employed to subordinate Black women. At the same time, however, that imagery was deployed to dismantle welfare programs that benefited a broad range of people, including white women and non-Black women of color. As Dorothy Roberts has succinctly pointed out, "white Americans . . . have been unwilling to create social programs that will facilitate Blacks' full citizenship and economic well-being, *even when those programs would benefit whites*."[2]

In the contemporary moment, the Reconstruction era continues to offer important insights into how political interests are defined. As W. E. B. Du Bois showed in his definitive history of the period, the events of Reconstruction demonstrate that white workers will often choose racial solidarity over class solidarity even when it undermines their long-term economic interests.[3] Du Bois's and Roberts's observations both raise the question of how different political interests are constituted in complex ways. Throughout this book I have shown how state policies that forced Black women to adhere to heteronormative ideals and engage in highly exploitative forms of labor brought together a wide range of interests and unified political opposition to public assistance. These policies simultaneously created impossible situations for Black women, just as they increased economic precarity and curtailed freedom for most people. Linking public assistance and unfreedom in the public imagination consolidated the privatization of structural inequalities. New political configurations that can disrupt that linkage and challenge its anti-Black foundations are necessary to realizing the wide-reaching visions of freedom that once animated freedpeople's desires.

Notes

Chapter 1. Welfare Reform

1 The promise to "end welfare as we know it" was a cornerstone of Bill Clinton's 1992 presidential campaign, and this often-repeated phrase became synonymous with the project of welfare reform in the mid-nineties. The shift from the language of ending poverty to the language of ending welfare was the culmination of decades of antiwelfare politics and encapsulates the significance of the transformations the law instituted.

2 Only two other women were onstage at the signing of the law: Janet Ferrel, a white former AFDC recipient from West Virginia, and Penelope Howard, a Black former AFDC recipient from Delaware. Neither of these women spoke at the ceremony, but they were referred to in Clinton's speech, along with Harden, as examples of the successes of welfare-to-work programs.

3 Lillie Harden, "Introductory Remarks at the Signing of the Personal Responsibility and Work Opportunity Reconciliation Act," August 22, 1996, available at http://www.c-span.org/video/?74541-1/welfare-reform-bill-signing.

4 Clinton, "Remarks on Signing," 2:1325.

5 Clinton, "Remarks on Signing," 2:1325.

6 Many progressive scholars avoid the term *welfare reform*, choosing instead to use terminology like *welfare deform* that highlights the negative impacts of PRWORA. While I agree with these scholars regarding the negative impacts of the law, throughout this book I use the terminology of *welfare reform* in order to emphasize the power of reformist strategies to strengthen oppressive institutions. Building on the work of abolitionist scholars like Angela Davis and Ruth Wilson Gilmore, my use of the word *reform* does not imply improvement but rather signifies a counterpoint to radical or transformational approaches to structural problems. A. Davis, *Are Prisons Obsolete?*; Gilmore, "Globalisation and US Prison Growth."

7 The Personal Responsibility and Work Opportunity Reconciliation Act of 1996, Pub. L. No. 104–193, 110 Stat. 2105 (1996).

8   On the fixation with protecting children, see Meiners, *For the Children?*

9   Bush, "Remarks to Welfare-to-Work Graduates," 935.

10 A. Gordon, *Ghostly Matters*, 8.

11 M. Jacqui Alexander, *Pedagogies of Crossing*, 190.

12 For examples of feminist histories of welfare, see L. Gordon, *Pitied but Not Entitled*; Mink, *Wages of Motherhood*; Gordon, *Women, the State, and Welfare*; Koven and Michel, *Mothers of a New World*; and Ladd-Taylor, *Mother-Work*. Scholars of race and the welfare state including Linda Faye Williams and Chad Alan Goldberg have made moves similar to mine in locating the Freedmen's Bureau in the history of the welfare state. L. Williams, *Constraint of Race*; Goldberg, *Citizens and Paupers*. However, it is rare for the Freedmen's Bureau to be engaged within feminist literature on the welfare state.

13 As Elsa Barkley Brown shows, "We need to recognize not only differences but also the relational nature of those differences. Middle-class white women's lives are not just different from working-class white, Black and Latina women's lives. It is important to recognize that middle-class women live the lives they do precisely because working-class women live the lives they do. White women and women of color not only live different lives but white women live the lives they do in part because women of color live the ones they do." E. Brown, "'What Has Happened Here,'" 298.

14 L. Gordon, *Pitied but Not Entitled*.

15 On maternalism and racial hierarchies, see Mink, *Wages of Motherhood*; and Ward, *White Welfare State*.

16 Andrea Smith, *Conquest*, 23; Lugones, "Heterosexualism and the Colonial/Modern Gender System."

17 As Seth Koven and Sonya Michel write, "Maternalism always operated on two levels: it extolled the virtues of domesticity while simultaneously legitimating women's public relationships to politics and the state, to community, workplace, and market place. Maternalist ideologies, while invoking traditional images of womanliness, implicitly challenged the boundaries between public and private, women and men, state and civil society." Koven and Michel, "Introduction: 'Mother Worlds,'" 6.

18 Amy Kaplan draws attention to the interconnectedness of these first two meanings of the term in her essay "Manifest Domesticity."

19 Many thanks to Charis Thompson for pointing me toward this third meaning of the term.

20 Bhattacharjee, "Public/Private Mirage."

21 C. Cohen, "Punks, Bulldaggers, and Welfare Queens."

22 Patterson, *Slavery and Social Death*.

23 Franke, "Becoming a Citizen."

24 Harris, "Whiteness as Property"; Sexton, "People-of-Color-Blindness."

25 Hall, "Race, Culture, and Communications," 17. For elaboration on Stuart Hall's characterization of racism, see Gilmore, "Fatal Couplings of Power."

26 Hunter, *To 'Joy My Freedom*.

27 On the right to their own lands, see Saville, *Work of Reconstruction*, 18–19. On the vote, see E. Brown, "Negotiating and Transforming"; and Rosen, *Terror in the Heart*. On freedom of movement, see Foner, *Reconstruction*, 82–84.

28 Foner, *Reconstruction*, 85.

29 Hunter, *To 'Joy My Freedom*.

30 Du Bois, *Black Reconstruction in America*, 30.

31 Lieberman, "Freedmen's Bureau and the Politics," 413–14.

32 Foner, *Reconstruction*, 248.

33 Du Bois, *Black Reconstruction in America*, 276–77; Du Bois, "Freedmen's Bureau."

34 Foner, *Reconstruction*, 233–37.

35 Farmer, "Because They Are Women," 166.

36 Du Bois, *Black Reconstruction in America*; A. Davis, *Are Prisons Obsolete?*, 22–39; Michelle Alexander, *New Jim Crow*; Lichtenstein, *Twice the Work*.

37 Bentley, *History of the Freedmen's Bureau*; Farmer, "Because They Are Women."

38 Quoted in Farmer, "Because They Are Women," 165–66.

39 Quoted in Farmer, "Because They Are Women," 167.

40 Franke, "Becoming a Citizen," 253.

41 Hartman, *Scenes of Subjection*, 116–17.

42 Hartman, *Scenes of Subjection*, 118.

43 Hartman, *Scenes of Subjection*, 125.

44 Gordon writes, "Following the ghosts is about making a contact that changes you and refashions the social relations in which you are located. It is about putting life back in where only a vague memory or a bare trace was visible to those who bothered to look. It is sometimes about writing ghost stories, stories that not only repair representational mistakes, but also strive to understand the conditions under which a memory was produced in the first place, toward a countermemory, for the future." A. Gordon, *Ghostly Matters*, 22.

45 M. Jacqui Alexander, *Pedagogies of Crossing*, 190.

46 M. Jacqui Alexander, *Pedagogies of Crossing*, 181–284.

47 Hartman, *Lose Your Mother*, 6.

48 Hall, "Problem of Ideology," 35–36.

49 Arondekar, *For the Record*, 4.

50 Arondekar, *For the Record*, 4.

51 Mahmood, *Politics of Piety*, 34.

52 A. McClintock, *Imperial Leather*, 45.

Chapter 2. Making State, Making Family

1 C. Cohen, "Punks, Bulldaggers, and Welfare Queens," 438.

2 Kapadia, "Up in the Air and on the Skin," 369.

3   Muñoz, *Cruising Utopia*, 25–26.

4   Shah, *Stranger Intimacy*.

5   R. Ferguson, *Aberrations in Black*, 3.

6   R. Ferguson, *Aberrations in Black*, 12.

7   Weber, "Politics as Vocation," 78.

8   Foucault, *History of Sexuality, Vol. 1*.

9   Poulantzas, *Political Power and Social Classes*.

10 On states' capacity to appear as above or encompassing of society, see J. Ferguson and Gupta, "Spatializing States."

11 Omi and Winant, *Racial Formation*, 56.

12 P. Collins, "It's All in the Family," 63.

13 Hong, *Ruptures of American Capital*, ix–x.

14 Hong, *Ruptures of American Capital*, x.

15 A. McClintock, *Imperial Leather*, 45.

16 W. Brown, *States of Injury*, 189.

17 P. Collins, "It's All in the Family," 65.

18 Edwards, *Gendered Strife and Confusion*.

19 P. Collins, "It's All in the Family," 66.

20 Tillmon, "Welfare Is a Women's Issue," 374.

21 Kandaswamy, "'You Trade in a Man.'"

22 Wolfe, *Settler Colonialism and the Transformation*, 2.

23 For more on settler colonialism as structure in the specific context of racial and gender formation in the United States, see Glenn, "Settler Colonialism as Structure."

24 Wolfe, "Settler Colonialism and the Elimination," 388.

25 King, *Black Shoals*, 65–68.

26 King, *Black Shoals*, 45.

27 Thavolia Glymph's study of relationships between white women and Black women within the space of the plantation home is a particularly good example of this. Glymph shows how white women employed vicious forms of violence against enslaved domestics in order to live up to the expectations of domesticity. Glymph, *Out of the House*.

28 Finley, "Decolonizing the Queer Native Body," 32. On the normalization of sexuality and Native genocide, see Morgensen, *Spaces between Us*; and Driskill et al., *Queer Indigenous Studies*.

29 L. Simpson, *As We Have Always Done*, 129.

30 L. Simpson, *As We Have Always Done*, 124.

31 A. McClintock, *Imperial Leather*, 36–44; M. Jacqui Alexander, *Pedagogies of Crossing*, 181–254.

32 Importantly, indigenous feminist scholarship offers an alternate conception of time. For example, Simpson's idea of resurgence eschews liberal progress narratives and instead links the future to the past. L. Simpson, *As We Have Always Done*.

33 Morgensen, "Settler Homonationalism," 117.

34 Andrea Smith, *Conquest*; Deer, *Beginning and End of Rape*.

35 Morgensen, *Spaces between Us*, 36–38.

36 Urban Indian Health Institute, *Missing and Murdered Indigenous Women*.

37 Rifkin, "Romancing Kinship."

38 Morgensen, "Settler Homonationalism," 113.

39 Caitlin Keliiaa documents the specifically gendered effects of allotment and boarding schools in her discussion of outing programs that placed Native girls as domestic workers in wealthy white homes in the San Francisco Bay Area. Keliiaa's analysis makes visible the relationship between the production of white domesticity and the confinement of and violence against Native girls. Keliiaa's history shows how the cultivation of domesticity within boarding schools was not about making Native girls into female citizens but rather about making them into domestic servants, much like the Freedmen's Bureau's efforts to force freedwomen into domestic work, described in chapter 4 of this book. Keliiaa, "Unsettling Domesticity."

40 Morgensen, "Settler Homonationalism," 116.

41 Andrea Smith and Kauanui, "Native Feminisms Engage American Studies"; Arvin, Tuck, and Morrill, "Decolonizing Feminism"; Kauanui, *Paradoxes of Hawaiian Sovereignty*; A. Simpson, *Mohawk Interruptus*; Barker, *Native Acts*; Goeman, *Mark My Words*.

42 Foucault, *"Society Must Be Defended."*

43 Stoler, *Race and the Education of Desire*; Morgensen, "Biopolitics of Settler Colonialism."

44 Foucault, *"Society Must Be Defended,"* 254.

45 Foucault, *"Society Must Be Defended,"* 255.

46 Morgensen, "Settler Homonationalism."

47 Finley, "Decolonizing the Queer Native Body," 34.

48 King, *Black Shoals*, xiii.

49 King, "New World Grammars."

50 See also Weheliye, *Habeas Viscus*.

51 King, *Black Shoals*, 25.

52 King, *Black Shoals*, 24.

53 Shah, *Stranger Intimacy*, 8–9.

54 As Dean Spade documents, the administrative apparatus of the welfare state is both founded on and deeply invested in reproducing binary constructions of gender. These practices strongly resemble earlier settler-colonial practices that sought to eliminate Native genders that did not conform to binary constructions. Spade, *Normal Life*.

55 Roberts, *Killing the Black Body*.

56 For examples of key feminist texts that conflate the public-private divide with a static, uniformly experienced division between the state and the home, see MacKinnon, *Toward a Feminist Theory*; and Pateman, *Sexual Contract*.

57 Camp, *Closer to Freedom*.

58 As Jennifer Morgan argues, at the most basic level, the plantation economy was impossible without Black women's reproduction. Morgan, *Laboring Women*.

59 Glymph, *Out of the House*.

60 Camp, *Closer to Freedom*, 7.

61 Camp, *Closer to Freedom*, 93–94.

62 A. Davis, "Reflections," 115.

63 A. Davis, "Reflections," 115.

64 On women claiming ownership of their bodies as a practice of freedom, see Hunter, *To 'Joy My Freedom*, 168–86.

65 Hammonds, "Toward a Genealogy"; Hine, "Rape and the Inner Lives."

66 E. Brown, "Negotiating and Transforming."

67 Hunter, *To 'Joy My Freedom*; Glymph, *Out of the House*. For twentieth-century examples of these same dynamics, see Nadasen, *Household Workers Unite*.

68 Haley, *No Mercy Here*, 156–94. In her discussion of Mothers Reclaiming Our Children, a Southern California activist group of mothers working to free their children from the prison system in the 1990s, Ruth Wilson Gilmore demonstrates that the opposite can also be true. These activists reconstructed the boundaries between public and private space in order to contest the carceral state. Gilmore, *Golden Gulag*, 181–240.

69 Bhattacharjee, "Public/Private Mirage."

70 Mitchell, "Limits of the State," 90.

Chapter 3. Marriage and Gendered Citizenship

1 Patterson, *Slavery and Social Death*.

2 Stanley, *From Bondage to Contract*, 6.

3 On kinship among the enslaved, see Stevenson, *Life in Black and White*; Franke, "Becoming a Citizen."

4 Hunter, *Bound in Wedlock*, 28.

5 Cott, *Public Vows*, 61.

6 Edwards, *Gendered Strife and Confusion*, 6.

7 Glymph, *Out of the House*.

8 On informal marriage practices, see Gutman, *Black Family in Slavery*; Hunter, *Bound in Wedlock*, 23–60.

9 Roberts, *Killing the Black Body*, 24; A. Davis, *Women, Race and Class*, 6–7.

10 A. Davis, *Women, Race and Class*, 7–10; Roberts, *Killing the Black Body*, 22–55; White, *Ar'n't I a Woman?*, 30–2.

11 On the invisibilization of queer sexualities in African American History, see Richardson, "No More Secrets." Omise'eke Natasha Tinsley notes the queerness of the Black Atlantic, pointing to the ways in which the violence of the Middle Passage and slavery fostered queer forms of love and companionship. Similarly, Gloria Wekker demonstrates a strong presence of same-sex sexuality

within working-class African diasporic cultures in order to "argue that same-sex sexuality has firm roots in African heritage." Tinsley, "Black Atlantic, Queer Atlantic"; Wekker, *Politics of Passion*, 78.

12 Patterson, *Slavery and Social Death*, 341–42.

13 A. McClintock, *Imperial Leather*, 189–90.

14 A. McClintock, *Imperial Leather*, 38.

15 Lugones, "Heterosexualism and the Colonial/Modern," 192.

16 A. McClintock, *Imperial Leather*, 49.

17 Bederman, *Manliness and Civilization*, 28.

18 B. Williams, *Women Out of Place*, 1–36.

19 Kandaswamy, "Gendering Racial Formation."

20 Both quoted in Stanley, *From Bondage to Contract*, 18, 24.

21 Quoted in Cott, *Public Vows*, 58.

22 Stanley, *From Bondage to Contract*, 24.

23 Franke, "Becoming a Citizen."

24 American Freedmen's Inquiry Commission, *Preliminary Report*, 9.

25 On the importance of Black women's reproductive labor under slavery, see A. Davis, "Reflections"; and Hartman, "Belly of the World."

26 J. P. Lee, "Report on Alexandria and Fairfax Counties," October 1866, Records of the Assistant Commission for the District of Columbia, 1865–69 (National Archives Microfilm Publication M1055, roll 13, frame 300), Bureau of Refugees, Freedmen, and Abandoned Lands-Record Group 105, National Archives, Washington, DC.

27 Thadeus K. Preuss, "Monthly Report of Operations from Oxford, Mississippi," August 31, 1867, Records of the Assistant Commissioner for the State of Mississippi, 1865–1869 (National Archives Microfilm Publication M826, roll 30, frames 147–48, BRFAL-RG 105, National Archives, Washington, DC.

28 Franke, "Becoming a Citizen."

29 For more on the perils of conflating marriage and freedom, see Franke, *Wedlocked*.

30 Frankel, *Freedom's Women*, 82; Edwards, *Gendered Strife and Confusion*, 32.

31 Stevens, *Reproducing the State*, xi.

32 Regosin, *Freedom's Promise*, 54–78.

33 Headquarters of the Assistant Commissioner of BRFAL of South Carolina, "General Order No. 14: Marriage Rules," 1866, Records of the Assistant Commissioner for the State of South Carolina, BRFAL, 1865–1870 (National Archives Microfilm Publication M869, roll 44, "Other Records"), BRFAL-RG 105, National Archives, Washington, DC.

34 H. Brown, *John Freeman and His Family*, 21.

35 Regosin, *Freedom's Promise*, 56.

36 H. Brown, *John Freeman and His Family*, 22.

37 Hartman, *Scenes of Subjection*, 116–17.

38 Hartman, *Scenes of Subjection*, 155.

39 H. Brown, *John Freeman and His Family*, 26.

40 Hartman, *Scenes of Subjection*, 156.

41 Hartman, *Scenes of Subjection*, 155–57.

42 Stevens, *Reproducing the State*, 10.

43 Stevens, *Reproducing the State*, 14.

44 Halberstam, *In a Queer Time and Place*, 5.

45 Edwards, *Gendered Strife and Confusion*, 32.

46 Edwards, *Gendered Strife and Confusion*, 6.

47 On the criminalization of movement, see Lichtenstein, *Twice the Work*; W. Cohen, *At Freedom's Edge*.

48 P. Marshal, "Inspection Report of Jefferson and Orleans Counties," January 31, 1866, Records of the Assistant Commissioner for the State of Louisiana, 1865–1869 (National Archives Microfilm Publication M1027, roll 28, frame 125), BRFAL-RG 105, National Archives, Washington, DC.

49 J. A. Mower, "Monthly Report of Operations and Conditions," August 31, 1867, Records of the Assistant Commissioner of the State of Louisiana, 1865–1869 (National Archives Microfilm Publication M1027, roll 27, frame 204), BRFAL-RG 105, National Archives, Washington, DC.

50 Shah, *Stranger Intimacy*, 11.

51 Mink, *Wages of Motherhood*.

52 Franke, "Becoming a Citizen," 252.

53 Samuel Thomas, *Digest of Orders and Instructions to Sub-commissioners Bureau of Refugees, Freedmen, and Abandoned Lands* (Vicksburg, MI: Freedmen's Bureau Press Print, 1866), 30–31 (National Archives Microfilm Publication M826, roll 30), BRFAL-RG 105, National Archives, Washington, DC.

54 American Freedmen's Inquiry Commission, *Preliminary Report*, 6.

55 Hartman, *Scenes of Subjection*, 116–18.

56 Quoted in Cott, *Public Vows*, 82.

57 William Spurgin, "Report of Operations," March 1, 1866, Records of the Assistant Commissioner for the District of Columbia, 1865–69 (National Archives Microfilm Publications M1055, roll 13, frame 332), BRFAL-RG 105, National Archives, Washington, DC.

58 A. K. Brown, "Report of Operations," October 10, 1868, Records of the Assistant Commissioner for the District of Columbia, 1865–69 (National Archives Microfilm Publications M1055, roll 13, frames 843–45), BRFAL-RG 105, National Archives, Washington, DC.

59 Frankel, *Freedom's Women*, 87.

60 American Freedmen's Inquiry Commission, *Preliminary Report*, 6–7.

61 Captain Lee, "Report of Operations," January 1, 1867, Records of the Assistant Commissioner for the District of Columbia, 1865–69 (National Archives Microfilm Publications M1055, roll 13, frames 420–22), BRFAL-RG 105, National Archives, Washington, DC.

62 Edwards, *Gendered Strife and Confusion*, 35.

63 Rutherford Allan, "Annual Report for the Fourth Subdistrict, Wilmington, North Carolina," September 25, 1867, Records of the Assistant Commissioner of the State of North Carolina, 1865–1870 (National Archives Microfilm Publication M843, roll 22, frames 54–57), BRFAL-RG 105, National Archives, Washington, DC.

64 Edwards, *Gendered Strife and Confusion*, 39.

65 Mink, *Wages of Motherhood*; L. Gordon, *Pitied but Not Entitled*; Canaday, *Straight State*, 91–136.

66 Edwards, *Gendered Strife and Confusion*, 145–83.

67 E. Brown, "Negotiating and Transforming."

68 Rosen, *Terror in the Heart*, 106–8.

69 Fraser and Gordon, "Genealogy of Dependency."

70 On the transition from sovereign power to biopower, see Foucault, *"Society Must Be Defended"*; and Foucault, *History of Sexuality, Vol. 1*.

71 Scott Lauria Morgensen points to a similar phenomenon in the way that heteronormativity and homonormativity have operated as a tool of settler colonialism and Native American genocide. Morgensen, "Settler Homonationalism."

72 Franke, "Becoming a Citizen."

73 M. McClintock, "Civil War Pensions."

74 A number of scholars have pointed to the Civil War pension system as an inaugural moment in the U.S. welfare state. Perhaps most notably, Theda Skocpol argues that a maternalist welfare state emerged in the United States out of claims made on behalf of soldiers and mothers, in contrast to the paternalist welfare states of Europe, which emerged from more universal claims rooted in labor activism. While useful, Skocpol's argument is also limited in that it does not truly grapple with the complexity of the historical period and the impact that race, in particular, had on the structure of pension programs. However, the point that Civil War pensions and the forms of social stratification they enabled laid the foundation for future welfare provision is an important one. Skocpol, *Protecting Soldiers and Mothers*.

75 Shaffer, "'I Do Not Suppose.'"

76 Krowl, "'Her Just Dues'"; Shaffer, "'I Do Not Suppose'"; Brimmer, "'Her Claim for Pension.'"

77 Shaffer, "'I Do Not Suppose,'" 140–41.

78 Regosin, *Freedom's Promise*, 40.

79 Affidavit of Adeline Mozee, March 16, 1891, Pension File of Adeline Mozee (Application No. 500,193), National Archives Record Group 15, National Archives, Washington, DC; and affidavit of Adeline Mozee, March 28, 1891, Pension File of Adeline Mozee (Application No. 500,193), NARG 15, National Archives, Washington, DC.

80 Krowl, "'Her Just Dues,'" 63.

81 Pension File of Mary Boaz (Certificate No. 197,692), NARG 15, National Archives, Washington, DC; Pension File of Lucretia Boaz (Application No. 364,532), NARG 15, National Archives, Washington, DC.

82 Pension File of Harriet Valley (Application No. 724622), NARG 15, National Archives, Washington, DC.

83 Quoted in letter from the Chief of the Law Division to the Chief of the Board of Review, June 30, 1906, pp. 2–3, Pension File of Harriet Valley (Application No. 724622), NARG 15, National Archives, Washington, DC.

84 Mississippi Constitution, art. XII, sec. 22, adopted in Convention on May 15, 1868, and ratified on December 1, 1869.

85 Letter from the Chief of the Law Division to the Chief of the Board of Review, June 30, 1906, p. 5, Pension File of Harriet Valley (Application No. 724622), NARG 15, National Archives, Washington, DC.

86 Letter from J. B. Cralle to the Assistant Secretary of the Interior, December 6, 1901, Pension File of Sallie Christy (Application No. 643348), NARG 15, National Archives, Washington, DC.

87 Pension Bureau, *Laws of the United States*, 62.

88 Pension File of Anna Hayden (Application No. 729789), NARG 15, National Archives, Washington, DC.

89 Pension File of Maria Bohannan (Application No. 402286), NARG 15, National Archives, Washington, DC.

90 Krowl, "'Her Just Dues,'" 63–64.

91 Krowl, "'Her Just Dues,'" 61.

92 Krowl, "'Her Just Dues,'" 60; Brimmer, "'Her Claim for Pension,'" 217–22.

93 M. McClintock, "Civil War Pensions," 477.

94 Deposition A of Anne M. Ross, December 16, 1903, Pension File of Anne M. Ross (Application No. 771125), NARG 15, National Archives, Washington, DC.

95 Deposition A of Anne M. Ross, 15.

96 Deposition A of Anne M. Ross, 19–20.

97 Deposition A of Anne M. Ross, 17.

98 Special Examiner's Report, December 29, 1903, p. 6, Pension File of Anne M. Ross (Application No. 771125), NARG 15, National Archives, Washington, DC.

99 Krowl, "'Her Just Dues,'" 49.

100 Special Examiner's Report, Pension File of Anne Ross, p. 4.

101 Deposition of Annie Russell, December 18, 1903, pp. 69–70, Pension File of Anne M. Ross (Application No. 771125), NARG 15, National Archives, Washington, DC.

102 Hunter, *To 'Joy My Freedom*.

Chapter 4. Domestic Labor and the Politics of Reform

1 Glenn, *Unequal Freedom*.

2 On citizenship as a burden, see Hartman, *Scenes of Subjection*, 115–163.

3 W. Cohen, *At Freedom's Edge*, 33.

4 As many scholars of carceral institutions have noted, the Thirteenth Amendment did not actually abolish slavery. Rather, it limited slavery to those con-

victed of a crime. As such, criminal justice institutions became a primary vehicle for reestablishing slavery (albeit in a different form) after the Civil War. Vagrancy laws were central to this project. A. Davis, *Are Prisons Obsolete?*, 22–39.

5 Jones, *Labor of Love*, 16.

6 W. Cohen, *At Freedom's Edge*.

7 Kerber, *No Constitutional Right*.

8 Kerber, *No Constitutional Right*, 51–55.

9 Kerber, *No Constitutional Right*, 58.

10 Shah, *Stranger Intimacy*. Similar constructions that link male vagrancy with deviant sexualities can be seen in Margot Canaday's discussion of the Federal Transient Program and New Deal–era relief. Canaday, *Straight State*, 91–134.

11 Farmer-Kaiser, *Freedwomen and the Freedmen's Bureau*, 90–91.

12 Farmer-Kaiser, *Freedwomen and the Freedmen's Bureau*, 88–91.

13 Hammonds, "Toward a Genealogy," 170.

14 Kerber, *No Constitutional Right*, 59.

15 Quoted in Kerber, *No Constitutional Right*, 50.

16 Rosen, *Terror in the Heart*, 43.

17 Kerber, *No Constitutional Right*, 58.

18 T. W. Mostyn, "Monthly Rations Report, Colony at Garland," July 1, 1866, Records of the Assistant Commissioner of the State of Alabama, 1865–1870 (National Archives Microfilm Publication M809, roll 19, frame 504), BRFAL-RG 105, National Archives, Washington, DC.

19 This is not to romanticize sex work but rather to underscore Tera Hunter's point that claiming ownership and enjoyment of one's own body was an important practice of freedom for Black women in the Reconstruction era. Hunter, *To 'Joy My Freedom*.

20 Farmer-Kaiser, *Freedwomen and the Freedmen's Bureau*, 84–92.

21 Jones, *Labor of Love*, 45, 59.

22 Quoted in Stanley, *From Bondage to Contract*, 189.

23 Quoted in Stanley, *From Bondage to Contract*, 189. }

24 Butler argues that "gender is an identity tenuously constituted in time, instituted in an exterior space through a stylized repetition of acts." In her formulation, gender in not the expression of an interior essence; rather, the appearance of interiority is produced through the repeated performance of gendered acts. The idea, then, that freedwomen were simply playing the lady complicates how we think about the gendered body, revealing the ways that race functioned as a limit in the constitution of gender. Butler, *Gender Trouble*, 179.

25 James Devine, "Annual Report of Huntsville Office," January 21, 1867, Records of the Assistant Commissioner of the State of Texas, 1865–1869 (National Archives Microfilm Publication M821, roll 20), BRFAL-RG 105, National Archives, Washington, DC.

26 John Brough, "Monthly Report for the State of Louisiana," November 18, 1867, Records of the Assistant Commissioner of the State of Louisiana, 1865–69

(National Archives Microfilm Publication M1027, roll 28), BRFAL-RG 105, National Archives, Washington, DC.

27 Kerber, *No Constitutional Right*, 62, 66.

28 American Freedmen's Inquiry Commission, *Preliminary Report*, 40.

29 Farmer-Kaiser, *Freedwomen and the Freedmen's Bureau*, 84–85.

30 Stanley, *From Bondage to Contract*, 9.

31 Samuel Thomas, "Advice to Freedmen," January 2, 1866, Records of the Commissioner of the State of Mississippi, 1865–69 (National Archives Microfilm Publication, M826, roll 28), BRFAL-RG 105, National Archives, Washington, DC.

32 Stanley, *From Bondage to Contract*, 36.

33 Thomas, "Advice to Freedmen."

34 "Labor Contract between A. P. Hopper and Jane Tallifern and Child," Records of the Assistant Commissioner for the State of Tennessee, 1865–69 (National Archives Microfilm Publication, M999, roll 21, frame 366), BRFAL-RG 105, National Archives, Washington, DC.

35 "Labor Contract between G. F. Smith and Lizzie Crofford," January 9, 1866, Records of the Assistant Commissioner for the State of Tennessee, 1865–69 (National Archives Microfilm Publication, M999, roll 20, frame 248), BRFAL-RG 105, National Archives, Washington, DC.

36 "Labor Contract between W. A. Dick and Isabella Dick," August 29, 1965, Records of the Assistant Commissioner for the State of North Carolina (National Archives Microfilm Publication M843, roll 34, frame 212), BRFAL-RG 105, National Archives, Washington, DC.

37 Frankel, *Freedom's Women*, 64.

38 For example, see Kevin Mumford's discussion of Black women's participation in sex work during the Great Migration. Mumford, *Interzones*, 93–119.

39 Frankel, *Freedom's Women*, 128–30; Jones, *Labor of Love*, 62.

40 Farmer-Kaiser, *Freedwomen and the Freedmen's Bureau*, 83–85.

41 "Labor Contract between Mary Galbreth and Willis M. Lauchlin," August 26, 1865, Records of the Assistant Commissioner for the State of North Carolina (National Archives Microfilm Publication M843, roll 34, frame 153), BRFAL-RG 105, National Archives, Washington, DC.

42 Hartman, *Scenes of Subjection*, 156.

43 Frankel, *Freedom's Women*, 64–65.

44 *Freedmen's Record* 1, no. 2 (February 1865): 17.

45 Harrison, *Washington during Civil War*, 61.

46 William Spurgin, "Report of Operations of Washington Office," November 1, 1865, Records of the Assistant Commissioner for the District of Columbia (National Archives Microfilm Publication M1055, roll 13, frame 307), BRFAL-RG 105, National Archives, Washington, DC.

47 On the development of the field of poverty knowledge in the twentieth century, see O'Connor, *Poverty Knowledge*.

48 Sarah Haley shows how this practice continued into the Jim Crow era with the hiring out of female prisoners as domestic workers in white homes. Haley, *No Mercy Here*.

49 Masur, *Example for All the Land*, 52–53.

50 J. J. Coats, "Report of Visiting Agent for One Month Previous to the Date," January 24, 1866, Records of the Assistant Commissioner for the District of Columbia (National Archives Microfilm Publication M1055, roll 14), BRFAL-RG 105, National Archives, Washington, DC.

51 Masur, *Example for All the Land*, 58.

52 Farmer-Kaiser, *Freedwomen and the Freedmen's Bureau*, 44.

53 Harrison, *Washington during Civil War*, 81.

54 Farmer-Kaiser, *Freedwomen and the Freedmen's Bureau*, 37.

55 Farmer-Kaiser, *Freedwomen and the Freedmen's Bureau*, 45–49.

56 William Spurgin, "Report of Operations of Washington Office," November 1, 1865, Records of the Assistant Commissioner for the District of Columbia (National Archives Microfilm Publication M1055, roll 13, frames 307–8), BRFAL-RG 105, National Archives, Washington, DC.

57 A. H. Lawrence, "Report on the Freedmen's Village," October 31, 1866, Records of the Assistant Commissioner for the District of Columbia (National Archives Microfilm Publication M1055, roll 13, frame 409), BRFAL-RG 105, National Archives, Washington, DC.

58 H. N. Howard, "Report on the Freedmen's Village," July 19, 1867, Records of the Assistant Commissioner for the District of Columbia (National Archives Microfilm Publication M1055, roll 13, frame 488), BRFAL-RG 105, National Archives, Washington, DC.

59 Faulkner, *Women's Radical Reconstruction*, 136.

60 Masur, *Example for All the Land*, 64.

61 Faulkner, *Women's Radical Reconstruction*, 136.

62 Faulkner, *Women's Radical Reconstruction*, 136–40.

63 Greenwood, *First Fruits of Freedom*, 122.

64 On comparisons to the slave trade, see Greenwood, *First Fruits of Freedom*, 122.

65 Spurgin, "Report of Operations of Washington Office," November 1, 1865 (M1055, roll 13, frame 307).

66 Greenwood, *First Fruits of Freedom*, 123.

67 William Spurgin, "Report of Operations from Office of Superintendent of Refugees, Freedmen of Washington and Georgetown from July 19–Aug. 4, 1865," August 4, 1865, Records of the Assistant Commissioner for the District of Columbia (National Archives Microfilm Publication M1055, roll 13, frames 261–62), BRFAL-RG 105, National Archives, Washington, DC.

68 William Spurgin, "Report of Operations," March 1, 1866, Records of the Assistant Commissioner for the District of Columbia (National Archives Microfilm Publication M1055, roll 13), BRFAL-RG 105, National Archives, Washington, DC.

69 Greenwood, *First Fruits of Freedom*, 124.

70 Marks, "Bone and Sinew of the Race," 152.

71 *Freedmen's Record* 1, no. 5 (1865): 80.

72 Howard Industrial School Association, *Second Annual Report*, 5.

73 Greenwood, *First Fruits of Freedom*, 124; Anna Lowell, "Report of the Operations of the Howard Industrial School," August 4, 1867, Records of the Assistant Commissioner for the District of Columbia (National Archives Microfilm Publication M1055, roll 14, frames 100–109), BRFAL-RG 105, National Archives, Washington, DC.

74 Howard Industrial School Association, *Second Annual Report*, 10.

75 Lowell, "Report of the Operations of the Howard Industrial School."

76 Lowell, "Report of the Operations of the Howard Industrial School."

77 Quoted in Faulkner, *Women's Radical Reconstruction*, 128.

78 Lowell, "Report of the Operations of the Howard Industrial School."

79 Many parallels exist between Rebecca Tolliver's plight and the continuing plight of Black mothers who have had their children taken from them by Child Protective Services due to systemic poverty. For more on this, see Roberts, *Shattered Bonds*.

80 Faulkner, *Women's Radical Reconstruction*, 118.

81 Greenwood, *First Fruits of Freedom*, 128.

Chapter 5. The Chains of Welfare

Epigraph: Florida Representative E. Clay Shaw is quoted in Subcommittee on Human Resources of the Committee on Ways and Means of the House of Representatives, *Hearings on Contract with America—Welfare Reform, Part 1*, 104th Cong., 1st sess., January 13, 1995, 6.

1 Throughout this chapter I use the general term *welfare* to refer to the AFDC and TANF programs more specifically. My intention in doing this is not to erase the broad forms of welfare support that a wide range of citizens benefit from but rather to mirror the way the term has been used in U.S. political discourse in the late twentieth century.

2 Clinton promised to "end welfare as we know it" throughout his 1992 Presidential campaign and used this language repeatedly in his efforts to get a welfare reform law passed throughout his first term as president.

3 On situating welfare reform in the United States within the larger global context of structural adjustment, see Chang, *Disposable Domestics*.

4 Hartman, *Lose Your Mother*, 6.

5 A. McClintock, *Imperial Leather*, 45.

6 Koven and Michel, *Mothers of a New World*; L. Gordon, *Pitied but Not Entitled*; Mink, *Wages of Motherhood*; Ladd-Taylor, *Mother-Work*.

7 Abramovitz, *Regulating the Lives of Women*, 188.

8 Mink, *Wages of Motherhood*, 34.

9 Mink, *Wages of Motherhood*, 33.
10 L. Gordon, *Pitied but Not Entitled*.
11 Mink, *Wages of Motherhood*.
12 Canaday, *Straight State*, 91–134.
13 Katznelson, *When Affirmative Action Was White*.
14 Lieberman, *Shifting the Color Line*, 121.
15 Mink, *Wages of Motherhood*, 142.
16 Lieberman, *Shifting the Color Line*, 124–25.
17 Lieberman, *Shifting the Color Line*, 151. For more on the production of a distinction between recipients of survivors' benefits and recipients of ADC, see Mink, *Wages of Motherhood*, 135–38.
18 Goodwin, "'Employable Mothers' and 'Suitable Work'"; Reese, *Backlash against Welfare Mothers*, 40.
19 Mink, *Wages of Motherhood*, 142–43.
20 Mink, *Wages of Motherhood*, 143–45.
21 Reese, *Backlash against Welfare Mothers*, 41–42.
22 Mink, *Wages of Motherhood*, 138–49.
23 Mittelstadt, "'Dependency as a Problem,'" 232–33.
24 Mittelstadt, "'Dependency as a Problem.'"
25 Piven and Cloward, *Poor People's Movements*, 264–362.
26 Milwaukee County Welfare Rights Organization, *Welfare Mothers Speak Out*, 17–24.
27 Mink, *Welfare's End*, 48–49.
28 Mink, *Welfare's End*, 50.
29 Mink, *Welfare's End*, 55.
30 Quoted in Goodwin, "'Employable Mothers' and 'Suitable Work,'" 267.
31 Goodwin, "'Employable Mothers' and 'Suitable Work.'"
32 Premilla Nadasen notes that this was often a point of contention between welfare mothers and many of the middle-class male organizers within the movement. Nadasen notes that in order to counter stereotypes about Black women on welfare, "the middle-class staff questioned the stereotypes by asserting that black women did, in fact, want to work, but the lack of jobs and problems of day care prevented them from seeking paid employment. When public hostility did not subside, the staff considered ways to divert attention from black women and shift the movement's political focus by organizing poor working men, who they believed would draw more sympathy as recipients of public assistance. The black women on welfare in the organization had a different approach. Since the movement's inception, they had put forth a critique of the way in which the AFDC program controlled the lives of poor women and articulated their concerns as mothers. They justified welfare assistance by arguing that as mothers, they were working and, therefore, contributing to society." Nadasen, *Welfare Warriors*, 236–37.
33 Tillmon, "Welfare Is a Women's Issue," 378.

34 Kornbluh, *Battle for Welfare Rights*; Nadasen, *Welfare Warriors*.

35 Tillmon, "Welfare Is a Women's Issue," 377.

36 This is a striking contrast to Black nationalist movements of the time that sought recognition of Black men's humanity by asserting their status as men. R. Ferguson, *Aberrations in Black*, 110–37.

37 The decline of the NWRO is usually attributed to internal conflicts within the organization, the inability to build an adequate organizational infrastructure to sustain a national organization, and the changing social and political context. For a fuller discussion of these factors, see Piven and Cloward, *Poor People's Movements*, 349–59; and Nadasen, *Welfare Warriors*, 193–230.

38 Moynihan, *Negro Family*.

39 O'Connor, *Poverty Knowledge*, 99–123; Briggs, *Reproducing Empire*, 162–92.

40 Omi and Winant, *Racial Formation in the United States*.

41 Goodwin, "'Employable Mothers' and 'Suitable Work'"; Rose, "Gender, Race," 328–29.

42 Rose, "Gender, Race," 329–30.

43 Peck, *Workfare States*, 91.

44 Mink, *Welfare's End*, 41.

45 Mink, *Welfare's End*, 41–42.

46 Quoted in Peck, *Workfare States*, 96.

47 Peck, *Workfare States*, 92–93.

48 Quadagno, *Color of Welfare*.

49 Gilens, *Why Americans Hate Welfare*.

50 Gilens, "How the Poor Became Black," 105.

51 Edin and Lein, *Making Ends Meet*.

52 Luker, *Dubious Conceptions*.

53 Roberts, *Killing the Black Body*, 218.

54 Lubiano, "Black Ladies, Welfare Queens," 335.

55 Lubiano, "Black Ladies, Welfare Queens," 336.

56 P. Collins, *Black Feminist Thought*, 76–77.

57 Hancock, *Politics of Disgust*.

58 Fraser and Gordon, "Genealogy of Dependency."

59 Shah, *Stranger Intimacy*, 8–9.

60 Subcommittee on Human Resources of the Committee on Ways and Means of the House of Representations, *Hearing on Contract with America—Welfare Reform*, 104th Congress, 1st sess., January 13, 1995, 7–8.

61 Plotkin and Scheuerman, *Private Interests, Public Spending*, 32.

62 Quoted in Josh Levin, "The Real Story of Linda Taylor, America's Original Welfare Queen," *Slate Magazine*, December 19, 2013, http://www.slate.com/articles /news_and_politics/history/2013/12/linda_taylor_welfare_queen_ronald _reagan_made_her_a_notorious_american_villain.html.

63 Briggs, *How All Politics Became Reproductive*, 51; Levin, "Real Story of Linda Taylor."

64 Additionally, Julilly Kohler-Hausmann highlights how the Linda Taylor story and the emphasis on welfare fraud linked antiwelfare discourse and anticrime discourse in ways that simultaneously supported the assault on welfare institutions and the growth of carceral institutions. Kohler-Hausmann, *Getting Tough*, 184–91.

65 Calavita, "New Politics of Immigration"; Chang, *Disposable Domestics*.

66 Representative Lamar Smith, speaking for the Personal Responsibility and Work Opportunity Reconciliation Act of 1996, 104th Cong., 2nd sess., July 31, 1996, *Congressional Record* H9401.

67 Quoted in Roberts, *Killing the Black Body*, 217.

68 Luker, *Dubious Conceptions*; Coontz, *Way We Never Were*.

69 Roberts, *Killing the Black Body*.

70 The Personal Responsibility and Work Opportunity Reconciliation Act of 1996, Pub. L. No. 104–193, 110 Stat. 2105 (1996).

71 Onwuachi-Willig, "Return of the Ring."

72 Onwuachi-Willig, "Return of the Ring," 1676.

73 Anna Smith, *Welfare Reform and Sexual Regulation*, 3.

74 Anna Smith, *Welfare Reform and Sexual Regulation*, 118.

75 Quoted in Boggess, Price, and Rodriguez, *What We Want to Give*, 4.

76 Boggess, Price, and Rodriguez, *What We Want to Give*.

77 Boggess, Price, and Rodriguez, *What We Want to Give*, 8.

78 D.-A. Davis, *Battered Black Women and Welfare*, 127–28.

79 Kerber, *No Constitutional Right*, 58.

80 Glenn, "From Servitude to Service Work."

81 Morgen, Acker, and Weigt, *Stretched Thin*, 125.

82 Marchevsky and Theoharis, *Not Working*, 128.

83 Hays, *Flat Broke with Children*, 39.

84 Hays, *Flat Broke with Children*, 44.

85 Marchevsky and Theoharis, *Not Working*, 117.

86 Marchevsky and Theoharis, *Not Working*, 132.

87 John McCormick, "The School of Hard Knocks," *Newsweek*, October 30, 2000, 46.

88 McCormick, "School of Hard Knocks," 46.

89 McCormick, "School of Hard Knocks," 46.

90 McCormick, "School of Hard Knocks," 46.

91 Adam Cohen, "Dressed for Success: Companies Are Teaching Their Welfare-to-Work Hires How to Look and Act the Part," *Time*, July 13, 1998, 38.

92 A. Cohen, "Dressed for Success," 39.

93 Marchevsky and Theoharis, *Not Working*, 125.

94 Hays, *Flat Broke with Children*, 38; D.-A. Davis, *Battered Black Women and Welfare*, 109.

95 D.-A. Davis, *Battered Black Women and Welfare*, 101.

96 D.-A. Davis, *Battered Black Women and Welfare*, 95–103.

97 D.-A. Davis, *Battered Black Women and Welfare*, 106–7.

98 Marchevsky and Theoharis, *Not Working*, 124.

99 Steven Greenhouse, "Many Participants in Workfare Take the Place of City Workers," *New York Times*, April 13, 1998.

100 Boris, "When Work Is Slavery," 36.

101 Robert McFadden, "Union Chief Calls Workfare 'Slavery,'" *New York Times*, April 19, 1998.

102 D.-A. Davis, *Battered Black Women and Welfare*, 99–103.

103 Marchevsky and Theoharis, *Not Working*, 133–35.

104 Mink writes, "The negation of care-giving by single mothers is the cardinal achievement of the new welfare law. The law does not prescribe outside work as a serious alternative to welfare, for it does not 'make work pay' with wage protections and social supports. Rather, the law prescribes outside work to make single mothers pay—pay for daring to be mothers though they be single and poor." Mink, *Welfare's End*, 108.

105 Southeast Asian Youth Leadership Project and Committee against Anti-Asian Violence, *Eating Welfare*. For a more detailed analysis of how Asian immigrants and refugees were impacted by welfare reform, see Fujiwara, *Mothers without Citizenship*.

106 J. Collins and Mayer, *Both Hands Tied*; Marchevsky and Theoharis, *Not Working*.

Conclusion

1 Muñoz, *Cruising Utopia*.

2 Roberts, *Killing the Black Body*, 244.

3 Du Bois, *Black Reconstruction in America*.

Bibliography

Abramovitz, Mimi. *Regulating the Lives of Women: Social Welfare Policy from Colonial Times to the Present*. Boston: South End, 1988.

Alexander, Michelle. *The New Jim Crow: Mass Incarceration in the Age of Colorblindness*. New York: New Press, 2012.

Alexander, M. Jacqui. *Pedagogies of Crossing: Meditations on Feminism, Sexual Politics, Memory, and the Sacred*. Durham, NC: Duke University Press, 2006.

Alexander, M. Jacqui, and Chandra Talpade Mohanty, eds. *Feminist Genealogies, Colonial Legacies, Democratic Futures*. New York: Routledge, 1997.

American Freedmen's Inquiry Commission. *Preliminary Report Touching the Condition and Management of Emancipated Refugees*. New York: John F. Trow, Printer, 1863. http://hdl.handle.net/2027/mdp.39015068800252.

Arondekar, Anjali. *For the Record: On Sexuality and the Colonial Archive in India*. Durham, NC: Duke University Press, 2009.

Arvin, Maile, Eve Tuck, and Angie Morrill. "Decolonizing Feminism: Challenging Connections between Settler Colonialism and Heteropatriarchy." *Feminist Formations* 25, no. 1 (Spring 2013): 8–34.

Barker, Joanne. *Native Acts: Law, Recognition, and Cultural Authenticity*. Durham, NC: Duke University Press, 2011.

Bederman, Gail. *Manliness and Civilization: A Cultural History of Gender and Race in the United States, 1880–1917*. Chicago: University of Chicago Press, 1996.

Bentley, George R. *A History of the Freedmen's Bureau*. Philadelphia: University of Pennsylvania Press, 1955.

Bhattacharjee, Anannya. "The Public/Private Mirage: Mapping Homes and Undomesticating Violence Work in the South Asian Immigrant Community." In *Feminist Genealogies, Colonial Legacies, Democratic Futures*, edited by M. Jacqui Alexander and Chandra Talpade Mohanty, 308–29. New York: Routledge, 1997.

Boggess, Jacquelyn, Anne Price, and Nino Rodriguez. *What We Want to Give Our Kids: How Child Support Debt Can Diminish Wealth-Building Opportunities for Struggling Black Fathers and Their Families*. Madison, WI: Center for Family Policy and Practice, 2014.

Boris, Eileen. "When Work Is Slavery." In *Whose Welfare?*, edited by Gwendolyn Mink, 36–55. Ithaca, NY: Cornell University Press, 1999.

Briggs, Laura. *How All Politics Became Reproductive Politics: From Welfare Reform to Foreclosure to Trump*. Oakland: University of California Press, 2017.

Briggs, Laura. *Reproducing Empire: Race, Sex, Science, and U.S. Imperialism in Puerto Rico*. Berkeley: University of California Press, 2002.

Brimmer, Brandi C. "'Her Claim for Pension Is Lawful and Just': Representing Black Union Widows in Late-Nineteenth Century North Carolina." *Journal of the Civil War Era* 1, no. 2 (2011): 207–36.

Brown, Elsa Barkley. "Negotiating and Transforming the Public Sphere: African American Political Life in the Transition from Slavery to Freedom." *Public Culture* 7, no. 1 (1994): 107–46.

Brown, Elsa Barkley. "'What Has Happened Here': The Politics of Difference in Women's History and Feminist Politics." *Feminist Studies* 18, no. 2 (Summer 1992): 295–312.

Brown, Helen E. *John Freeman and His Family*. Boston: American Tract Society, 1864.

Brown, Wendy. *States of Injury*. Princeton, NJ: Princeton University Press, 1995.

Bush, George W. "Remarks to Welfare-to-Work Graduates, June 4, 2002." In *Public Papers of the Presidents of the United States: George W. Bush 2002: January 1 to June 30, 2002*, 933–36. Washington, DC: Government Printing Office, 2004.

Butler, Judith. *Gender Trouble: Feminism and the Subversion of Identity*. New York: Routledge, 1990.

Calavita, Kitty. "The New Politics of Immigration: 'Balanced-Budget Conservatism' and the Symbolism of Proposition 187." *Social Problems* 43, no. 3 (1996): 284–305.

Camp, Stephanie M. H. *Closer to Freedom: Enslaved Women and Everyday Resistance in the Plantation South*. Chapel Hill: University of North Carolina Press, 2004.

Canaday, Margot. *The Straight State: Sexuality and Citizenship in Twentieth-Century America*. Princeton, NJ: Princeton University Press, 2011.

Chang, Grace. *Disposable Domestics: Immigrant Women Workers in the Global Economy*. Cambridge, MA: South End, 2000.

Cimbala, Paul A., and Randall M. Miller, eds. *The Freedmen's Bureau and Reconstruction*. 2nd ed. New York: Fordham University Press, 1999.

Clinton, William J. "Remarks on Signing the Personal Responsibility and Work Opportunity Reconciliation Act and an Exchange with Reporters, August 22, 1996." In *The Public Papers of the Presidents of the United States: William J. Clinton*, 2: 1325–28. Washington, DC: Government Printing Office, 1996.

Cohen, Cathy J. "Punks, Bulldaggers, and Welfare Queens: The Radical Potential of Queer Politics?" *GLQ: A Journal of Lesbian and Gay Studies* 3, no. 4 (1997): 437–65.

Cohen, William. *At Freedom's Edge: Black Mobility and the Southern White Quest for Racial Control, 1861–1915*. Baton Rouge: Louisiana State University Press, 1991.

Collins, Jane L., and Victoria Mayer. *Both Hands Tied: Welfare Reform and the Race to the Bottom in the Low-Wage Labor Market*. Chicago: University of Chicago Press, 2010.

Collins, Patricia Hill. *Black Feminist Thought: Knowledge, Consciousness, and the Politics of Empowerment*. New York: Routledge, 1991.

Collins, Patricia Hill. "It's All in the Family: Intersections of Gender, Race, and Nation." *Hypatia* 13, no. 3 (1998): 62–82.

Coontz, Stephanie. *The Way We Never Were: American Families and the Nostalgia Trap*. New York: Basic Books, 1993.

Coryell, Janet L., Thomas H. Appleton Jr., Anastatia Sims, and Sandra Giola Treadway, eds. *Negotiating Boundaries of Southern Womanhood*. Columbia: University of Missouri Press, 2000.

Costa, Mariarosa Dalla, and Selma James. *The Power of Women and the Subversion of the Community*. 3rd ed. Bristol: Falling Wall, 1975.

Cott, Nancy F. *Public Vows: A History of Marriage and the Nation*. Cambridge, MA: Harvard University Press, 2002.

Davis, Angela Y. *Are Prisons Obsolete?* New York: Seven Stories, 2003.

Davis, Angela Y. "Reflections on the Black Woman's Role in the Community of Slaves." In *The Angela Y. Davis Reader*, edited by Joy James, 111–28. Malden, U.K.: Blackwell, 1998.

Davis, Angela Y. *Women, Race and Class*. New York: Random House, 1981.

Davis, Dána-Ain. *Battered Black Women and Welfare Reform: Between a Rock and a Hard Place*. Albany: State University of New York Press, 2006.

Deer, Sarah. *The Beginning and End of Rape: Confronting Sexual Violence in Native America*. Minneapolis: University of Minnesota Press, 2015.

Driskill, Qwo-Li, Chris Finley, Brian Joseph Gilley, and Scott Lauria Morgensen, eds. *Queer Indigenous Studies: Critical Interventions in Theory, Politics, and Literature*. Tucson: University of Arizona Press, 2011.

Du Bois, W. E. B. *Black Reconstruction in America, 1860–1880*. New York: Free Press, 1998. First published 1935 by Harcourt, Brace.

Du Bois, W. E. B. "The Freedmen's Bureau." *Atlantic Monthly* 87 (1899): 354–65.

Edin, Kathryn, and Laura Lein. *Making Ends Meet: How Single Mothers Survive Welfare and Low-Wage Work*. New York: Russell Sage Foundation, 1997.

Edwards, Laura F. *Gendered Strife and Confusion: The Political Culture of Reconstruction*. Urbana: University of Illinois Press, 1997.

Elia, Nada, David M. Hernández, Jodi Kim, Shana L. Redmond, Dylan Rodríguez, and Sarita Echavez See, eds. *Critical Ethnic Studies: A Reader*. Durham, NC: Duke University Press, 2016.

Farmer, Mary. "Because They Are Women: Gender and the Virginia Freedmen's Bureau's 'War on Dependency.'" In *The Freedmen's Bureau and Reconstruction: Reconsiderations*, edited by Paul A. Cimbala and Randall M. Miller, 161–92. New York: Fordham University Press, 1999.

Farmer-Kaiser, Mary. *Freedwomen and the Freedmen's Bureau: Race, Gender, and Public Policy in the Age of Emancipation*. New York: Fordham University Press, 2010.

Faulkner, Carol. *Women's Radical Reconstruction: The Freedmen's Aid Movement*. Philadelphia: University of Pennsylvania Press, 2006.

Ferguson, James, and Akhil Gupta. "Spatializing States: Toward an Ethnography of Neoliberal Governmentality." *American Ethnologist* 29, no. 4 (2002): 981–1002.

Ferguson, Roderick A. *Aberrations in Black: Toward a Queer of Color Critique*. Minneapolis: University of Minnesota Press, 2003.

Finley, Chris. "Decolonizing the Queer Native Body (and Recovering the Native Bull-Dyke): Bringing 'Sexy Back' and Out of the Native Studies Closet." In *Queer Indigenous Studies: Critical Interventions in Theory, Politics, and Literature*, edited by Qwo-Li Driskill, Chris Finley, Brian Joseph Gilley, and Scott Lauria Morgensen, 31–42. Tucson: University of Arizona Press, 2011.

Foner, Eric. *Reconstruction: America's Unfinished Revolution, 1863–1877*. Updated ed. New York: Harper Perennial Modern Classics, 2014.

Foucault, Michel. *The History of Sexuality, Vol. 1: An Introduction*. Translated by Robert Hurley. New York: Vintage, 1978.

Foucault, Michel. *"Society Must Be Defended": Lectures at the Collège de France, 1975–1976*. Translated by David Macey. New York: Picador, 2003.

Franke, Katherine. "Becoming a Citizen: Post-bellum Regulation of African American Marriage." *Yale Journal of Law and the Humanities* 11 (1999): 251–309.

Franke, Katherine. *Wedlocked: The Perils of Marriage Equality*. New York: New York University Press, 2017.

Frankel, Noralee. *Freedom's Women: Black Women and Families in Civil War Era Mississippi*. Bloomington: Indiana University Press, 1999.

Fraser, Nancy, and Linda Gordon. "A Genealogy of Dependency: Tracing a Keyword of the U.S. Welfare State." *Signs* 19, no. 2 (1994): 309–36.

Fujiwara, Lynn. *Mothers without Citizenship: Asian Immigrant Families and the Consequences of Welfare Reform*. Minneapolis: University of Minnesota Press, 2008.

Gilens, Martin. "How the Poor Became Black: The Racialization of American Poverty in the Mass Media." In *Race and the Politics of Welfare Reform*, edited by Sanford Schram, Joe Soss, and Richard Fording, 101–30. Ann Arbor: University of Michigan Press, 2003.

Gilens, Martin. *Why Americans Hate Welfare: Race, Media, and the Politics of Antipoverty Policy*. Chicago: University of Chicago Press, 2000.

Gilmore, Ruth Wilson. "Fatal Couplings of Power and Difference: Notes on Racism and Geography." *Professional Geographer* 54, no. 1 (2002): 15–24.

Gilmore, Ruth Wilson. "Globalisation and US Prison Growth: From Military Keynesianism to Post-Keynesian Militarism." *Race and Class* 40, no. 2–3 (1999): 171–88.

Gilmore, Ruth Wilson. *Golden Gulag: Prisons, Surplus, Crisis, and Opposition in Globalizing California*. Berkeley: University of California Press, 2007.

Glenn, Evelyn Nakano. "From Servitude to Service Work: Historical Continuities in the Racial Division of Paid Reproductive Labor." *Signs: Journal of Women in Culture and Society* 18, no. 1 (1992): 1–43.

Glenn, Evelyn Nakano. "Settler Colonialism as Structure: A Framework for Comparative Studies of U.S. Race and Gender Formation." *Sociology of Race and Ethnicity* 1, no. 1 (2015): 52–72.

Glenn, Evelyn Nakano. *Unequal Freedom: How Race and Gender Shaped American Citizenship and Labor.* Cambridge, MA: Harvard University Press, 2002.

Glymph, Thavolia. *Out of the House of Bondage: The Transformation of the Plantation Household.* New York: Cambridge University Press, 2008.

Goeman, Mishuana. *Mark My Words.* Minneapolis: University of Minnesota Press, 2013.

Goldberg, Chad Alan. *Citizens and Paupers: Relief, Rights, and Race, from the Freedmen's Bureau to Workfare.* Chicago: University of Chicago Press, 2008.

Goodwin, Joanne L. "'Employable Mothers' and 'Suitable Work': A Re-evaluation of Welfare and Wage-Earning for Women in the Twentieth-Century United States." *Journal of Social History* 29, no. 2 (1995): 253–74.

Gordon, Avery. *Ghostly Matters: Haunting and the Sociological Imagination.* Minneapolis: University of Minnesota Press, 1997.

Gordon, Linda. *Pitied but Not Entitled: Single Mothers and the History of Welfare, 1890–1935.* Cambridge, MA: Harvard University Press, 1995.

Gordon, Linda, ed. *Women, the State, and Welfare.* Madison, WI: University of Wisconsin Press, 1990.

Greenwood, Janette Thomas. *First Fruits of Freedom: The Migration of Former Slaves and Their Search for Equality in Worcester, Massachusetts, 1862–1900.* Chapel Hill: University of North Carolina Press, 2010.

Gutman, Herbert George. *The Black Family in Slavery and Freedom, 1750–1925.* 1st ed. New York: Pantheon Books, 1976.

Halberstam, J. Jack. *In a Queer Time and Place: Transgender Bodies, Subcultural Lives.* New York: New York University Press, 2005.

Haley, Sarah. *No Mercy Here: Gender, Punishment, and the Making of Jim Crow Modernity.* Chapel Hill: University of North Carolina Press, 2016.

Hall, Stuart. "Race, Culture, and Communications: Looking Backward and Forward at Cultural Studies." *Rethinking Marxism* 5, no. 1 (1992): 10–18.

Hall, Stuart. "The Problem of Ideology: Marxism without Guarantees." In *Stuart Hall: Critical Dialogues in Cultural Studies,* edited by David Morley and Kuan-Hsing Chen, 24–45. New York: Routledge, 1996.

Hammonds, Evelynn M. "Toward a Genealogy of Black Female Sexuality: The Problematic of Silence." In *Feminist Genealogies, Colonial Legacies, Democratic Futures,* edited by M. Jacqui Alexander and Chandra Talpade Mohanty, 170–82. New York: Routledge, 1997.

Hancock, Ange-Marie. *The Politics of Disgust: The Public Identity of the Welfare Queen.* New York: New York University Press, 2004.

Harris, Cheryl I. "Whiteness as Property." *Harvard Law Review* 106, no. 8 (1993): 1707–91.

Harrison, Robert. *Washington during Civil War and Reconstruction: Race and Radicalism.* New York: Cambridge University Press, 2011.

Hartman, Saidiya V. "The Belly of the World: A Note on Black Women's Labors." *Souls* 18, no. 1 (2016): 166–73.

Hartman, Saidiya V. *Lose Your Mother: A Journey along the Atlantic Slave Route.* New York: Farrar, Straus and Giroux, 2007.

Hartman, Saidiya V. *Scenes of Subjection: Terror, Slavery, and Self-Making in Nineteenth-Century America.* New York: Oxford University Press, 1997.

Hays, Sharon. *Flat Broke with Children: Women in the Age of Welfare Reform.* New York: Oxford University Press, 2004.

Hine, Darlene Clark. "Rape and the Inner Lives of Black Women in the Middle West." *Signs* 14, no. 4 (1989): 912–20.

Hong, Grace Kyungwon. *The Ruptures of American Capital: Women of Color Feminism and the Culture of Immigrant Labor.* Minneapolis: University of Minnesota Press, 2006.

HoSang, Daniel Martinez, Oneka LaBennett, and Laura Pulido, eds. *Racial Formation in the Twenty-First Century.* Berkeley: University of California Press, 2012.

Howard Industrial School Association. *Second Annual Report of the Howard Industrial School Association.* Cambridge, MA: Riverside, 1868.

Hunter, Tera W. *Bound in Wedlock: Slave and Free Black Marriage in the Nineteenth Century.* Cambridge, MA: Belknap Press of Harvard University Press, 2017.

Hunter, Tera W. *To 'Joy My Freedom: Southern Black Women's Lives and Labors after the Civil War.* Cambridge, MA: Harvard University Press, 1997.

James, Joy, ed. *The Angela Y. Davis Reader.* Malden, U.K.: Blackwell, 1998.

Jones, Jacqueline. *Labor of Love, Labor of Sorrow: Black Women, Work, and the Family from Slavery to the Present.* New York: Vintage, 1985.

Kandaswamy, Priya. "Gendering Racial Formation." In *Racial Formation in the Twenty-First Century*, edited by Daniel Martinez HoSang, Oneka LaBennett, and Laura Pulido, 23–43. Berkeley: University of California Press, 2012.

Kandaswamy, Priya. "'You Trade in a Man for the Man': Domestic Violence and the U.S. Welfare State." *American Quarterly* 62, no. 2 (2010): 253–77.

Kapadia, Ronak. "Up in the Air and on the Skin: Drone Warfare and the Queer Calculus of Pain." In *Critical Ethnic Studies: A Reader*, edited by Nada Elia, David M. Hernández, Jodi Kim, Shana L. Redmond, Dylan Rodríguez, and Sarita Echavez See, 360–74. Durham, NC: Duke University Press, 2016.

Kaplan, Amy. "Manifest Domesticity." *American Literature* 70, no. 3 (1998): 581–606.

Katznelson, Ira. *When Affirmative Action Was White: An Untold History of Racial Inequality in Twentieth-Century America.* New York: W. W. Norton, 2006.

Kauanui, J. Kehaulani. *Paradoxes of Hawaiian Sovereignty: Land, Sex, and the Colonial Politics of State Nationalism.* Durham, NC: Duke University Press, 2018.

Keliiaa, Caitlin. *Unsettling Domesticity: Native Women Challenging U.S. Indian Policy in the San Francisco Bay Area, 1911–1931.* Berkeley: Institute for the Study of Societal Issues, 2017. https://escholarship.org/uc/item/3md8r7hh.

Kerber, Linda K. *No Constitutional Right to Be Ladies: Women and the Obligations of Citizenship*. New York: Hill and Wang, 1998.

King, Tiffany Lethabo. *The Black Shoals: Offshore Formations of Black and Native Studies*. Durham, NC: Duke University Press, 2019.

King, Tiffany Lethabo. "New World Grammars: The 'Unthought' Black Discourses of Conquest." *Theory and Event* 19, no. 4 (2016).

Kohler-Hausmann, Julilly. *Getting Tough: Welfare and Imprisonment in 1970s America*. Princeton, NJ: Princeton University Press, 2019.

Kornbluh, Felicia. *The Battle for Welfare Rights: Politics and Poverty in Modern America*. Philadelphia: University of Pennsylvania Press, 2007.

Koven, Seth, and Sonya Michel. "Introduction: 'Mother Worlds.'" In *Mothers of a New World: Maternalist Politics and the Origins of Welfare States*, edited by Seth Koven and Sonya Michel, 1–42. New York: Routledge, 1993.

Koven, Seth, and Sonya Michel, eds. *Mothers of a New World: Maternalist Politics and the Origins of Welfare States*. New York: Routledge, 1993.

Krowl, Michelle. "'Her Just Dues': Civil War Pensions of African American Women in Virginia." In *Negotiating Boundaries of Southern Womanhood*, edited by Janet L. Coryell, Thomas H. Appleton Jr., Anastatia Sims, and Sandra Giola Treadway, 48–70. Columbia: University of Missouri Press, 2000.

Ladd-Taylor, Molly. *Mother-Work: Women, Child Welfare, and the State, 1890–1930*. Urbana: University of Illinois Press, 1994.

Lichtenstein, Alexander C. *Twice the Work of Free Labor: The Political Economy of Convict Labor in the New South*. New York: Verso, 1996.

Lieberman, Robert. "The Freedmen's Bureau and the Politics of Institutional Structure." *Social Science History* 18, no. 3 (1994): 405–37.

Lieberman, Robert C. *Shifting the Color Line: Race and the American Welfare State*. Cambridge, MA: Harvard University Press, 2001.

Lubiano, Wahneema. "Black Ladies, Welfare Queens, and State Minstrels: Ideological War by Narrative Means." In *Race-ing Justice, Engendering Power: The Anita Hill-Clarence Thomas Controversy and the Construction of Social Reality*, edited by Toni Morrison, 323–62. New York: Pantheon, 1992.

Lugones, María. "Heterosexualism and the Colonial/Modern Gender System." *Hypatia* 22, no. 1 (Winter 2007): 186–209.

Luker, Kristin. *Dubious Conceptions: The Politics of Teenage Pregnancy*. Cambridge, MA: Harvard University Press, 1997.

MacKinnon, Catharine A. *Toward a Feminist Theory of the State*. Cambridge, MA: Harvard University Press, 1989.

Mahmood, Saba. *Politics of Piety: The Islamic Revival and the Feminist Subject*. Princeton, NJ: Princeton University Press, 2005.

Marchevsky, Alejandra, and Jeanne Theoharis. *Not Working: Latina Immigrants, Low-Wage Jobs, and the Failure of Welfare Reform*. New York: New York University Press, 2006.

Marks, Carole. "The Bone and Sinew of the Race: Black Women, Domestic Service and Labor Migration." *Marriage and Family Review* 19, no. 1–2 (1993): 149–73.

Masur, Kate. *An Example for All the Land: Emancipation and the Struggle over Equality in Washington, D.C.* Chapel Hill: University of North Carolina Press, 2010.

McClintock, Anne. *Imperial Leather: Race, Gender, and Sexuality in the Colonial Contest.* New York: Routledge, 1995.

McClintock, Megan J. "Civil War Pensions and the Reconstruction of Union Families." *Journal of American History* 83, no. 2 (1996): 456–80.

Meiners, Erica R. *For the Children? Protecting Innocence in a Carceral State.* Minneapolis: University of Minnesota Press, 2016.

Milwaukee County Welfare Rights Organization. *Welfare Mothers Speak Out: We Ain't Gonna Shuffle Anymore.* New York: W. W. Norton, 1972.

Mink, Gwendolyn. *The Wages of Motherhood: Inequality in the Welfare State, 1917–1942.* Ithaca, NY: Cornell University Press, 1995.

Mink, Gwendolyn. *Welfare's End.* Ithaca, NY: Cornell University Press, 1998.

Mink, Gwendolyn, ed. *Whose Welfare?* Ithaca, NY: Cornell University Press, 1999.

Mink, Gwendolyn and Rickie Solinger, eds. *Welfare: A Documentary History,* New York: New York University Press, 2003.

Mitchell, Timothy. "The Limits of the State: Beyond Statist Approaches and Their Critics." *American Political Science Review* 85, no. 1 (1991): 77–96.

Mittelstadt, Jennifer. "'Dependency as a Problem to Be Solved': Rehabilitation and the American Liberal Consensus on Welfare in the 1950s." *Social Politics: International Studies in Gender, State and Society* 8, no. 2 (2001): 228–57.

Morgan, Jennifer L. *Laboring Women: Reproduction and Gender in New World Slavery.* Philadelphia: University of Pennsylvania Press, 2004.

Morgen, Sandra, Joan Acker, and Jill Weigt. *Stretched Thin: Poor Families, Welfare Work, and Welfare Reform.* Ithaca, NY: Cornell University Press, 2009.

Morgensen, Scott Lauria. "The Biopolitics of Settler Colonialism: Right Here, Right Now." *Settler Colonial Studies* 1, no. 1 (2011): 52–76.

Morgensen, Scott Lauria. "Settler Homonationalism: Theorizing Settler Colonialism within Queer Modernities." *GLQ: A Journal of Lesbian and Gay Studies* 16, no. 1–2 (2010): 105–131.

Morgensen, Scott Lauria. *Spaces between Us: Queer Settler Colonialism and Indigenous Decolonization.* Minneapolis: University of Minnesota Press, 2011.

Morley, David, and Kuan-Hsing Chen, eds. *Stuart Hall: Critical Dialogues in Cultural Studies,* New York: Routledge, 1996.

Morrison, Toni, ed. *Race-ing Justice, Engendering Power: The Anita Hill-Clarence Thomas Controversy and the Construction of Social Reality.* New York: Pantheon, 1992.

Moynihan, Daniel Patrick. *The Negro Family: The Case for National Action.* Washington, DC: Office of Policy Planning and Research, US Department of Labor, 1965.

Mumford, Kevin J. *Interzones: Black/White Sex Districts in Chicago and New York in the Early Twentieth Century.* New York: Columbia University Press, 1997.

Muñoz, José Esteban. *Cruising Utopia: The Then and There of Queer Futurity.* New York: New York University Press, 2009.

Nadasen, Premilla. *Household Workers Unite: The Untold Story of African American Women Who Built a Movement.* Boston: Beacon, 2016.

Nadasen, Premilla. *Welfare Warriors: The Welfare Rights Movement in the United States*. New York: Routledge, 2004.

O'Connor, Alice. *Poverty Knowledge: Social Science, Social Policy, and the Poor in Twentieth-Century U.S. History*. Princeton, NJ: Princeton University Press, 2002.

Omi, Michael, and Howard Winant. *Racial Formation in the United States: From the 1960s to the 1990s*. 2nd ed. New York: Routledge, 1994.

Onwuachi-Willig, Angela. "The Return of the Ring: Welfare Reform's Marriage Cure as the Revival of Post-bellum Control." *California Law Review* 93, no. 6 (2005): 1647–96.

Pateman, Carole. *The Sexual Contract*. Stanford, CA: Stanford University Press, 1988.

Patterson, Orlando. *Slavery and Social Death: A Comparative Study*. Cambridge, MA: Harvard University Press, 1982.

Peck, Jamie. *Workfare States*. New York: Guilford, 2001.

Pension Bureau. *Laws of the United States Governing the Granting of Army and Navy Pensions Together with the Regulations Relating Thereto*. Washington: Government Printing Office, 1916.

Piven, Frances Fox, and Richard Cloward. *Poor People's Movements: Why They Succeed, How They Fail*. New York: Vintage, 1977.

Plotkin, Sidney, and William E. Scheuerman. *Private Interests, Public Spending: Balanced-Budget Conservatism and the Fiscal Crisis*. Boston: South End, 1999.

Poulantzas, Nicos. *Political Power and Social Classes*. London: Verso Books, 1975.

Quadagno, Jill. *The Color of Welfare: How Racism Undermined the War on Poverty*. New York: Oxford University Press, 1996.

Reese, Ellen. *Backlash against Welfare Mothers: Past and Present*. Berkeley: University of California Press, 2005.

Regosin, Elizabeth Ann. *Freedom's Promise: Ex-Slave Families and Citizenship in the Age of Emancipation*. Charlottesville: University Press of Virginia, 2002.

Richardson, Mattie Udora. "No More Secrets, No More Lies: African American History and Compulsory Heterosexuality." *Journal of Women's History* 15, no. 3 (2003): 63–76.

Rifkin, Mark. "Romancing Kinship: A Queer Reading of Indian Education and Zitkala-Sa's American Indian Stories." *GLQ: A Journal of Lesbian and Gay Studies* 12, no. 1 (2006): 27–59.

Roberts, Dorothy. *Killing the Black Body: Race, Reproduction, and the Meaning of Liberty*. 1st ed. New York: Pantheon Books, 1997.

Roberts, Dorothy. *Shattered Bonds: The Color of Child Welfare*. New York: Basic Civitas Books, 2002.

Rose, Nancy. "Gender, Race and the Welfare State: Government Work Programs from the 1930s to the Present." *Feminist Studies* 19, no. 2 (1993): 318–42.

Rosen, Hannah. *Terror in the Heart of Freedom: Citizenship, Sexual Violence, and the Meaning of Race in the Postemancipation South*. Chapel Hill: University of North Carolina Press, 2008.

Saville, Julie. *The Work of Reconstruction: From Slave to Wage Laborer in South Caro-lina 1860–1870*. Cambridge: Cambridge University Press, 1994.

Schram, Sanford, Joe Soss, and Richard Fording, eds. *Race and the Politics of Wel-fare Reform*. Ann Arbor: University of Michigan Press, 2003.

Sexton, Jared. "People-of-Color-Blindness: Notes on the Afterlife of Slavery." *Social Text* 28, no. 2 (103) (2010): 31–56.

Shaffer, Donald R. "'I Do Not Suppose That Uncle Sam Looks at the Skin': African Americans and the Civil War Pension System, 1865–1934." *Civil War History* 46, no. 2 (2000): 132–47.

Shah, Nayan. *Stranger Intimacy: Contesting Race, Sexuality, and the Law in the North American West*. Berkeley: University of California Press, 2011.

Simpson, Audra. *Mohawk Interruptus: Political Life across the Borders of Settler States*. Durham, NC: Duke University Press, 2014.

Simpson, Leanne Betasamosake. *As We Have Always Done: Indigenous Freedom through Radical Resistance*. Minneapolis: University of Minnesota Press, 2017.

Skocpol, Theda. *Protecting Soldiers and Mothers: The Political Origins of Social Policy in the United States*. Cambridge, MA: Harvard University Press, 1995.

Smith, Andrea. *Conquest: Sexual Violence and American Indian Genocide*. Cam-bridge, MA: South End, 2005.

Smith, Andrea, and J. Kehaulani Kauanui. "Native Feminisms Engage American Studies." *American Quarterly* 60, no. 2 (2008): 241–49.

Smith, Anna Marie. *Welfare Reform and Sexual Regulation*. New York: Cambridge University Press, 2007.

Southeast Asian Youth Leadership Project and Committee against Anti-Asian Vio-lence. *Eating Welfare: Asians and Welfare in New York City*. Bronx, NY: Youth Leadership Project, 2001. VHS.

Spade, Dean. *Normal Life: Administrative Violence, Critical Trans Politics and the Limits of Law*. Boston: South End, 2011.

Stanley, Amy Dru. *From Bondage to Contract: Wage Labor, Marriage, and the Market in the Age of Slave Emancipation*. Cambridge: Cambridge University Press, 1998.

Stevens, Jacqueline. *Reproducing the State*. Princeton, NJ: Princeton University Press, 1999.

Stevenson, Brenda E. *Life in Black and White: Family and Community in the Slave South*. New York: Oxford University Press, 1996.

Stoler, Ann Laura. *Race and the Education of Desire: Foucault's History of Sexuality and the Colonial Order of Things*. Durham, NC: Duke University Press, 1995.

Tillmon, Johnnie. "Welfare Is a Women's Issue." 1972. In *Welfare: A Documentary History*, edited by Gwendolyn Mink and Rickie Solinger, 373–79. New York: New York University Press, 2003.

Tinsley, Omise'eke Natasha. "Black Atlantic, Queer Atlantic: Queer Imaginings of the Middle Passage." GLQ: *A Journal of Lesbian and Gay Studies* 14, no. 2–3 (2008): 191–215.

Urban Indian Health Institute. *Missing and Murdered Indigenous Women and Girls*. Seattle: Urban Indian Health Institute, 2018. https://www.uihi.org/wp-content

/uploads/2018/11/Missing-and-Murdered-Indigenous-Women-and-Girls -Report.pdf.

Ward, Deborah E. *The White Welfare State: The Racialization of U.S. Welfare Policy.* Ann Arbor: University of Michigan Press, 2005.

Weber, Max. "Politics as Vocation." In *From Max Weber: Essays in Sociology,* edited by H. H. Gerth and C. Wright Mills, 77–156. New York: Oxford University Press, 1946.

Weheliye, Alexander G. *Habeas Viscus: Racializing Assemblages, Biopolitics, and Black Feminist Theories of the Human.* Durham, NC: Duke University Press, 2014.

Wekker, Gloria. *The Politics of Passion: Women's Sexual Culture in the Afro-Surinamese Diaspora.* New York: Columbia University Press, 2006.

White, Deborah Gray. *Ar'n't I a Woman? Female Slaves in the Plantation South.* New York: W. W. Norton, 1999.

Williams, Brackette, ed. *Women Out of Place: The Gender of Agency and the Race of Nationality.* New York: Routledge, 1996.

Williams, Linda Faye. *The Constraint of Race: Legacies of White Skin Privilege in America.* University Park: Penn State University Press, 2004.

Wolfe, Patrick. "Settler Colonialism and the Elimination of the Native." *Journal of Genocide Research* 8, no. 4 (2006): 387–409.

Wolfe, Patrick. *Settler Colonialism and the Transformation of Anthropology: The Politics and Poetics of an Ethnographic Event.* London: Continuum, 1998.

Index

dency, 12, 84–87, 103, 117–18; and the domestic sphere, 145; and freedwomen, 120, 148; norms of, 77, 93–94; respectable, 136; and the welfare queen, 22; white, 73

feminism, 55, 100, 138, 191, 194; histories, 5–9, 79, 103, 108, 153, 193, 198n12; Native, 44; scholarship, 27, 33–34, 50, 52, 200n32. *See also* Black feminist scholarship; methodology of the book

Ferguson, Roderick, 31

Finley, Chris, 41, 45

food stamps, 174, 189. *See also* Temporary Assistance to Needy Families (TANF)

forced labor, 3–5, 9–10, 152, 154, 193–95; and family values, 178–91; and limitation of freedom, 26–28, 110–11, 116–17; and state austerity, 17; and welfare reform, 48, 162

Foucault, Michel, 44–45, 86

"founding fathers" metaphor, 35–36

Fourteenth Amendment, 162

Franke, Katherine, 19, 79

Fraser, Nancy, 172

Frasier, E. Franklin, 166

Freedman's Village, 137

Freedmen's Bureau, significance to project, 5–20

Freedmen's Record (journal), 133, 141

freedom, definition of, 3–4, 11

free labor, 13–15, 18, 25, 81, 124, 127, 140, 187

Geary, John, 105

gender norms, 37, 65, 68, 84, 121. *See also* femininity; heteropatriarchy; masculinity

gender roles, 10, 43, 84, 155–56; and citizenship, 7, 12; heteronormative, 12, 49, 67, 98, 107, 137, 144, 164

Georgia, 55, 162

Georgia State Constitution, 162

Giuliani, Rudy, 189

Glenn, Evelyn Nakano, 183

Goldberg v. Kelly, 162

Gordon, Avery, 4, 20, 199n44

Gordon, Linda, 157, 171–72

Greater Avenues for Independence (GAIN), 184–86, 188

Greenwood, Janette Thomas, 140

Halberstam, Jack, 74

Haley, Sarah, 54, 209n48

Hall, Stuart, 23

Hancock, Ange-Marie, 170–71

Harden, Lillie, 1–3, 8, 190, 197n2

Hargrove, Hattie, 189

Harper's Weekly (magazine), 59–61

Hartman, Saidiya, 19–20, 22, 72–73, 110, 153

Hays, Sharon, 185

heteropatriarchy, 7, 30–44, 63, 65, 103, 190, 195; defining kinship, 12, 17, 95; and freedpeople, 47, 55–56, 72–74, 83–85, 117–20; naturalization of, 49–50; and the welfare state, 154–55, 157, 167, 178–80

hierarchies, 41, 49, 155, 180; gender, 9, 26, 56–58, 62, 84–85, 121, 153; naturalizing, 34–39; racial, 7, 9, 26, 62, 89, 102–3, 111, 173

Hill Collins, Patricia, 33, 37

Hong, Grace Kyungwon, 33

Howard, Charles, 139

Howard, H. N., 137

Howard, Oliver Otis, 13–14

Howard Industrial School, 141–43

Hunter, Tera, 13, 54, 63, 101

Illinois: Chicago, 174

immigration, 38, 156, 166, 175, 183, 189; white, 120, 141. *See also* migration

inclusion, 20, 36, 53, 68, 86, 126, 139, 144; legal, 6–7, 173; racial, 193, 195

indigenous peoples, 39–42, 49, 200n32. *See also* Native Americans

intersectionality, 33, 49

Jim Crow, 16, 53, 55, 209n48

Job Opportunities and Basic Skills program, 168

job readiness, 184–87

John Freeman and His Family (instructional text), 71–73

Johnson, Andrew, 14–15

Johnson, Yvette, 187

Kelley, William, 81

Kerber, Linda, 111–12, 120

Keynesian economics, 15

King, Tiffany Lethabo, 40, 45–46

King v. Smith, 162

kinship, 53–54, 57, 90, 93, 95, 148, 194–95;
heteronormative, 10, 32, 36, 61–64, 72,
76, 88, 155, 180; nonheteronormative, 17,
27, 35, 38–40, 68, 83, 101–2; privatization
of, 42–44; recognition of, 12, 74–76, 80.
See also family values; heteropatriarchy;
private sphere

Krowl, Michelle, 99

Ku Klux Klan, 16

Latin America, 175

Latinas, 159, 174, 189–90, 198n13

Lawrence, A. H., 137

Lee, J. P., 67, 82, 203n26

Lein, Laura, 169

Lewis, Oscar, 166

liberalism, 50–51, 55, 85, 113, 116, 122, 126–
27, 146–47; and freedom, 11–12, 19–26,
61–62, 78–79; and the individual, 69–76,
94, 101–3; narratives of, 6, 10, 200n32; and
personhood, 28, 30–32, 45–48, 122, 132,
195; racial, 5, 166; and welfare, 168–70,
184. *See also* neoliberalism

Lieberman, Robert, 158–59

Louisiana, 78, 119, 159, 162; Donaldsonville,
96

Lowell, Anna, 141–42, 144

low-wage labor, 2–3, 9, 122, 135, 152, 154,
162, 178, 188–93; market for, 5, 169,
182

Lubiano, Wahneema, 170

Lugones, María, 64

Luker, Kristin, 170

Madison, Nathan, 96

Mahmood, Saba, 24–25

Marchevsky, Alejandra, 184–85, 188–89

*Marriage of a Colored Soldier at Vicksburg by
Chaplain Warren of the Freedmen's Bureau*
(Waud), 60

marriage-promotion programs, 24–28, 56,
66–67, 86, 102, 136; to counter vagrancy,
16–18, 39, 46–47, 75–80, 84, 110, 117,
120–21, 148; and PRWORA, 3–5, 9, 152,
154–60, 179–82

Marshal, P., 78

masculinity, 6, 59, 77, 79, 113, 145; and
citizenship, 36, 81, 106, 112; and independence, 12, 17, 48, 73, 84–87, 103, 119–20.
See also emasculation

Massachusetts, 144; Cambridge, 141; Worcester,
140

maternalism, 3, 6–8, 144, 163, 192, 198n17,
205n74; movements, 27, 36; politics, 38,
154–158; reformers, 108, 135, 138, 156,
160, 191

McClintock, Anne, 34–35

McClintock, Megan, 95

methodology of this book, 5–10, 21–34,
153–54, 193–96

Mexico, 166

migration, 46, 109; north, 132–44

military service, 59, 87–90, 144, 166. *See also*
soldiers

Mink, Gwendolyn, 156, 168

Mississippi, 67, 69, 80, 91, 123

Mississippi River, 96

Mississippi State Constitution, 91

Missouri: Kansas City, 187

Mitchell, Timothy, 56

Morgen, Sandra, 184

Morgensen, Scott Lauria, 41–43, 45, 49,
205n71

Moynihan, Daniel Patrick, 165–66, 168

Mozee, Adeline, 89

Muller v. Oregon, 156

Muñoz, José Esteban, 30

Murray, Charles, 176

naming conventions, 25, 66, 70–74, 88, 95

natal alienation, 63, 74, 83, 102. *See also*
social death

national identity, 5, 10, 23, 31, 33–35

National Welfare Rights Organization
(NWRO), 38, 161, 163–64, 167, 178

Native Americans, 39–51, 65, 79, 171, 201n39;
genocide of, 26, 34, 36, 57, 205n71. *See also*
indigenous peoples

Native studies, 40

neoliberalism, 17, 20, 180. *See also* austerity;
deindustrialization

New Deal, 1, 18, 28, 156–61, 163–64, 180,
192, 194; in contrast to Freedmen's Bureau,
49, 56, 84, 119, 148

New England Freedmen's Aid Society, 133

New Jersey, 162

Newsweek (magazine)186

New York City, 189; Bronx, the, 190

New York state, 162, 189

North Carolina, 69, 75, 82

Omi, Michael, 33, 166

Omnibus Budget Reconciliation Act, 167–68

Onwuachi-Willig, Angela, 180

Oregon, 184

palimpsest, concept of, 4, 21–22

paternafare, 181–82

pathologization, 2, 37, 153, 170, 181; of gender
and sexuality, 22–23, 30, 78, 114, 194

Patterson, Orlando, 11–12, 64

pauperization, 15, 17, 136, 139, 141

Pennsylvania, 81, *106*

Pension Bureau, 89–93, 99, 103

Percy, Charlie, 96

Personal Responsibility and Work Opportunity Reconciliation Act (PRWORA), 1, 8,
167–69, 197n6; and barriers to mothering, 190–91; compared to the Freedmen's
Bureau, 178–85; and the "family cap,"
176; and forced labor, 3–4, 9, 188–89; and
immigrants, 175; as solution to women's
poverty, 152; and the workfare worker, 154.
See also welfare reform

personhood, 24–25, 74, 76; legal, 61, 69–70,
131; liberal, 28, 31, 102–3, 122, 132, 177, 195

Plotkin, Sidney, 173

policing, 4, 47, 95, 110, 115, 128, 160, 164, 177;
of vagrancy, 26, 31, 50–51, 53, 57

post–Civil War era, 4, 11–13, 16, 25, 61–62,
102, 140, 147, 156, 183

poverty, 2, 8, 135, 137, 149, 157, 186–87, 210n79;
culture of, 78, 165–70, 174, 177, 179–81, 184;
discourse about, 30, 197n1; due to welfare,
151–52; postwar era, 160–61; urban, 147

Pratt, Richard, 43

Preuss, Thadeus, 67

privacy, 7, 9, 33, 38, 94, 130, 132, 181; and citizenship, 27, 86, 103; and domestic sphere,
77, 80; right to, 53–54, 56–57, 61–62,
146–49; and vagrancy, 121, 126, 177

private sphere, 9, 47, 61, 63, 77, 83; and contracts, 126, 128; for freedpeople, 79, 114; and
the heteropatriarchal family, 32–33; meaning of, 53–54, 61; and the state, 51, 56–57;
and vagrancy, 120–21, 178; and women, 131,
144. *See also* public-private divide

progress, 20–22, 31, 43; evolutionary, 64;
liberal narratives of, 10, 23, 61, 200n32;
racial, 25, 62, 67, 102

Progressive Era, the, 18, 28, 103, 119, 138–39,
166, 194; and mothers' pensions, 5–6, 108,
135, 148

Project Success, 2. *See also* Arkansas

prostitutes, 28, 53, 99–100, 175–76; and the
Freedmen's Bureau, 67, 78; and vagrancy,
48, 108–9, 113–17, 121–22, 126, 128–29,
132, 145

public-private divide, 34, 50–58, 155

public sphere, 50–58, 61, 83–84, 103, 172, 183;
compared to private, 61, 63, 76–77, 130–32;
and freedwomen, 114–18, 144–47, 176–77;
liberal constructions of, 26, 126; and vagrancy, 121–22. *See also* public-private divide

Puckett, James, 92

Puerto Rico, 166

Quadagno, Jill, 168

queerness, 3, 62, 64, 101, 107, 202n11; definition of use, 10, 24, 30–31; indigenous,
39–42; of welfare queen figure, 3, 29, 34, 195

queer of color critique, 29, 31, 39

www.ingramcontent.com/pod-product-compliance
Lightning Source LLC
Chambersburg PA
CBHW071737270326
41928CB00013B/2714